Ellen E. Dickinson

New Light on Mormonism

Ellen E. Dickinson
New Light on Mormonism
ISBN/EAN: 9783337250607
Printed in Europe, USA, Canada, Australia, Japan
Cover: Foto ©Lupo / pixelio.de

More available books at **www.hansebooks.com**

New Light on Mormonism

BY

MRS. ELLEN E. DICKINSON

WITH INTRODUCTION

BY

THURLOW WEED

NEW YORK
FUNK & WAGNALLS
10 AND 12 DEY STREET
1885

All Rights Reserved

Entered, according to Act of Congress, in the year 1885, by
FUNK & WAGNALLS,
In the Office of the Librarian of Congress at Washington, D. C.

PREFACE.

The rapid growth of Mormonism and the grave political aspect it has assumed render it one of the most important topics of current reform.

The time seems ripe for giving to the public its true origin, and for the re-telling of an old story, with the addition of facts and circumstances that have not hitherto been printed.

A deeper interest may be felt in this attempt to cut to the very root of this monstrous parasite upon our American civilization, by my stating here that the Rev. Solomon Spaulding, the author of the romance called "The Manuscript Found," from which the "Book of Mormon" was formulated, was my mother's uncle by marriage; that this romance was for a long time in the house of my grandfather, William Harvey Sabine, near Syracuse, New York, and that it contained no suggestion of polygamy.

With the intention of writing these pages I visited Mrs. McKinstry, the daughter and only child of the Rev. S. Spaulding, in Washington, D. C., in 1880, and she then made a sworn statement as to her father's authorship of the work which has been used with such disastrous effect by crafty men. (Appendix No. 1.)

This venerable lady at the time mentioned was seventy-seven years of age, but in sound health and possessed of excellent memory. She resided for fifty years at Munson, Mass., where she is favorably known, as well as her son, Dr. McKinstry, of Long Meadow, near Springfield, Mass., and her son-in-law, Mr. Seaton, chief clerk of the Census Bureau, Washington, D. C.

With Mrs. McKinstry's full consent to follow up the subject, several localities in Ohio and Central New York were visited by the writer in the autumn of 1881, and with the gleanings thus obtained, the family traditions, the letters written by aged people conversant with the topic and roused into action through the publishing of the statement referred to in the *Century Magazine* (then *Scribner's*), the following pages have been written. It is the only attempt of the Rev. S. Spaulding's relatives to set this matter in its proper light, a duty long delayed to the memory of an upright man.

ELLEN E. DICKINSON.

AUTHORS CONSULTED AT THE ASTOR LIBRARY.

GUNNISON, STENHOUSE,
HYDE, GREEN,
KIDDER, TUCKER,
CASWELL, Gov. ELI H. MURRAY,
AMERICAN ENCYCLOPÆDIA.

INTRODUCTION.

No. 12 West Twelfth Street,
New York, July 9, 1882.

In my boyhood I resided in Onondaga Hollow (now Valley), and was acquainted with William H. Sabine, the grandfather of Mrs. Ellen E. Dickinson, the author of this book, and well remember his residence, in which the Spaulding manuscript is said to have been kept for some years. I have not read this book myself, as my health will not permit it; but in conversation with Mrs. Dickinson I have become satisfied that she has introduced considerable original material, and has gathered from books already published a large amount of interesting matter relating to the subject of Mormonism.

This seems to be the time to publish a narrative of the *early history of Mormonism*. The subject is exciting great interest at present; and as no books have been published relating to it for many years, the present generation has slight acquaintance with it.

With my knowledge of Joseph Smith and one of his first followers, Phelps, a Canandaigua printer, it has been for more than half a century the occasion of surprise and regret that such vulgar impostors should have obtained a following, which is even now drawing proselytes by the thousand from Europe.

Thurlow Weed.

CONTENTS.

CHAPTER I.
Sketch of the Life of Solomon Spaulding and his Authorship of a Romance which he called "The Manuscript Found" 13

CHAPTER II.
Following the Fate of "The Manuscript Found" from the Year 1816 to 1834... 19

CHAPTER III.
Sketch of Joseph Smith's Early Life—The Printing of the "Book of Mormon".. 28

CHAPTER IV.
Sketch of Sidney Rigdon—Interview with General and Mrs. Garfield, at Mentor—Description of the Mormon Temple at Kirtland, Ohio... 47

CHAPTER V.
Interview with D. P. Hurlburt, at Gibsonburg, Ohio, and with E. D. Howe, at Painesville, Ohio, in 1880................. 62

CHAPTER VI.
Visit to Conneaut, Ohio, in 1880—Reminiscences of Rev. S. Spaulding and the First Mormon Conference, in 1834....... 77

CHAPTER VII.
The Mormons in Missouri...................................... 82

CHAPTER VIII.

The Mormons at Nauvoo—Description of the Temple—The Death of the Prophet.................................. 94

CHAPTER IX.

Brigham Young's Election to the Presidency—Expulsion of the Mormons from Nauvoo, in 1846.......................... 113

CHAPTER X.

The Early Political Situation of the Mormons in "The Land of the Honey Bee"—The Mountain Meadow Butchery—The Influence of the Mormons Over the Indians................ 122

CHAPTER XI.

Polygamy in Utah—The Granting of Woman's Suffrage in 1871—The Edmunds' Bill—Sketch of Brigham Young...... 140

CHAPTER XII.

John Taylor Elected as Successor to the Second Prophet—The Trial of Rudger Clawson, Jr., for Bigamy—Salt Lake City—Its Beautiful Location—The Tabernacle and Public Buildings—Mormon Conferences—The Freedom of the Ballot in Utah—The Present Generation of Mormons—Predictions Regarding the Future of Mormonism—Far-seeing Mormons Preparing a Rendezvous for the Victims of the Edmunds' Law.. 167

CHAPTER XIII.

The Doctrines of Mormonism—Hierachical Organization—The "Book of Mormon"—Church Polity—The Faith of the Latter-Day Saints—Their Modes of Worship............... 200

CHAPTER XIV.

The Josephites—Epitome of the Faith and Doctrines of the Reorganized Church of Jesus Christ of Latter-Day Saints—David Whitmer—The Debate at Kirtland, Ohio, in 1884, Concerning the "Book of Mormon"—The Revelation on Celestial Marriage Given to Joseph Smith in 1843.......... 215

APPENDIX.. 237

INDEX... 269

NEW LIGHT ON MORMONISM.

CHAPTER I.

Sketch of the Life of Solomon Spaulding and his authorship of a romance which he called "The Manuscript Found."

SOLOMON SPAULDING was born at Ashford, Conn., in 1761, of a highly respectable family of English extraction, some of whose members served as officers in the Revolutionary War.

He was educated at the Plainfield, Conn., Academy and at Dartmouth College, where he graduated in 1785, subsequently studying theology, and preached for a few years in some obscure New England town, but retired from the ministry, it is said, in consequence of ill-health. Soon after leaving Dartmouth he married Miss Matilda Sabine, of Pomfret, Conn. Next we hear of Mr. Spaulding at Cherry Valley, N. Y., where he became principal of an academy, and remained until, through the persuasion of his brother, John Spaulding, he removed to a little town in Ohio, west of Buffalo, called at the time Salem, but now known as Conneaut, Ashtabula Co. Here the Spauldings, with Mr. Henry Lake, were owners of an iron foundry, and were engaged in successful business until the War of 1812, which ruined them financially.

Solomon Spaulding, being an invalid, remained much of the time in his own house, reading and writing. He was a peculiar man, of fine education, especially devoted to historical study, the writing of essays and romances, and given to talking to his neighbors of what he had read and written.

He was greatly superior to the people generally with whom he came in contact in that part of the country, both in mental capacity and education, possessed a commanding personal appearance—being over six feet in height—and had a pleasing, intelligent countenance. With all these advantages he was naturally looked upon as a man of consequence, and his opinions and conversation were listened to with earnest consideration by his acquaintances and neighbors.

He was in the habit of frequently reading to them something he had written for their amusement and benefit, and these unique entertainments made a vivid and lasting impression upon those who were so fortunate as to attend them.

In close proximity to the Spaulding residence there were some earth-mounds; they greatly interested him, and in order to have one of them investigated he had a large and vigorous tree cut down, which, on examination, turned out to be one thousand years old. Buried within the mound were various evidences of a prehistoric race, relics of a civilized condition, mingled with human bones, which were portions of gigantic skeletons. This discovery very greatly excited him and fired his imagination. He had been the very first person, it is said, to speculate and write on the origin of the various earth-mounds in the Mississippi Valley and that region, and had long had a theory as to the peopling of this country by a race which had inhabited the whole Continent, possessing the refinements of civilization, and which had, in some unaccountable manner, perished. The relics secured by his workmen seemed to confirm this idea; here he found tangible proofs that his theories and conversations on the subject were not the mere vagaries of a distorted and fanciful imagination, and he immediately began to write a new romance.

The extreme antiquity of the relics belonging to the race whose history he professed to give led him to adopt the most antique style of composition, and so he imitated the Scriptures, as the most ancient book in the world; and his knowledge of the classics and histories of the olden times enabled him to introduce the odd names which were noticed by his friends, and which were afterward easily distinguished by them. In common with all antiquarians, Mr. Spaulding was aware that the mound-builders are supposed to have been very religious, as well as superstitious; but as to the nature of their religion and superstitions it is impossible to determine aught, save their striking similiarity to the religion of the modern Indians, and to that of the ancient Magi of Persia, before the days of Zoroaster.

Mr. Spaulding conceived the idea that among the prehistoric mementoes discovered by his workmen some golden plates covered with hieroglyphical writing had been found, and that he merely translated the story of a people whose wanderings and sufferings had been thereon inscribed, and of which he had deciphered the interpretation. He altered the plot of his novel after writing a portion of it. The emigrant Jews, whose story he professed to narrate, were, in the first instance, fitted out at Rome for their travels; but after reflection he started them from Jerusalem, with Levi and his four sons, under divine direction. Years after, when his manuscript romance was eagerly sought for at Harlwich, N. Y., the rejected beginning of his story was found.

Mr. Spaulding was a rapid writer, and as he progressed with his romance from day to day, he read it to his wife and neighbors, all of whom were greatly impressed with its peculiarities. He called it "The Manuscript Found"—that is, a written history of a lost people, found in an earth-mound. It purported to be an account of the peopling of America by the lost tribes of Israel, the tribes and their leaders having very singular names; among them, *Mormon, Moroni, Lamenite*, and *Nephi*—names found nowhere else in literature. So much interest was awakened by this romance, and it was such a distinction, at the time, to write a book, that he determined to publish it. (Mr. Spaulding laughingly remarked to Nathan Howard, a neighbor, that probably in a century from that time his account of the early inhabitants of America would be accepted as a veritable history.) For this purpose he removed to Pittsburg, where he had a friend named Patterson, a publisher, to whom he gave his manuscript for inspection, hoping he would print it, believing that its publication would not only establish him as a successful author, but give him, in addition, a comfortable competence. The war had blasted all his hopes of bettered fortune at Conneaut; but he now felt sanguine of success if his book could reach the public in proper form. A young printer, named Sidney Rigdon, was in Mr. Patterson's printing house; he had been there but a short time, and, from many indisputable facts, it is believed he had followed Mr. Spaulding from Conneaut, or its immediate neighborhood, and having heard him read "The Manuscript Found," and announce his plan for its publication, devised a treachery toward both author and publisher, which the world has reason to remember. This same Sidney Rigdon figured prominently twenty years later as a preacher among the Mormons. After weeks of delay, during which time Mr. Spaulding's manuscript was left carelessly lying about in the office of the printing house, Mr. Patterson decided not to publish it. He admitted its cleverness, and said to the author, "Polish it up, finish it, and you will make money out of it." It is probable that Mr. Spaulding did not attempt to find another publisher, as he was disheartened and impecunious. It was a very different matter to publish a book at that time from the present era of books and bookmaking. Within a few months he seems to have abandoned his attempt to have his romance printed, and took his family to Amity, Washington Co., Penn., where he at one time kept a store, and then a public-house, and again became the centre of an admiring circle of listeners to his talk and writings. The author has recently received a letter (see Appendix No. 2) from a very aged man, still living near Amity, who distinctly remembers Solomon Spaulding and his "Manuscript Found." This same Mr. Miller testifies that he often heard the romance read, remembers many particulars in it, citing a description in the story where, before a battle, one of the armies painted their faces with red paint to distinguish them from their enemies, and that he afterward read the same description in the same connection in the "Book of Mormon." Mr. Miller remembers distinctly, too, that Mr. Spaulding accused Rigdon of copying his manuscript while it was in Mr. Patterson's office, giving his reasons for such a belief. In 1816 Mr. Spaulding died of consumption at Amity, and was there buried in the village graveyard.

His friend Miller tells how he nursed him in his long

illness, made his coffin, helped to bury him, and settled up his slender estate. At this time "he stooped forward a little, had a sober visage, was reserved in conversation, and very candid apparently in his dealings," and "I think he was a very good man," adds the narrator of this unfortunate author's last experiences.

The humble head-stone which marks his grave has been almost entirely chipped away by relic hunters of our own and foreign lands; but there is a promise that the Historical Society of Washington Co., Penn., will replace it with a handsome and suitable monument at no distant day.

CHAPTER II.

Following the fate of "The Manuscript Found" from the year 1816 to 1834.

IMMEDIATELY after Solomon Spaulding's death at Amity, Penn., in 1816, Mrs. Spaulding and her daughter removed to the residence of William H. Sabine at Onondaga Valley (called "Hollow" at the time), N. Y., taking with her all her personal effects. According to the remembrances of certain persons now living, Mrs. Spaulding was greatly esteemed by "Squire Sabine," as he was familiarly known. She was his only sister, and a woman of intelligence, refinement, and many virtues, and he invited her to make a prolonged visit at his house in consequence of her impoverished condition. Mr. Sabine was a lawyer of distinction and wealth, a graduate of Brown University, and known throughout central New York for his legal abilities and probity of character.* He was the personal friend of Judge Conkling of Utica (father of Roscoe Conkling), of Judge Strong of Onondaga Co., and of Judge Miller of Cayuga Co. (the father-in-law of William H. Seward), and of all the leading men of that part of the State, one of the most prominent of whom was Judge Joshua Forman, his brother-in-law and partner, whose name will always be associated with the history of our country in

---

* It may also be stated that Mr. Sabine accepted a military commission, and was promoted to the rank of Captain, and in 1811 withdrew from the service. He was a strong Federalist, and was candidate for the Assembly in 1815, 1816, and 1817.

connection with his instrumentality in the construction of the Erie Canal and originating the banking system called the "Safety Fund Act," during the administration of Martin Van Buren as Governor of the State of New York, which subsequently became a law in this State, and in 1860 was adopted by the general government, and is now in general use.*

Squire Sabine's house remains in perfect preservation, is still owned by the family; and Mrs. McKinstry, in talking of it two years since, described its rooms and surroundings as she saw them in 1816 and 1817, which correspond very closely to their present condition.

Among Mrs. Spaulding's belongings which she conveyed to the old homestead was a hair-covered trunk, of a kind much used in those days, filled with her deceased husband's writings, which she had preserved—sermons, essays, novels, and a manuscript, which she and all the family were familiar with, under the title of "The Manuscript Found." Mrs. McKinstry, Mr. Spaulding's daughter, says that she perfectly remembers this trunk and its contents; that it was in the garret of the house; that she and her cousins (one of them the mother of the writer) had access to it and frequently looked it through. She remembers one set of papers or manuscripts an inch thick, closely written and tied up with some of the stories which she recognized as having been written by her father, and read to her by him at Conneaut. One of these stories was called "The Frogs of Wyndham," and she repeated it to the writer recently, giving an imitation of her father's comic recitation of it. One of the manuscripts she distinctly remembers to have seen had the title "The Manuscript Found."

---

* See *Magazine of American History*, June, 1882.

As she was between eleven and twelve years of age at this time, and precocious, she well understood what she saw and read. The trunk containing the manuscript is understood to have been in Mr. Sabine's house nearly three years. While it was there Mrs. Anna T. Redfield, still living in Syracuse, N. Y., eighty-three or four years of age, of sound mind and memory, and of high social position (see Appendix No. 3), was a resident in Mr. Sabine's family.

She also remembers hearing a great deal of a manuscript which Mrs. Spaulding said was written by her deceased husband, and the comments made upon it by Mr. Sabine and the neighbors, and their all agreeing that it was a wonderful story, both in style and substance. In after years, in seeing the "Book of Mormon," she found names and incidents in it which she heard in connection with the Spaulding manuscript at Onondaga Valley. The writer has often heard members of her family say that Joe Smith was at one time their servant or hired man. Probably it was while Mrs. Spaulding was at Onondaga Valley.

Smith was in Onondaga County about the time mentioned, as his name (according to Gunnison) appears in the criminal records of 1817. He was about eighteen or nineteen years old, possibly twenty, when he was in the Onondaga County Jail for "vagrancy and debt," and this jail was then at Onondaga Hill, two miles from Mr. Sabine's house. An old man remembered that Smith was about this time employed to "locate" water with sticks of witch-hazel, the "divining-rods" in the vicinity of Syracuse and Onondaga Valley, and there is a local tradition that he was employed to look for gold in what is supposed to be an earth-mound, a conical-shaped hill, between Syracuse and Onondaga Valley, with his "seer-stone."

There is no reason to doubt that Joe Smith was once in the employ of Mr. Sabine as a teamster and man for out-door work, taking his meals in the kitchen, and hearing the talk of the house.

Some authors on Mormonism have said Smith stole the Spaulding manuscript while at Mr. Sabine's; this statement is not correct. He heard of it, and from his knowledge of it was afterward prepared to use what he knew of the matter in getting up one of the greatest delusions in the history of modern times.

Joseph Sabine, Esq., of Syracuse, son of William H. Sabine, now deceased, twice wrote his recollections for New York newspapers of the family traditions in relation to Mr. Spaulding, his romance, its being in his father's house, and of Joe Smith's residence at Onondaga Valley.

In 1820 Mrs. Spaulding married Mr. Davison of Hartwick, near Cooperstown, N. Y. Mrs. McKinstry says she vividly remembers seeing the hair trunk and looking over its contents in a closet in Mr. Davison's house, at Cooperstown, where it had been removed, and noticing its important feature, "The Manuscript Found;" but the two ladies, mother and daughter, in their new relations and new home, did not give the same attention to Mr. Spaulding's literary legacy that they had while in Mr. Sabine's house.

In 1828 Matilda Spaulding married Dr. A. McKinstry, of Munson, Hampden Co., Mass., and her mother followed her a little while afterward to make a visit, which, for some family reasons (on the part of Mrs. Davison), eventuated in her remaining there permanently until her death. She placed her furniture, and with it the old Spaulding trunk of manuscripts, in the custody of a cousin at Hartwick, named Jerome Clark.

Here it must be remembered that the facilities for travel and transportation were then very different from the present expeditious methods by railway and express. Fifty years ago journeys were slowly and expensively accomplished; and in leaving her effects with a cousin she felt they were safe, and that she would return for them; and she had not the remotest suspicion of the use to be made of one of the manuscripts by fraudulent men almost immediately after her departure from Hartwick.

Soon after Mrs. Davison went to Munson the whole country was filled with an agitation in regard to a new religious faith called Mormonism; and the report that it was founded on Solomon Spaulding's romance, "Manuscript Found," quickly followed, to the immense surprise of Mrs. Davison, Mrs. McKinstry, and every one connected with the author of that remarkable and unfortunate novel. Then a report was directly carried to these ladies, that a great meeting of Mormons had been held at Conneaut, Ohio, and that on one occasion, when the "Book of Mormon" was read before the assemblage, John Spaulding and Mr. Lake, the former partners of Solomon Spaulding, and many other persons who were present, recognized its similarity to the story called "The Manuscript Found," with which they had been so familiar years before (see statements 4th and 5th, Appendix) in that very locality.

She was not a little excited over what she heard of the Mormons, and Mrs. McKinstry says she remembers how her mother talked on the subject, expressing a firm conviction that Sidney Rigdon had copied the manuscript, which had been in Mr. Patterson's office in Pittsburg. She also said at this time that Mr. Spaulding had assured her that he recovered his original manuscript when Mr.

Patterson refused to publish it; and she never wavered or doubted in this belief.

That the Mormons agreed with her in this conviction, and felt that their exposure and ruin were certain if the Spaulding manuscript remained in existence, is proved by the trick which they practised to get it into their possession. Previous to this time, when the Mormon fraud was inaugurated at Palmyra, the report of it naturally reached Hartwick; and some one who was acquainted with the fact that Spaulding's writings were in the hands of Jerome Clark applied to him requesting to see them, and he refused. He probably allowed persons interested, whom he could trust, to look over the contents of the old trunk. A son of this Mr. Clark, now residing in Sonoma, California (see Appendix No. 6), wrote to the author that when he sold his father's farm near Hartwick, in 1864, the old trunk known to the family as having belonged to the Spauldings was still in the garret. Mrs. George Clark also remembers "that Mrs. Davison once while visiting them gave her a manuscript to read written, as she said, by Mr. Spaulding, as a pastime to while away the days of sickness." From these letters of the Clarks it appears that Mrs. Davison spent some time with them at Hartwick "nearly fifty years ago, and went from there direct to Munson, Mass."

Later, she sent word to these relatives to sell the furniture which they had stored for her, but the trunk remained. Mrs. McKinstry states that her mother fully intended to return to Hartwick. Certain events occurred to prevent it, which are not necessary to be related here.

It will be subsequently seen that "The Manuscript Found" was stolen from her.

Onondaga Valley, Hartwick, and Palmyra, being contiguous in central New York, the story of the Spaulding manuscript was familiar to many people, as well as to the residents of Conneaut, where the first great conference of the Mormons was held.

Of the professed converts to Mormonism, so long as it suited a scheme he had to make money out of it, was one Dr. D. P. Hurlburt, a man of good address and fine personal appearance. He was sent by a committee, as he at the time represented the matter, to visit Mrs. Davison at Munson, Mass., and ask permission to carry "The Manuscript Found," written by Solomon Spaulding, to Conneaut, in order to compare it with the "Book of Mormon."

Further on in these pages there is an account of an interview with this Dr. Hurlburt, who was still living at Gibsonburg, Ohio, in November, 1880.

The perfect familiarity of the Mormon leaders with the history of the Spaulding manuscript at the time is proved by Dr. Hurlburt's method to obtain it. His visit to William H. Sabine, at Ononodaga Valley, to procure a letter of introduction to Mrs. Davison, with a request from him to let Hurlburt have the manuscript, was a subtle and clever contrivance, undoubtedly suggested by Joseph Smith, who was acquainted with his former employer's peculiarities, his probity of character, and unquestionable willingness to assist in proving the "Book of Mormon" to be a plagiarism of Spaulding's romance.

In the year 1834 Dr. Hurlburt, after procuring a letter of introduction to Mrs. Davison from her brother, William H. Sabine, at Onondaga Valley, proceeded in his nefarious scheme for obtaining the original Spaulding "Manuscript Found." When he appeared at Munson, Mass., equipped with this letter and the request it contained, that Mrs. Davison should write an order to Jerome Clark to give him the manuscript, both Mrs. Davison and Mrs. McKinstry distrusted his motives at once.

With a woman's quick perception of character, they each had an intuition, from something in his personal appearance, that he was deceptive, and that he visited them for no good purpose. He told them that he had been a convert to Mormonism, but was now convinced of its fallacies and plagiarisms, and had come to them to ask their assistance in exposing the shameful imposition to the world.

With all his honeyed words, Mrs. Davison disliked the man. She was careful to have her daughter with her during the interview, and so unwilling was she to yield to her brother's request to loan the manuscript, that she requested Dr. Hurlburt to stay over night that she might reflect thoroughly upon the matter; and it was only after his protracted waiting, and his repeated and apparently sincere assurances that he would in due season return the manuscript, that she at last gave him the order to Jerome Clark, at Hartwick, to deliver it into his temporary keeping.

This unfortunate surrender, Mrs. McKinstry says, her mother regretted to her dying day, since it was entirely against her better judgment, and that she only yielded in deference to her brother's demand, as she had great respect for his opinion.

Very soon after Hurlburt left Munson the ladies heard directly from Mr. Clark, that he had given him "The Manuscript Found," and that he "opened the old trunk for the purpose."

Lieutenant Gunnison, in his "History of Mormonism," says that Clark either by accident or design retained a part of the manuscript, which accounts for the report that years after a quire of paper was found in the trunk with Spaulding's first attempt at the romance.

So far we have traced "The Manuscript Found" to the care of Hurlburt, who gave his most unqualified and sacred promise to return it to its proper owner; but from the time it was intrusted to his keeping, no member of Mrs. Davison's family has ever seen it.

A few weeks after Jerome Clark placed it in Hurlburt's hands, at Hartwick, Mrs. Davison and her daughter, as well as other members of the family, learned that a manuscript, said to be the one Hurlburt had received, was shown and read at Conneaut; but this report was never completely verified.

Mrs. Davison made repeated requests by letter to Hurlburt to return her property, but he never responded by message or letter to her demands, or noticed her appeals in any manner, and entirely ignored the matter.

CHAPTER III.

Sketch of Joseph Smith's early life and the printing of the "Book of Mormon."

Mormonism was founded by Joseph Smith, Jr., in the year 1830, at Palmyra, N. Y. He has been called "the American Mahomet," and he himself declared the "Book of Mormon" to be the Bible of the Western Continent, and the word Mormon to be derived from several languages, and to mean "more good." He was born at Sharon, Vt. The date of his birth is not accurately known, but is supposed to be about the year 1800, possibly a little earlier. His father's name was Joseph, and his mother's maiden name was Lucy Mack, and both were of Scotch descent. They had nine children—Hyrum, Alvin, Joseph, Samuel, Harrison, William, Don Carlos, Sophronia, Catherine, and Lucy.

The family removed to Palmyra, central New York, while Joseph was still a lad of nine or ten years of age. Mrs. Smith was a woman who was full of odd conceits and superstitions, while possessing a great deal of natural talent, and she ruled her husband, who was a weak character.

Before the family left Vermont the parents had agreed that one of their several children was to be or would be a prophet; and as Joseph resembled his mother more than the others in a certain mental quickness and in his powers of dissimulation, they settled upon him as the "genius" of the household.

It is said that Joseph at an early age could read, but

not write; and when quite young committed these lines to memory from the story of Captain Kidd, the notorious pirate, which seemed to give him great pleasure:

> "My name was Robert Kidd
> As I sailed, as I sailed;
> And most wickedly I did
> As I sailed, as I sailed."

The Smiths lived two or three miles from the town of Palmyra, then in Ontario County, now Wayne, and were the terror and torment of the neighborhood. They seemed to have no regular occupation, to have been "everything by turns, and nothing long." The father was a cooper by trade, and he dug wells and worked on the neighboring farms when he could; he also peddled beer and ginger bread, doing a thriving business on training days. The whole family made baskets and maple sugar, and raised and sold garden stuff, at odd times, and the mother washed by the day; but her employers were careful to have the clothes in before dark, as experience had taught them they would disappear if left on the lines over night. The youthful Joseph assisted generally, and was an adept in robbing hen-roosts and orchards; indeed, from all accounts, the Smiths were considered a thoroughly disreputable family.

A certain superstitious feeling concerning them also existed in the minds of their more ignorant neighbors on account of the reputation Mrs. Smith had for "telling fortunes" (see Appendix No. 9).

Mr. Seth W. Chapman at present owns the property that was then known as the Smith farm. What is now the dining-room of the dwelling was the living-room of the numerous Smiths, with two attic chambers above and a cellar underneath. Later a bedroom was added on the ground floor.

Very early Mrs. Smith instructed her son Joseph to set up a claim for miraculous powers, which he willingly adopted. While he was watching the digging of a well, or himself digging it, he found, or pretended to find, a peculiarly shaped stone that resembled a child's foot in its outlines. It has been said that this little stone, afterward known as the "peek stone" and the "Palmyra seer stone," had been in the possession of Mrs. Smith's family for generations, and that she merely presented it to Joseph when he was old enough to work miracles with it; and that he hid it in the earth to find it again when it was convenient. As has been written, this "seer stone" was "the acorn of the Mormon oak."

From that time on Joseph Smith fooled the credulous residents of the sparsely settled vicinity with the "peeker" in his white stove-pipe hat, which he held close to his face; he saw very remarkable sights—buried treasures of gold and silver, etc.; he could trace stolen property, tell where herds of cattle had strayed, and where water was to be found. With the "peek stone" he carried a rod of witch-hazel, to assist in the discovery of water; and between the stone and the rod he eked out a precarious subsistence.

A personage of this peculiar type was sure to find followers; and "Joe Smith," as he was called, soon became the head of a band that slept during the day and wandered in the night-time to such places as they were directed to by their leader to dig for hidden treasures.

Joe laid down certain laws to his "phalanx" in their operations; and if they disobeyed his rules, the charm of the proceeding was broken. So it frequently happened, when he assured his friends that they were close to the coveted prize, if the commanded silence, which may have lasted for hours, was broken by the slightest manifestation of gratified pleasure, he declared the gold, or silver, had been "spirited away," and he must again "follow the lead of the witch-hazel and 'peek stone' to see where it had 'located.'" When Joe wanted fresh meat for his family, he gave out that it would be necessary to insure the success of the "diggers," as these worthies were called, by having a black sheep killed, as a sacrificial offering, before going to work.

This state of affairs continued for some time, and his reputation extended to the adjacent counties, which he often visited. He disappeared for four years, which are involved in mystery; but he is known to have been during that time in both Onondaga and Chenango counties, as his name appears in the criminal records of both as a vagabond.

It must have been during this absence from Ontario (now Wayne) County that he was employed by William H. Sabine, Esq., at Onondaga Valley, in 1819 or 1820. Smith, by his own statement, at one time worked for a man by the name of Stowell, near Hartwick, where the trunk containing Spaulding's manuscript and other writings was at the time deposited. He is also known to have been in Broome County, and at Harpersville, Penn., visiting some relatives of his mother's.

At that time there was a peddler named Parley P. Pratt, afterward distinguished for his connection with Mormonism, who was familiar with the affairs of the day, and knew everybody of the slightest note in western New York and northern Ohio. He frequently extended his trips into northern Pennsylvania. His family resided at Mentor, Ohio. Sidney Rigdon made mysterious journeys to Pennsylvania; but exactly when and where Smith, Rigdon, and Pratt met, it is now impossible to determine. There is conclusive evidence, however, that they did meet, Pratt being, it is supposed, the medium of Rigdon's and Smith's knowledge of each other, the first having copied the Spaulding romance at Pittsburg, and soon after retiring from his trade "to study the Scriptures," as he said, and avowing his intention to become a preacher. His ostensible residence was also at Mentor, Ohio, and it is an established fact that he visited Pittsburg and the interior of Pennsylvania.

Smith is known to have had a copy of the Spaulding manuscript in his possession about the year 1820, or at the time these three worthies met, as it is certain that the scheme of the great Mormon fraud was determined about this period between Smith and Rigdon, and arrangements made to develop it as quickly as circumstances would permit and money could be procured for the purpose.

Smith was wandering through the country during these years of mystery a portion of the time, and was occasionally seen at Palmyra. He heard the theories (as it was a common topic of conversation at the time) that were afloat to account for the peopling of America; the traditions collected from the Indians; the Hebrew traditions among them; the discovery of ruined cities and temples in Central America; the relics of pottery, bricks, and stumps of axe-cut trees, buried far beneath the surface of the Mississippi Valley. He had the wit to understand when Rigdon said a book elucidating such theories would pay, especially with the addition of the biblical language of the Spaulding manuscript and its quaint romance.

Either there, or elsewhere, he pretended to be interested in the great revivals that were common at the time in the churches of the different religious denominations. In 1821 there was a revival in the Methodist,

Baptist, and Presbyterian churches at Palmyra, and some of the Smith family declared they were " converted." The mother, three of the brothers, and a sister joined the Presbyterian communion. Joe asserted his partiality for the Methodists, but ultimately declared he could not decide which was right. He said that his mind was greatly exercised by what he heard first in one church and then in another, and that he gave himself up to prayer for days, " agonizing," that the truth might be made known to him among all the conflicting opinions that he heard among these different sects ; that suddenly his chamber became illuminated, an angel appeared and conversed with him, instructed him in the ways of righteousness, and informed him there was *no true Church on earth.*

He was further told that his prayers were heard, that he was " dearly beloved of the Lord, and should be commissioned a priest after the order of Melchisedec—organizing a church of faithful persons in that line to receive the Lord, in the Millennium."

In a second visit the angel informed him " that the truth should SPRING OUT OF THE EARTH ;" that he would be led to the Hill Cumorah, near Palmyra, and receive from out of the ground holy and prophetic records concerning a family of Jews that emigrated from Jerusalem in the time of Zedekiah, and were miraculously led across the Eastern Ocean.

Beyond question his mind was strangely exercised by the popular religious movement that swept through the country at the time, and his naturally imaginative and superstitious nature was briefly impressed by the eloquence of the revivalists. He became familiar with scriptural expression, and followed the inclination of those about him to listen to any new-fangled doctrine.

While at Harpersville, Penn., in 1826, he married Emma, the daughter of Isaac Hale, a well-to-do farmer of the vicinity, who was greatly opposed to the "peeker," as he called Joe Smith, who was making himself notorious by his strange talk on religious topics and his pretensions to be able to work miracles, as well as to locate gold and silver. Numerous tricks were played on Smith by the unbelieving, and his father-in-law threatened to shoot him if he returned to his house after clandestinely marrying his daughter.

The Smith family were still very poor and still given to disreputable methods for a living.

In 1826 Joe Smith returned to Palmyra, and began to act his *rôle* in bringing before the public, with very great caution, the well-contrived Mormon scheme to delude the ignorant and superstitious. At dinner-time, one day, he told his family that in crossing through a grove he found a book in some white sand. They asked to see it, appearing to believe him; but he said that the angel who told him of its locality had forbidden him to show it without authority, and that any person thus looking on it would surely die.

Having a certain amount of magnetic influence, Smith gathered a few dissolute followers about him. He began to talk to them of some golden plates he had been directed in a vision to dig for in the vicinity, and went about with them to "locate" the treasure. He had a reputation among his admirers of also "casting out devils" and healing the sick.

Mrs. Smith, Joe's wife, owned a six-acre lot[*] near the hill that was soon to become famous, four miles from

---

[*] This was probably not Joseph's wife's house, but the house already described, now belonging to Mr. Seth Chapman.

Palmyra, on which there was a small log house, partly finished, having a stove-pipe running through the roof to answer for a chimney. This hill is at present known as "Gold Bible Hill." It is conical in shape, smooth and green to the very top, from which there is a picturesque view of hills and dales in all directions. From its peculiar form and isolation it is somewhat suggestive of an extinct volcano. It is owned by William T. Sampson, Commander in the United States Navy. In 1826 Joe and his wife were established in the primitive log house, which was visited by Sidney Rigdon, who spent three or four months there; and a number of other men came, and, after lingering a while, left with an air of mystery.

The neighbors became suspicious, and thought a band of counterfeiters were at work under Smith's direction; while he talked of wonders about to be performed "at the hill." There is a tradition that the boys of the vicinity believed a giant would come out of the hill and crush Palmyra and all those who ridiculed the talk of Joe Smith and his revelations. To his adherents Smith said he had been shown the box in which "the golden plates" were concealed, and had tried many times to open it, but was struck back by an invisible blow coming from Satan, who had been at his elbow, and accused him of avarice and ambition, and that he was obliged to repent and humiliate himself for that great event. He said that angels visited him frequently, and while he boldly confessed himself a great sinner, and owned that he had led an unworthy life, "the Lord had chosen him and forgiven all his sins; and for His own inscrutable purpose made him, weak and erring as he might have been, the instrument of His glory."

His interviews with the angel "Maroni" were frequent. One of these interviews lasted all night, and at daybreak, in going home, he was so exhausted that, in attempting to climb a fence he fell over it, and for a long time was unconscious. He beheld the angel standing over him when his senses returned, and he was directed to tell his father all that had been communicated, and his father said, "Follow the angel's direction, as he is a messenger from God."

Smith related that, after hearing a sermon from the text, "If any of you lack wisdom, let him ask of God that giveth unto all men and upbraideth none, and it shall be given him;" that he went into the woods, knelt down and began to pray. A thick darkness covered him, and he thought he was about to be destroyed; but suddenly a pillar of light arose just over his head, and he saw two personages bright and full of glory beyond description. One of them called him by name and, pointing to the other, said, "This is my beloved son."

His neighbors have testified that he made contradictory statements as to the locality where "the golden plates" were to be found; but at last, on the night of September 22, 1827, amid thunder and lightning and a grand display of celestial pyrotechnics, while Smith and the chosen were fervently praying, an angel came out of a chasm in Cummorah Hill, opened for this particular occasion, and delivered a box to Smith's care, who said he saw legions of devils struggling with the angel, to keep back the prize. The name of the angel who delivered the box was Moroni, and he informed Smith that the fate of the early inhabitants of America was written on golden tablets within the box, which could only be read by the aid of some wonderful stone spectacles called "*Urim and Thummim*," delivered with the plates.

Smith's story of his *first view* of the plates, several years previous, is that, following the direction of the angel, he went to the Hill Cummorah and on the west side, near the top, he found a box, that was only partly concealed by loose bits of rock and earth. He removed the obstructions with a lever. The box was made of stones held together with cement. On partly opening it he saw the plates and the *Urim* and *Thummim*.*

He attempted to take them out, and was forbidden by the "Voice," and told that four years from that time was the period fixed to receive them; but he must visit the place each year, on the anniversary of that occasion. He followed this advice, and the angel met him, giving him instructions touching "the Lord's purpose in the last days, and in what manner His kingdom was to be constituted."

This precious box was carried to Smith's cabin. He opened it in secret, but said it contained not only the six golden tablets eighteen inches square, held together by rings at the back, and the stone spectacles, but the sword of Laban and a "breastplate," which had been brought from Jerusalem.

The tablets, he announced, were covered with hieroglyphics, which he alone had the power to read with the spectacles; and a little low chamber of his house was made a translating room, Smith standing in one corner behind a blanket which screened him from the curiosity of his scribe, Oliver Cowdrey, who had been a schoolmaster, and Reuben Hale, his brother-in-law, an admirer of the "Peeker." Smith said the inscriptions were in a new language, which he called "reformed Egyptian." While the translation was going on, he came to a part of the narrative that informed him that baptism by immer-

---

* Urim and Thummim mean "light" and "perfection," or the "shining and the perfect," according to an accepted Biblical lexicograph.

sion for the remission of sins had been taught and commanded by the ancient inhabitants of America, and, anxious to learn his "privileges," the translator, with Cowdrey, retired to the woods "to inquire further of the Lord."

While they were praying John the Baptist appeared in a "cloud of light," and, laying his hands on them, ordained them. The neighbors heard Smith was writing a book which he called at the time "The Gold Bible," this idea being suggested by the report that a gold Bible had about this time been dug up somewhere in Canada.

As the work progressed the people sometimes called to see how it was getting along, and they were allowed to feel the manuscript as it reposed in a pillow-case, but no one was allowed to see it.

The translating process, it was reported, was simple, as a copy of the hieroglyphics was taken down from the plates, and then Smith dictated to those who copied on paper.

So much was said at Palmyra of the golden plates, that certain persons contrived a plan to capture them, and a writ for debt was served on Smith as a pretence. To avoid this, he placed the plates, long before prepared by himself and Rigdon, when they met in Pennsylvania, in a bag of beans, and tried to escape, but was overtaken and searched by the sheriff, who was not bright enough to look in the bean bag. "If he had looked" (says the narrator of this incident), "he would doubtless have found not only the plates, but a copy of Spaulding's manuscript."

After this failure of Smith's enemies to capture the golden plates, he and Cowdrey returned to their work, which was slowly accomplished. Meanwhile Smith added to his reputation by his first great miracle, performed on one Newell Knight, who was besieged by devils, his limbs and visage being distorted by pain. Smith commanded the evil spirits to leave him in the name of Christ, and Knight said, "I see them going right through the roof."

This established the fact, in the minds of certain people, that Smith had indeed a divine mission to perform, and that he had, as he affirmed, visits from angels and communications with them. But he was very poor, and so was Rigdon, or the world would have been stirred with Mormonism sooner.

Martin Harris, a farmer of the vicinity, a man of some considerable means, became acquainted with Smith, and being told by him that the Lord commanded him to assist in bringing out the book, yielded, as he afterward acknowledged, in the hope of making money. He made trouble afterward by telling what he had heard of the Spaulding manuscript in connection with Mormonism, and, on that account, was denied certain honors which he coveted.

In 1828 (as Abigail Harris, the sister-in-law of Martin Harris, testified in 1833), while Martin and his wife Lucy were at her house on a visit, during a conversation about the new faith's being devised by Smith, Lucy said it was "all a delusion;" to which her husband answered, "What if it is all a lie? Let me alone, and I'll make some money out of it."

The translation was suspended ten months by the abstraction of several sheets by Mrs. Harris, who could not be induced, by threat or cajolement, to give them up. In this way one hundred and sixteen pages of Smith's and Rigdon's work were lost, and the problem was how to replace them. Smith said he was denied the gift of translation, and eighteen months' labor was thus lost. Joseph had a "revelation." He was told that Satan had inspired Harris and his wife to get possession of the manuscript.

Mr. and Mrs. Harris separated, and divided their property, on her refusal to join the Mormons. She remained at Palmyra until her death; he followed Smith, and, after various misfortunes, died in want.

Professor Anthon, in a letter dated New York, February 17, 1834, relates that a paper presented to him as a transcript of the characters " on the golden plates" was, in fact, a singular scroll, having crooked characters in columns, which had evidently been arranged by some person who had before him at the time a book containing various alphabets, Greek, Hebrew, and Roman letters being inverted or placed sideways and placed in perpendicular columns. The whole ended in a rude delineation of a circle divided into various compartments, decked with strange marks copied " after the Mexican calendar given by Humboldt." During the period between September, 1829, and March of 1830, the " Book of Mormon" was published in the third story of a building in the main street of Palmyra, now known as Exchange Row.

Martin Harris contributed $3000 for this purpose. The foreman in the office at the time was Mr. Pomeroy Tucker, who has since written an interesting work on Mormonism. Major J. H. Gilbert (who is still living, and has contributed a valuable paper, No. 10, to be found in the Appendix) was a compositor in this office at the same time. This was at the printing establishment of E. B. Graudin, editor of the *Wayne Sentinel*.

Mr. Thurlow Weed, then editor of the *Anti-Masonic Inquirer* in Rochester, had already refused to do Smith's printing in 1829. The " copy" was on ruled paper and in Cowdrey's handwriting. Hyrum Smith brought it to the printing-office, producing it from a tightly buttoned overcoat. One day's supply was given at a time.

One David Whitmer of Richmond, Mo., it is said, has this manuscript copy. He is the sole survivor of the original "three witnesses," as they were called, who testified to the genuineness of the "Book of Mormon," and he may, it is believed, awaken "the saints" some time by publishing a fac-simile edition of the original translation.

Major Gilbert, mentioned above (as will be seen in the Appendix No. 9), has an unbound copy of the "Book of Mormon," which he kept, sheet by sheet, as it came from the press. The venerable owner and printer relates how the manuscript was brought to him little by little, badly spelled, grammatically imperfect, and without punctuation. He asked to be allowed to alter it. At first, he says, Smith was unwilling, but afterward permitted him to correct the proof, in the evening, as fast as it was printed, to facilitate its completion. In these corrections of proof Major Gilbert used some private marks, which he made with a blue pencil, which he says he could recognize at a glance.

The book was sold at first for $1.50 a copy, and soon the Smiths had money enough to buy a horse and other luxuries. Before Harris responded to Smith's proposal to raise funds to publish his "translation," two or three printing-houses in other towns had been visited for such purpose by Smith or his agents.

Mr. Thurlow Weed has testified to this circumstance, but said later that he was mistaken as to the year 1825; that it must have been two or three years later.

The publication of the book created an intense excitement in central and western New York. Certain questions of a religious nature were being agitated at the time, and the public mind was prepared for a new religious sensation. Smith's father and three brothers were his first converts. The first edition of the "Book of Mormon" was of several hundred pages, with an appendix, in which there was a statement signed by "three witnesses"—Oliver Cowdrey, David Whitmer and Martin Harris—who were at the time professed believers, and said, "We declare with words of soberness that an angel of God came down from heaven, and he brought and laid down before our eyes, that we beheld and saw, the plates and the engravings thereon." Several years after these "three witnesses" quarrelled with Smith, renounced Mormonism, and avowed the falsity of the above statement.

Soon after the book appeared, the church was organized at the house of Peter Whitmer in Fayette, Seneca Co., N. Y., with six members—Joseph Smith, Jr., Oliver Cowdrey, Hyrum Smith, Peter Whitmer, Jr., Samuel H. Smith, and David Whitmer.

Immediately the Holy Ghost fell on Cowdrey, and he "prophesied," and Smith "stood up and prophesied."

They had a happy time together, but, owing to the "unbelievers" about them, kept their baptism, ordination, and rejoicings a secret for a time.

These members were called "elders," Cowdrey baptizing Joseph Smith, and Smith baptizing the rest. They said it was eighteen hundred years to a day since the resurrection of Christ. They professed to believe it was the "Church of Christ" once more restored to the earth, holding the keys of authority, and power to bind, and loose, and to seal, on earth and in heaven.

The following Sunday Cowdrey preached his first sermon on this "dispensation," and "the principles of the gospel as revealed to Joseph." Mrs. Joe Smith was baptized, and given the new name of "Electra Cyria," or "Daughter of God."

The following June (1830) the first Mormon conference was held at Fayette, and there were thirty professed Mormons present, showing that converts to the new faith were not rapidly made ; but " the gifts" began to mainfest themselves. Smith was heard to say about this time, that he had " got everything ready to fix the fools."

The religious teachings of the " Book of Mormon" show the influence of the doctrinal questions that were being agitated in central New York in 1830—Calvinism, Universalism, Methodism, Millerism, Romanism and other forms of belief. Smith and Rigdon were inclined to be Millerites. They had at first vague ideas of the church they were about to establish. Millerism was attracting great attention at the time, so they settled on that doctrine, and that the Millennium was close at hand ; that the Indians were to be converted ; and that America was to be the final gathering-place of the saints, who were to assemble at the New Jerusalem, somewhere in the interior of the Continent. With the " Book of Mormon" as their text, they began to exhort.

Sidney Rigdon preached the first Mormon sermon in what is at present the Hall of the Young Men's Christian Association, at Palmyra, taking a text from " the first Book of Nephi"—part of the " Book of Mormon"— "*And the angel spake unto me, saying, These last records which thou hast seen among the Gentiles shall establish the truth of the first, which is of the twelve Apostles of the Lamb ; and shall make known the plain and precious things which have been taken away from them, and shall make known to all kindreds, tongues, and peoples that the Lamb of God is the eternal father and Saviour of the world, and that all men must come to Him, or they cannot be saved.*" The preacher ventured to try to establish the theory that the Bible and the "Book of Mormon" are one in importance and inspiration. He said that he was "God's Messenger," to proclaim this truth, etc.

This sermon made so much disturbance, that no "regular preaching" was afterward attempted by the Mormons in the immediate vicinity.

In June (1831) two elders were sent West to preach and found churches, wherever people would listen to them. They made numerous converts. Rigdon was already preparing the way, to tell of the new revelation in the vicinity of Mentor, Ohio. Palmyra being contiguous to Hartwick and Onondaga Valley, where the Spaulding manuscript was familiar to many people, the similarity of the two was discussed. Smith had a "revelation" that Palmyra was not a place for the "Saints" to prosper in, or be recognized, and he talked vaguely of the New Jerusalem in the West, and announced that it was time for the faithful to remove with him to Kirtland, Ohio, that locality having been agreed upon between himself and Rigdon; and so the Mormons made "The First Hegira" in their tragical pilgrimage to the West— a tedious journey in 1832—as they moved onward in wagons, carrying their household goods with them. Smith was already called a "prophet." His family followed him.

On this journey to Ohio a sister of Joseph was delivered of a lifeless female child, which, before its birth, it had been foretold would astonish the Gentile world as a second advent of a "triune humanity." The mother was unmarried, and the birth of the babe was to be miraculous; but it became pretty well understood that Rigdon was its father.

In the year of the first Hegira, 1831, the "work" had extended over several of the States, and a large number of converts had been made by the captivating and fiery eloquence of Cowdrey, Rigdon, Orley P. Pratt, and others; the more intelligent and the better educated in the cause had been sent out for that purpose.

These missionaries had no compensation, and this was one secret of their successful preachings. They braved every danger, "faced a frowning world," rejoiced in tribulation, blessed the saints, cursed their enemies, and sang and shouted Glory Hallelujah!

There had been as yet no whisper of polygamy. The Mormons were generally hated, but increased with astonishing rapidity after the year 1830.

They were a community which had all goods in common, and this fact threw a fascination over the new faith to thousands of uneducated and illiterate people. They heard scriptural expressions used by the leaders, and had but a vague idea of what it was they professed; there was a novelty about the movement that captivated them, and they were willing to be led on by insinuating men.

In the year 1832 Smith professed to have had seventy-five "visions" or "revelations." As the analysis of the "Book of Mormon" will show, it is merely a narrative of a people who in an early age inhabited America, its whole construction being Hebraic, and a servile copy of that of the Spaulding manuscript. There was no instruction in it for the conduct of the "Latter-Day Saints." At first neither Smith nor Rigdon, nor their immediate followers, knew what spiritual commands they required. But as events developed their needs, the angel Moroni, the same who delivered the golden plates, appeared to Smith from time to time, until he was killed at Nauvoo in 1846.

It is a remarkable coincidence that the "Book of Mormon" was printed fourteen years after " The Manuscript Found" was written by Solomon Spaulding at Conneaut, and it was fourteen years from the time the Mormons left Palmyra for " Sheinar," as they called Kirtland, to the time of Smith's death.

Some of the people who remember Smith at Palmyra have described him as given to strong drink, and to have been " thoroughly disreputable." Mr. Thurlow Weed remembers his personal appearance in 1830, and says: " He was tall and awkward in his manner, showed his low origin, and was impudent and bold." At one time Smith affirmed that he was as good as " Jesus Christ," and he was given to showing his abundant self-esteem and egotism on all occasions.

Of the many reminiscences of the Mormons in Palmyra, is that of the trick that Stephen H. Harding, since Governor of Utah, when a mischievous lad, played on one Calvin Stoddard, who was a convert of Joseph's, and felt he " had a call " to preach the new faith. One dark, stormy night Harding rapped thrice on Stoddard's doorstep, and cried in a deep, sepulchral voice : " Calvin Stoddard, the angel of the Lord commands that before another going down of the sun thou shalt go forth among the people and preach the gospel of Nephi, or thy wife shalt be a widow and thy children orphans, and thy dust shalt be cast to the four winds of heaven."

Stoddard no longer hesitated as to his duty, but joined " the new faith," so ridiculed at the time, but which has since become such a mischievous power.

CHAPTER IV.

Sketch of Sidney Rigdon—Interview with General and Mrs. Garfield at Mentor, Ohio—Description of the Mormon Temple at Kirtland. — Interview with General and Mrs. Garfield at Mentor in 1880, concerning the Mormons.—Description of the Mormon Temple at Kirtland, Ohio.

SIDNEY RIGDON was born in Alleghany Co., Penn. He had a fair English education, as well as a knowledge of Latin, Greek, and Hebrew. At an early age he was a printer by trade, and is known to have been in Conneaut, Ohio, at the time Spaulding read his "Manuscript Found" to his neighbors. Major Gilbert is of the opinion that Rigdon took notes on such occasions for after use.

Everybody who saw this intelligent, well-educated, and erratic young printer, then and later in life, was impressed with his unusual ability and capacity for trickery; and it is easy to believe the report that he followed or preceded Spaulding to Pittsburg, knowing all his plans, in order to obtain his manuscript, or to copy it, while it was in Patterson's printing-house—an easy thing to do, as the fact of the manuscript being left carelessly in the office for months is not questioned.

Mr. Spaulding (as already stated) told his wife and intimates in the last years of his life that a young printer in Patterson's office, named Rigdon, had copied his manuscript while it was there; *but he never said that he stole the original copy.* Spaulding died in 1816. In 1817 or 1818 Rigdon, when about twenty-three or twenty-four years of age, became an orthodox preacher, but soon gave utterance to strange doctrines, which were recognized later as derived from Spaulding's manuscript. He wandered about through the interior and northern part of Pennsylvania, preaching here and there, as opportunity afforded, and then abandoned the practice, as he said "to study the Bible."

In this interval he met Joseph Smith, as it is believed, through the ubiquitous tin peddler, Orley B. Pratt. For two years he dogged the footsteps of Smith, was frequently in Palmyra and its vicinity, and was the master mind in the preparations for this "Peeker" and money-digger in the discovery of the golden plates in Cummorah Hill.

While these preparations were being slowly made, through lack of funds, Rigdon became a Campbellite preacher at Mentor, Ohio.

Mr. F. Rudolph, father of Mrs. Garfield (see Appendix No. 11), knew Sidney Rigdon very well, and from him the statement comes that "during the winter previous to the appearance of the 'Book of Mormon' Rigdon was in the habit of spending weeks away from his home, going no one knew where, and that he often appeared very preoccupied, and would indulge in dreamy, imaginative talk, which puzzled those who listened." When the "Book of Mormon" appeared, and Rigdon joined in the advocacy of the new religion, the suspicion was at once aroused that he was one of the framers of the new doctrines, and probably was not ignorant of the authorship of the "Book of Mormon."

Rigdon was versatile in his gifts, had a keen wit, was shrewd, given to discussion on theological and scientific topics, and was considered wily and unprincipled.

The followers of this remarkable man were now being

prepared for some new *ism*, and his preaching was talked of far and near.

Of course the excitement concerning Joe Smith and his new Mormon doctrines at Palmyra, and through central and western New York, spread into northern Ohio; and when "The First Hegira" took place, in 1832, and the Mormons were at Conneaut, Rigdon was prepared to meet them and to affect to be converted to the new faith.

Near his residence in Kirtland there had been for some time previous a few families belonging to his congregation who had formed themselves into a community or common-stock society; they had become fanatical, and were daily looking for some wonderful event to take place in the world. They were prepared to embrace Mormonism, or any other *ism*. Seventeen of these people believed the whole story which was related to them of the finding of the plates, and were all baptized in one night.

At this time Rigdon said he had never been satisfied in his religious yearnings, and that at night he had often been unable to sleep, walking and praying for more light and comfort in his religion. But while in the midst of this agony he heard of the revelations to Joe Smith, and his soul suddenly found peace, as they filled all his aspirations. In 1831 the Mormons settled at Kirtland, Lake Co., three miles from Mentor, and here Rigdon joined them. He had no property to offer them, but from this time openly advocated their doctrines, preaching to crowds of people who gathered to hear his eloquent discourse, and over whom he seemed to have a wonderful power, and such influence that it is felt to the present day in that vicinity. A Presbyterian clergyman of Painesville, Ohio, informed the writer in November, 1880, that all the northern part of the State is permeated with the doctrines of the early Mormons. A graphic account of

Rigdon's power as an advocate of his new faith has been made by Judge John Barr, of Cuyahoga Co., Ohio.

In 1830, while Rigdon and Cowdrey were preparing the way for Mormonism, he was at Mayfield, not far from Kirtland, and one Sunday morning went to hear Rigdon and Cowdrey on the revelations of Mormonism. The roads were crowded with people going in the same direction. The services were held in a church. Cowdrey, a very eloquent man, opened with prayer, and gave an account of the finding of the golden plates of Nephi. Rigdon followed with an account of his own conversion. He was seemingly very much affected ; was listened to with rapt attention ; and at the close of his harangue very earnestly inquired if any one desired to come forward to be baptized. Only one man, a disreputable old fellow, named Cahoon, who had been some time a member of a Shaker community in the vicinity, and had lived on public charity in general, came forward for immersion.

This was afterward performed in a clear pool of the Chagrin River, near a bridge, at two o'clock in the afternoon of the same day, a great number of people gathering to witness the ceremony. Rigdon stood in the pool, which was shallow, and after a suitable address and prayer Cahoon came forward and was duly immersed.

Rigdon then, while still standing in the water, made a wonderfully eloquent exhortation. The crowd became greatly affected, and he asked converts to come and be baptized in the new faith, thirty accepting the invitation, while the preacher continued his discourse. While this exciting scene was transpiring, Judge Barr says the faces of the crowd expressed the most intense emotion. Mr. Card, afterward prosecuting attorney of Cuyahoga County, was with him, and was so affected by Rigdon's talk that he begged his friend to lead him away. "He was so pale," says Judge Barr, "I thought he would faint, although naturally a stoical man ; and after we were a mile away on our return, during which time we had not exchanged a word, he said, 'If you had not been there, I should have gone into the water ; the impulse was irresistible.'"

Rigdon often swooned, really or in affectation, which added to the impression he made on an easily excited multitude. When the Mormons went to Kirtland Rigdon said it was "the border of the inheritance of the Saints, which extended to the Pacific."

One thousand Mormons, the converts of Rigdon and Pratt, greeted Smith on his arrival at Kirtland. People from every part of "the lake region" flocked there, "ecstatics," men and women, falling to the floor groaning, and weeping, and pointing toward the heavens, to the "cloud of witnesses" they saw, uttering strange words, sometimes rushing out of doors and running to the fields to mount stumps, whence they gesticulated wildly, or to pick up stones on which a message was written, which disappeared as soon as it was deciphered.

Some writer has said that "Rigdon's ardor at this time was equal to Smith's genius."

This "outpouring of the spirit" did not please the prophet, so he ordered moderation, and said these manifestations were not the work of the spirit, and cautioned the faithful to beware. In 1832 Brigham Young, a native of Vermont, joined the Mormons at Kirtland, and was ordained an elder.

At a conference of elders, on May 3, 1833, the name of "Mormons" was repudiated, and that of "Latter-Day Saints" was adopted. The first presidency consisted of Smith, Rigdon, and F. G. Williams.

In May, 1835, the first missionaries, from the "Twelve

Apostles," went forth to foreign lands to make proselytes, among whom being Orson Hyde, Brigham Young, and Heber C. Kimball; Rigdon remained at Kirtland, and the same year issued a volume which he called "The Book of Doctrines and Covenants," and "Lectures on Faith," both of which were immediately adopted by the converts.

A professor of Hebrew having joined them, all the male adults studied that language industriously.

The Mormons remained at Kirtland seven years. Rigdon was considered the ablest man of the whole membership. At one time he said he was commanded by a vision to visit Queen Victoria, and to hurl her from her throne if she refused his gospel.

In 1837 he was president of a "wild-cat" bank at Kirtland, which he originated (Smith being cashier), and he manipulated a great many schemes to obtain money and goods both in Cleveland and in New York, the bubble bursting with loss and annoyance to many sufferers. Both Smith and Rigdon, after being tarred and feathered, fled to an advance settlement of Mormons called "Far West," in Missouri.

In 1840 the Mormons moved to Nauvoo, Ill. In 1844, when Smith was killed, Rigdon was tricked out of his leadership by Brigham Young; and, refusing to recognize his authority, was excommunicated and delivered to the devil, "to be buffeted in the flesh for a thousand years." After his departure from Nauvoo the Danite band was ordered to "*fan*" him and others who left to keep their mouths closed; also to intimidate members of the community who were inclined to desert.

In three years after Rigdon had openly joined the Mormons at Kirtland, Mormon societies were established in Canada, Missouri, Illinois, Ohio, Virginia, New York, Vermont, New Hampshire, Massachusetts, and in nearly all of the Northern, Middle, and some of the Southern States.

At one time during his residence at Kirtland, Alexander Campbell, his former associate and patron, challenged him to a public debate, in which he declared he would show the shameless pretension and manifest imposture of the Mormon scheme; but Rigdon prudently declined.

Rigdon once said that Kirtland was to be the eastern border of the " promised land," *and from thence it would extend to the Pacific Ocean.*

On this land the New Jerusalem was to be built, the City of Refuge, where all true Mormons were to assemble, to escape the destruction of the world, which was shortly to take place.

After his expulsion from Nauvoo he returned to Pittsburg, led a life of utter obscurity and vagrancy, wandering at times through the scenes where he had formerly preached with so much power, and dying at Friendship, a village in Alleghany Co., N. Y., July 14, 1876. Even in his extreme old age he is described by several persons as being remarkable in his personal appearance, intelligence, and memory.

The statement, that Rigdon with Smith's assistance prepared the plates to be used later at Cummorah Hill, while at Great Bend, Penn., is undoubtedly true. The absence of both individuals from their accustomed haunts was substantiated by several persons familiar with the matter at the time, and by the Rev. Peter Bridgeman, who died a few years since at Cortlandt, N. Y. Smith, too, at the time (1826) was heard to use the words "Mormon" and "Nephi" before he met Rigdon, proving his previous acquaintance with the Spaulding manuscript.

No one believes that Joe Smith was capable of formulating the "Book of Mormon" from "The Manuscript

Found." He was merely the tool of the very clever and unscrupulous Rigdon in this extraordinary and nefarious scheme.

During the visit to Ohio to collect material for this work, the author had an interesting interview with General and Mrs. Garfield at their home in Mentor. Dr. H. M. Field, of the New York *Evangelist*, had provided a letter of introduction. It was just after General Garfield's election to the Presidency, and happened to be his birthday. There was a family gathering, and at the mid-day dinner, and afterward in the drawing-room, of the general, his wife, his mother, and an elderly physician, long a resident of the neighborhood, and all being familiar with Rigdon, the Mormons, and Mormonism, the talk naturally ran in that direction.

The general was greatly interested in the account of the visit to Gibsonburg; he said his farm had once been owned by a Mormon, that the Mormons gathered at the village of Mentor before going to Kirtland, three miles away, and that Rigdon lived long in the neighborhood.

Mrs. Garfield repeated some reminiscences of her father's (Mr. F. Rudolph) in connection with Rigdon, and of his being a member of his church and studying Greek with him. General and Mrs. Garfield, as is well known, belonged to the Campbellite Church, in which Rigdon was in early life a minister.

The general related an anecdote of Joe Smith. He had been preaching at Kirtland some doctrine (a hint of polygamy) that was a surprise to the people of the neighborhood. The same night several men went to his house, dragged him out of bed, tarred and feathered him, and rode him on a rail; and, according to a Mormon historian, "his spirit left his body, but afterward regained possession." A child who was in bed with

Smith was also dragged out, and the exposure caused its death.

This created a sympathy for the prophet for the time being. The Kirtland Temple, the general said, is owned at present by Joe Smith's son, a number of Mormons still residing near it, the " true Mormons," or Josephites, as they call themselves, who profess to abhor polygamy.

Both the general and Mrs. Garfield were sure that Rigdon returned to his professed belief in the Campbellite doctrines after he left the Mormons in Illinois, and that he preached again in that neighborhood.

When General Garfield was at Salt Lake City, on a return trip from California, he visited Brigham Young and asked how he happened to choose that place for settlement.

"Why," said Young, "we were travelling along, and I was lying in a wagon, and all of a sudden I called out, 'Halt! the Lord says "stop here;"' and there on that hill" (pointing to one) " an angel of the Lord stood, and pointed down this valley, and said, ' Stay there.' "

"While we were talking" (continued the General) " the train I was coming away in commenced to move, and Young called to the engineer, stretching out his hand, ' Wait awhile for General Garfield,' and it did wait." Brigham Young he considered a man of immense will power and great intelligence.

General Garfield expressed his utter abhorrence of the Mormons and their doctrines, and hinted at his future course concerning them after his inauguration.

Kirtland is three miles from Mentor, on a branch of the Chagrin River, and twenty-two miles east from Cleveland, in a remarkably fine country.

The Mormons on their arrival purchased a square mile, which was laid out in half-acre lots; and in addition they bought a number of farms, the "church farm" being described as half a mile down in an exquisitely beautiful valley.

They evidently expected to remain there, as they erected a number of substantial houses and their beautiful Temple, which Smith called "the School of the Prophets."

The advent of so many strangers in the midst of a quiet village was a matter of wonder to the hitherto peaceful residents, and they looked on in astonishment, as did all northern Ohio, when the Mormons built their church, which was commenced in 1832 and finished in 1836, the entire cost being $40,000.

The site occupied measures eighty feet by sixty. On the eastern side is a square tower, one hundred and twenty-five feet in height, which is surmounted by a domed belfry. There are two lofty stories above a basement, and the shingled roof is relieved by a number of dormer windows.

The architectual proportions are good, and the building has but slight resemblance to the meeting-houses common to the rural portion of Ohio, the windows being Gothic, and filled with small panes of glass, thus affording a pleasing contrast to the solid walls of stone and stucco. There are thirty Gothic, three Venetian, three dormer, one circular, and two square windows. The dome of the steeple is one hundred and ten feet high, and the bell ninety feet from the ground.

Although the edifice is fifty years old, it is in good preservation, considering the neglect with which it has been treated, and it might be very easily restored to its former beauty. It is at present somewhat picturesque, with its walls streaked with iron-rust, the moss-grown shingles, the eaves filled with wasp and bird nests, and the chimneys betokening a mild decay. Many tourists visit the temple. The keys are kept by an old woman named Electry Stratton, whose father was a Mormon, and she charges a small fee for showing it to visitors.

Approaching the temple through the yard surrounding it, an inscription is seen high up on the front wall in golden letters upon a white tablet, which reads : " House of the Lord, built by the Church of Christ, 1834." The temple faces to the east. The entire front of the first story of the building consists of solid green doors, which open into a vestibule that terminates on each side in a semi-circular stairway. A flood of light enters the vestibule through a great square window above it.

At the right, under the stairway, is the temple "Register Room," containing a record of visitors. On the left, under the stairs, is the library. The ladies' entrance is on the right, the gentlemen's on the left. Between these doors are the inscriptions : *Laus Deo. Cruxmila anchora. Magno est Veritas et prevalebit.*

The whole of the first story is occupied by the auditorium. The windows at each end are very beautiful, and a row of wooden pillars at the sides gives the effect of galleries on entering the room. The space between the rows is arched toward the centre of the ceiling. One of the pillars contains a windlass, which, in the occupancy of the place by the Mormons, controlled some canvas curtains from above—a large curtain that fell in grooves between the high-backed pews, in such a manner as to separate the men from the women—while the smaller curtain was at right angles with the other, and when desirable it could be lowered, so as to divide the men and women into separate class-rooms. Thus the auditorium could be quartered, or halved, and made either eastward or westward, by changing the movable benches from one side of the pews to the other. The pulpits are in clusters of threes, in three tiers, at either end of the room, and are very richly carved. The eastern cluster was devoted to the "Avonic Priesthood," including the "Levitical Priesthood," and used in the administration of the temporal affairs of the church. Each of the three pulpits in the upper tier has three letters on the front, "B. P. A.," meaning "Bishop Presiding over Avonic Priesthood." The middle tier has the letters "P. A. P.," "Presiding Avonic Priesthood." The lower tier has the letters "P. A. T.," "Presiding Avonic Teacher." The smaller pulpit below is labelled "P. A. D.," "Presiding Avonic Doorkeeper."

The pulpits at the west end are built up against an outer window, having red and white glass in the arched transom. These were used by the spiritual leaders, or the "Melchisedec Priesthood," Joe Smith's seat being in the highest tier. This tier of pulpits is marked "M. P. C.," "Melchisedec President of Councillors;" "M. P. H.," "Melchisedec Presiding High-Priest." The lower tier is "M. H. P.," "Melchisedec High-Priest." Curtains were arranged so as to divide the priesthood, as well as congregation, and they could at will shut themselves in for consultation, but could not hide themselves from their superiors in ecclesiastical rank.

Remnants of these movable curtains are still hanging. A small desk before and below the Melchisedec pulpit has three letters on it, "M. P. E.," "Melchisedec Presiding Elder."

The letters are made of red curtain calico, and the desk, as well as all the pulpits above, are now covered with calico; but in their days of splendor rich velvet draperies enhanced the beauty of the carved wood, and the lettering on the pulpits was in gold.

The gilt mouldings have all been carried off by relic-hunters, but there are still several mottoes on the walls which remain intact, such as "No cross, no crown," "The Lord reigneth, let the people rejoice," "Great is our Lord and of great power." "Holiness to the Lord" is written over the ten Melchisedec pulpits.

The auditorium will hold six hundred people. Under Rigdon's, Pratt's, and Cowdrey's exhortations, as well as Smith's, relays of people occupied it in a single service. Smith was in the habit of saying from his high pulpit, "The truth is good enough without dressing up; but Brother Rigdon will now proceed to dress it up." The high pews in the corners were for "the best singers in Israel."

A story is told how a crazy woman would get into one of them and blow a horn when "the Saints" displeased her. In the upper story is a second auditorium, very similar to the one described, only smaller and lower, which was used as a school for the prophets. Here Latin and Greek were taught under the tutorship of Rigdon and his assistant professor of languages. The desks are no longer there, but the places they occupied are shown by marks on the floor.

One of the pillars in this room bears a remarkable inscription to this effect, "The Salt Lake Mormons."

When Joseph Smith was killed on June 27, 1844, Brigham Young assumed the leadership of the church, telling the people, in the winter of 1846, that "all the God they wanted was him," and "all the Bible they wanted was his heart." He led or drove about two thousand people to Utah in 1847, starting for Upper California and landing at Salt Lake, where, in 1852, he presented polygamic revelation to the people. The true church remained disorganized until 1860, when

Joseph Smith took the leadership or presidency of the church at Amboy, Ill.

"We (thirty thousand) have no affiliation with the Mormons whatever. They are to us an obsolete people, working all manner of abomination before God and man. We are no part or parcel of them in any sense whatever. Let this be distinctly understood. We are not Mormons. Truth is truth wherever it is found."

In the vestibule of the temple there is a photograph of Joseph Smith, Jr., and over it is written, "Joseph Smith, Jr., M. P. C., President of the Reorganized Church of I. C. and L. D. S." The garret of the temple was used formerly as a series of school-rooms for the young Mormons. There are mysterious closets, or, as Mr. F. G. Mather (in *Lippincott's Magazine* for August, 1880) calls them, "cubby-holes," in several parts of the building. In one of them was kept the body of "Joseph the son of Jacob," a roll of papyrus in his hand announcing this fact to the Saints.

When the temple at Kirtland was dedicated there was a great assemblage there, the Mormons spending the day in fasting and prayer. The members of the priesthood washed their bodies with pure water, and perfumed themselves with *eau-de-cologne*. They also washed each other's feet, and anointed each other with holy oil, pronouncing a benediction in the name of the Lord. In the evening they met to receive the long-expected endowment, when they first broke their fast by what they called the "Lord's Supper," in which they ate a light wheaten bread, and freely partook of wine, the prophet telling them it would not hurt them. A spirit of prophecy ensued in which they blessed their friends and cursed their enemies. An eye-witness of this strange scene says of it: "If I should be so unfortunate as to go to the regions of despair, I never expect to hear language more awful or more becoming the infernal pit."

In 1835 Smith issued a command at Kirtland, that his three or four hundred elders "should seek learning, study the best books, and get a knowledge of kingdoms, countries, and languages;" and a Jew by the name of Seixas was hired to teach languages.

The Temple has been used within a few years as an Odd Fellows' lodge. At the present time it is owned by Joseph Smith, Jr., and a Mr. Fortescue, who derived their title from a Mr. Huntley, a purchaser under a mortgage sale against the Prophet. This Joseph Smith, Jr., is a son of the Prophet; he was born at Kirtland in 1832, and was twelve years of age when his father was shot at Nauvoo. He has been a farmer, school-teacher, or director and justice of the peace. He has been the editor of *The Latter Day Saints' Herald* at Plano, Ill.

When Smith, the Prophet, and Rigdon fled in the night from Kirtland, the Mormons were divided into Rigdonites, Strangites, and various sects, and scattered to several localities; but a few families remained, of whom some aged members are still living who are full of reminiscences of their remarkable experiences in early life in connection with the beginning of Mormonism.

The Methodists at Kirtland now use what was the Theological Seminary of the Mormons for their church, and the residences of Rigdon and Smith are well preserved and are close to the quaint edifice described, for which the Prophet said he had a special revelation as to plan and architecture.*

---

* Several Mormons now resident in Utah who remember the dedication of the Temple at Kirtland, declare that angels were seen in the auditorium, and that a babe two months old cried out: "Glory Hallelujah!"

CHAPTER V.

Interview with D. P. Hurlburt at Gibonburg, Ohio, and with E. D. Howe, at Painesville, Ohio, in 1880.

In the year 1878 Mrs. McKinstry gave a gentleman residing in Utah, who is gathering material for an elaborate history of Mormonism, permission to question Dr. Hurlburt concerning the Spaulding manuscript. He made no response, although there was abundant evidence that he received the request. It is also known that he received other requests of the same character, which he has never acknowledged.

In 1834 Mrs. Davison heard that Hurlburt sold the manuscript to the Mormons for a sum of money, which he used in purchasing the farm near Gibsonburg, Ohio (about twelve miles from Fremont), where he now resides, and that the Mormons burned the manuscript at Conneaut. A second report was to the effect that Hurlburt sold it with the sworn agreement that it should not be given to the world until after his death. There are circumstances which support both theories; but the author's opinion, after a careful study of the matter, is, that Hurlburt made a copy of the original manuscript, which he sold to E. D. Howe, of Painesville, to use in writing the book "Mormonism Unveiled," and sold the original to the Mormons, who destroyed it. The life of Hurlburt since his return from his errand of duplicity to Munson shows conclusively that he wishes to hide himself from the world, and that he is burdened with a secret which he does not intend shall come to light through any act or revelation of his own.

THE INTERVIEW WITH DR. HURLBURT.

In August of 1880 the author had an article published in *Scribner's Magazine* on the "Book of Mormon," and in the November following visited Dr. Hurlburt at his home, near Gibsonburg, Ohio, in company with Oscar Kellogg, Esq., of Norwalk, a well-known lawyer of the vicinity. (Appendix, see Mr. Kellogg's letter, No. 7.) From notes written immediately after this visit, while staying in Mr. Kellogg's house, and while every detail and circumstance was fresh in the writer's mind, a description of the interview with Hurlburt will be here given.

In advance, it must be stated that Hurlburt had not the remotest anticipation of this visit, and that it was an entire surprise to him and his family. It was on November 13th, 1880, a cold, cheerless day, that Mr. Kellogg and myself made the journey from Fremont to Gibsonburg. A more forlorn country and worse roads it would be difficult to find in any portion of the United States; indeed, save for the telegraph wires and a line of railway that passes through Gibsonburg, one could imagine one's self at the antipodes, while traversing the melancholy twelve miles between Fremont and Dr. Hurlburt's house, which is a mile from the railway station at Gibsonburg.

Driving up to the front of a small white-painted cottage some distance from the road, we alighted without attracting attention. It was noon-time, and, stepping on the piazza, we heard within sounds that gave evidence of the midday meal and conversation. Rapping at the door, it was opened by an old woman, who had just risen from a table, where sat an old man, a young girl, and a young man, who were still engaged in eating. Advancing into the room, after excuses for so intruding,

I asked the old man, who, with the others, now rose from the table:

"Is this Dr. D. P. Hurlburt?"

"Yes," he replied.

I gave him a letter, saying that it was from the Hon. John Rice, of Fremont; and as he seemed very much agitated, I inquired:

"Shall I read it to you?"

"Yes," he again replied.

The letter mentioned the writer as seeking information regarding Mormonism. In short, it was a letter introducing Mr. Kellogg and myself, written by Dr. Hurlburt's physician, Dr. Rice, who had said to me that Hurlburt was in a precarious condition of health, and whatever I had to ask of him had better not be delayed, and that I had better see him at once.

Dr. D. P. Hurlburt died in 1882, two years after the interview described.

By the time I began the letter we were all seated, save Hurlburt, who remained standing; and when I had finished reading he was shaking violently, as with palsy, and very greatly agitated. I was struck with his appearance. He was still a very handsome old man, even in his shabby clothing and amid his plain and homely surroundings, having a fine, ruddy complexion, expressive eyes, long, abundant gray hair, and a figure of excellent proportions. He looked at us both curiously, then with difficulty burst out:

"I don't know what has made folks so curious about Mormonism lately. I think it is an article in a magazine published last summer. Why, I haven't heard anything about the Mormons in forty years till now; and there's a man named Craig, in Alleghany City, and one named Cobb, in Salt Lake City (above alluded to), and another named Patterson, in Pittsburg, all writing to me about a manuscript they say I got from Mrs. Davison, at Munson, Mass., in 1834; I have not answered one of these folks."

"Well, Mr. Hurlburt, did you get the manuscript from Mrs. Davison?" I asked.

"Yes," he replied, shaking still more violently— "yes, I got one she gave me an order for."

"Mr. Hurlburt" (for I dropped the Dr.), I remarked, getting up, and looking him steadily in the eye, "I am the person who wrote the magazine article you have just mentioned, the great-niece of Solomon Spaulding and the granddaughter of William H. Sabine, who gave the order for 'The Manuscript Found,' which you presented to Mrs. Davison at Munson, Mass., in 1834."

He started, appeared to be alarmed, trembled excessively, and after a little gasped out in a faint voice:

"Is that so?"

Mrs. Hurlburt, a sweet-faced, sad-eyed old woman, who had admitted Mr. Kellogg and myself, came close to me, and, gently stretching out her hand toward me, said:

"Well, we will tell you what we know; we are willing to tell you."

"I hope you will," I replied, "as I have come from New York on purpose to see you on this subject, and if there is any one who ought to have the truth concerning 'The Manuscript Found,' it is our family."

Then I turned to Hurlburt, and asked:

"Are you the Hurlburt who visited Mrs. Davison, my great-aunt, in 1834?"

"Yes," he replied.

"Did you get 'The Manuscript Found' at her order in Hartwick, N. Y., from Jerome Clark?"

"Yes; I got what they said was Spaulding's manuscript."

"For what purpose?"

"I was sent there by a man named E. D. Howe, of Painesville, Ohio. He wrote a book called 'Mormonism Unveiled,' and he wanted to compare the Spaulding manuscript with the 'Book of Mormon.'"

"Did he think Mrs. Davison had the original manuscript?"

"Yes, he thought so."

"Did you give him the manuscript you got at Hartwick?"

"Yes, I did."

Here Mrs. Hurlburt, who listened intently to this talk, went to a bureau and found a letter, which she handed to me, Hurlburt helping her to do so. I closely watched and listened to see if there was anything said between them. Their heads and hands were in close proximity as they bent over the drawer; and although I could hear nothing distinctly, I believe and always shall believe that he conveyed instructions to his wife as to her further conduct in the matter.

The letter was from E. D. Howe, of Painesville, the aged author of the book "Mormonism Unveiled." Its purport was that he had seen the magazine article alluded to, and after a criticism on the statements made in it, he told Hurlburt that the manuscript which he (Hurlburt) had given to him, in 1834, was burned, with other of his papers, in his office, etc.

After reading it I again looked significantly at both Mr. and Mrs. Hurlburt, and asked:

"Do you believe the manuscript was burned?"

"Well, he says it was," Hurlburt replied, greatly disturbed.

" Was it Spaulding's manuscript that was burned ?"

Hurlburt waited a moment before answering, his wife looking at him with a pleading, sad expression of countenance.

" Mrs. Davison thought it was ; but when I just peeped into it here and there, and saw the names Mormon, Maroni, Lamenite, Nephi, I thought it was all nonsense ; why, if it had been the real one, I could have sold it for $3000 ; but I just gave it to Howe because it was of no account."

" Had you any right to do so ? You borrowed it, solemnly promising to return it to Mrs. Davison."

He grew still more disturbed, and replied :

" Well, I forgot most all about it."

" Did you intend to return it ?" I asked, very slowly. Instead of answering, he told his wife to bring him another letter from the bureau, a kind of statement which he had made to send to Mr. Patterson, of Pittsburg, but would give to me. After reading it, I remarked :

" Then you know the history of the Spaulding manuscript ?"

" Oh, yes, all about it !"

" Were you a Mormon ?"

" No," he quickly answered.

" Yes, you were," interposed his wife.

" Well, I suppose I was about a year," said Hurlburt, reluctantly.

" Were you at Conneaut in 1834, at the time the Mormons met there and had their meeting ?"

" Why, certainly," he replied ; " the Mormons sent me to get the manuscript from Mrs. Davison."

" I thought you said Howe sent you."

" Well, when I found the manuscript amounted to nothing, I gave it to Howe," he replied, looking guilty.

Mr. Kellogg, who had been observing everything in our conversation, but letting me (as we had agreed before entering the house) do the talking, here said :

"Mr. Hurlburt, this lady has come a great distance to see you, and you ought to tell her what she desires to learn."

"You're a lawyer, I guess," remarked the old man, eying Mr. Kellogg.

"Yes, from Norwalk; my name is Oscar Kellogg, and I think you were once on the jury in a case I tried."

"Well, I thought I had seen you when you came in; is this lady a relative of yours?"

"Yes, my wife's cousin; she is staying with us."

"And you came over here from Norwalk with her to see me?"

"Yes, I came to help her, if she needs my assistance."

"Mr. Hurlburt," I resumed, "do you know where 'The Manuscript Found' is at the present time?"

The old lady went close to Hurlburt, touched his shaking arms, looked up in his face, and said:

"Tell her what you know."

His face became perfectly scarlet, and his trembling increased. He turned (for during this entire interview he stood up, a most pitiable object in his infirmity, as he became more and more agitated, in the evidently fierce conflict he was going through not to betray himself or to allow his wife to unburden her heart of her knowledge), and looked at both Mr. Kellogg and myself, and almost screamed:

"Why, you must be crazy to ask such a question. Did I not say I gave it to E. D. Howe, and he says in the letter you read from him it was burned up in his printing house. Why, lady, if I knew where it was, I would give $1000 and my farm besides for it."

"You know," I laughingly said, "the report is you were paid $300 by the Mormons for the manuscript, and with that money bought this farm."

He smiled for the first time, and replied:

"Why, the Mormons hated me; they threatened me. I had a fight with Joe Smith, and had to have him bound to keep the peace with me."

"Why did they hate you?"

"Well, it was something about that book, 'Mormonism Unveiled.'"

"Mr. Hurlburt, you retain your memory perfectly?"

"Yes, I'm right up here" (pointing to his head), "but this trembling goes to my heart. I shall go pretty soon."

He brought me a picture of himself, taken ten years ago.

"Please let me have it," I said, holding it in my hand, hoping to bring it away with me for further use.

"No; I'll have it copied for you," he answered, evidently divining my meaning.

"You know," I continued, "you are and will be remembered; your part in this Spaulding matter makes you known. You cannot help it, and the world may desire to see how you look."

He had grown calmer, but this speech of mine, by which, with a little flattery, I had hoped to gain my object, seemed to agitate him again greatly, and he said:

"No, I don't care to be known at all; I will write to you, and help you to get facts about Mormonism; but I don't want to be talked about."

Making one more effort to get at the truth, I said, very earnestly:

"Oh, Mr. Hurlburt, it all lies in a nutshell, and you

can crack it. Do you think Solomon Spaulding wrote the story from which the Mormons made their book?"

"Yes; and no question about it."

"Well, then, where is the manuscript?"

"I think it was copied by Rigdon, and he kept the original, and Mrs. Davison had the copy."

"But Mrs. McKinstry has sworn that her mother had what her father knew to be the original; and if the exact copy, it would have answered Howe's purpose."

Hulburt seemed nonplussed; he remained quiet, as if entirely unable or unwilling to continue the argument, and his wife, who was constantly watching him, said, with a meaning look at him:

"Why, don't you see the one he got from Mrs. Davison wa'n't no good?"

"Why did he not return it, then?"

"Well, Howe said he would; but then it got burned up."

As a final experiment, I said:

"There is a man in Illinois who is said to have the original manuscript, and that you, Mr. Hurlburt, sold it to him with the promise he would not use it *in your lifetime.*"

The old man again screamed:

"'Tain't so; it is not the original one."

Then, seeming to see that he had somewhat betrayed himself, he turned to Mr. Kellogg with:

"You said you knew this lady."

"Yes," replied Mr. Kellogg, "she is just who she represents herself to be."

"Well," said Hurlburt, turning in a sort of a defiant way to me, "if I talk all day I can't tell you any more; but I'll write to you."

The interview was over evidently. Both Mr. and

Mrs. Hurlburt asked us to have dinner, and the old lady urged us again and again to stay over night, "to talk it over by and by." I have since deeply regretted that we did not do so, as it has occurred to me that she intended in some way to give me information, which she dared not give in the presence of her husband; but the old distrust of Hurlburt which Mrs. Davison had was so strong within me, that even with Mr. Kellogg's protection, and willingness to remain, I could not persuade myself to do so.

We two women stood a little apart, and she said:

"I'll write to you; give me your address; I'll tell you what *I* know."

After thanking her, I asked if she was Hurlburt's only wife when he was a Mormon. A little flush came into her pale cheeks, and she replied:

"Well, he wa'n't a Mormon long; and I was his first wife."

We had no further chance for private words; and, as Mr. Kellogg and I agreed after we left the house, Hurlburt assumed a triumphant expression as we bade them good-day. We further agreed in the impression that certainly they had well feigned a part they were so unexpectedly called upon to act; and that beyond a shadow of doubt Hurlburt, after getting the genuine Spaulding romance at Munson, destroyed it or saw it destroyed by the Mormons at Conneaut, in 1834, after his being paid for his share of this transaction.

I may add that it has been told me that the general impression at the time of this sale and afterward, which prevailed in the minds of those most familiar with the subject in Ohio, was that Hurlburt became a Mormon with the intention of making money, and that his mission to Munson was the culmination of his projects in that direction. Hurlburt sent me the statement he promised. (No. 8, in the Appendix.)

The reader will see it contradicts several of his verbal statements made in his own house, and it amounts, in fact, to nothing, being a studied and deliberate affair with which he hoped to satisfy me and other inquirers on the same subject.

INTERVIEW WITH E. D. HOWE.

After visiting Hurlburt, the author saw E. D. Howe, at Painesville, Ohio. He admitted writing the letter shown by Hurlburt, and said that a manuscript was given to him by Hurlburt, in 1834, which "*had no connection with Mormonism.*"

He agreed to give Hurlburt five hundred copies of his book ("Mormonism Unveiled"), which agreement he kept, and that was the last he ever saw of him.

The manuscript he received from Hurlburt he said was "lying around" his printing-office for twenty years; he "considered it of no account, and did not know what became of it."

I asked if he did not agree to return it to Mrs. Davison, to which he replied:

"Perhaps I did; but it wa'n't of no account, so I did not think of it."

"You used it in your 'Mormonism Unveiled'?"

"Well, yes; there it was of some use."

I then told him what Hurlburt had said of Howe's connection with the matter.

He grew very red in the face, and remarked:

"Well, Hurlburt is not to be relied on."

I asked if he would make a sworn statement that the words "Mormon, Maroni, Nephi, and Lamenite" were not in the manuscript which Hurlburt gave him by agreement.

"No, I will not swear to it; but I'll answer questions, and my word is as good as Hurlburt's any day."

"You ought, for your own sake, to make a statement to answer him."

He made an odd reply.

"Hurlburt was always an unreliable fellow; he went lecturing in this neighborhood."

"Mr. Howe, did you send Hurlburt to get 'The Manuscript Found'?"

"Yes, I did, and the idea was proposed to me by him."

"Do you think the manuscript was burned in your office?"

"I don't know; it got lost," he replied.

"The whole matter, then, is between you and Hurlburt. Is there a possibility that the original Spaulding manuscript will yet come to light?"

"No, I don't think so," he replied, earnestly; "the Mormons had too much at stake to let it exist."

"Then you think Hurlburt destroyed it?"

"I believe he had two manuscripts—the original one and another—the one he gave me, which had no resemblance to the 'Book of Mormon.'"

"Do you think Spaulding wrote a story from which Rigdon and Smith made the 'Book of Mormon'?"

"*Certainly* I *do*," emphasizing the words.

He then told me a little of Rigdon's life, which I will hereafter use. Mr. Howe is very old—nearly ninety—but certainly of sound mind and memory; and although he was seemingly agitated during our conversation, he was not more so than such an unexpected visit would naturally occasion any one to be under the same circumstances; and he carefully considered his answers before making them. An unmistakable expression of relief settled upon his countenance as the interview closed.

Upon making an inquiry in Painesville as to the character of the author of "Mormonism Unveiled," nothing of a very satisfactory nature was elicited from several highly respected citizens of the town. At best it was to the effect that Mr. Howe had always had the reputation of being a sharp-witted, shrewd man, and that his declining years had not robbed him of his predominating qualities.

A clergyman of Painesville, in speaking of the traces that Mormonism had left in that vicinity, remarked that "time alone would obliterate the demoralization that had followed in the wake of the Saints; that whole families were sceptics in religious faith who had been church members before their conversion to the doctrines advocated so eloquently by Sidney Rigdon and other Mormon preachers, and who had later apostatized."

A very remarkable circumstance occurred to the writer on the day following the interview with E. D. Howe, at his residence in Painesville. At midday, on reaching the railway station with the intention of proceeding to Conneaut, Ohio, that afternoon, I personally attended to checking the one large trunk I had with me at the time. It was an odd trunk as to its outward appearance, and had my initials distinctly printed on either end. As it was a way train, I settled myself as comfortably as possible by a window, and was reading until we reached the next station—in fact, until the train was just moving on; then, by chance looking up, I was amazed to see my trunk being wheeled away on a truck across the platform. The conductor was standing at the door on the platform of the car. I ran to him and shouted, "That is my trunk being taken away; do stop the train and get it again!"

"Your trunk!" he replied; "no, it cannot be. You ladies always fancy your luggage is lost, or carried away, or something."

"But don't you see it is not like other trunks, and my initials, E. E. D., are on it? I beg you at least to stop the train, and let me get off." I screamed at him, greatly excited at my helplessness and the situation.

But the train moved on, and the conductor, with a derisive smile, said: "Now, to convince you of your mistake, let me take your check, and I'll soon return with the baggage-master to prove your trunk is still in his care."

I gave him the check, knowing how futile his errand was. After some twenty minutes or more, he came back with another man, whom he said was the baggage-master, and between them they admitted that my trunk had been taken from the train; there had been some unusual carelessness, but it would be all right; the conductor would send a telegram from the next station to have it sent on. Both men seemed annoyed and confused.

"When will my trunk reach me?" I asked.

"Well," said the conductor, "the truth is, I've got to first telegraph to Cleveland, to the office of the company, and then an order will be sent along the line until it is found, and at best you cannot get it before ten o'clock to-night."

This was not very reassuring. At the second station beyond he came in, showing me a telegram from the station where the trunk was taken from the train. It read to the effect that such a trunk was there, and would be detained until the order arrived to forward it to Conneaut. Arriving at the residence of Mr. Henry Lake, in Conneaut, and telling the family of the occurrence, they considered it very unusual—in fact, had never heard of anything like it before. Both Mr. and Mrs. Lake went to the station with me at ten o'clock, and the trunk was taken from the train on its arrival at that hour. My friends insisted that both the station-master and baggage-master of the train should be with me when opening the trunk, to see if its contents had been disturbed. The lock, a good sound one, I found had been forced open, the heavy straps alone holding it together. At a glance, on lifting the cover, it was evident that everything in the trunk had been turned over, just as though its contents had been pulled out and thrown in again by hasty and inexperienced hands. A later investigation the same night proved that not one single item had been stolen, although there were valuable articles of various descriptions in the trunk. *My papers connected with the interview with Hurlburt, Howe, and General Garfield—in fact, all the notes taken in this trip on the subject of Mormonism, were in my hand-satchel, and had been carefully guarded.* On writing to an official connected with the Lake Shore Railroad, relating all the facts of the case, his reply was to the effect that so long as nothing had been stolen from the trunk, it was proof conclusive that the breakage of the lock and its detention at the way station were merely accidental. He regretted the circumstance, but was of the opinion that there was no legal redress for it.

CHAPTER VI.

Visit to Conneaut, Ohio, in 1880—Reminiscences of Rev. Spaulding and the First Mormon Conference, in 1834.

IN connection with the visit at Mentor and Painesville, after the interview with Hurlburt at Gibsonburg, the author stopped at Conneaut, Ashtabula Co., Ohio, where the Rev. S. Spaulding resided, in 1812, and wrote the story which was made the foundation of the Mormon fraud. Some description of the town as it looks to-day may be interesting to the reader.

Conneaut is also interesting in its connection with the first great conference of Mormons, in the year 1834, when Hurlburt was sent to procure "The Manuscript Found" from Mrs. Davison, at Munson, Mass., "to compare it with the 'Book of Mormon.'"

The village of Conneaut is a mile from Conneaut Station, on the Lake Shore Railroad. It is the county-seat, and in its thrift and general appearance greatly resembles a New England town of the best type. At the eastern side of the village is the broad ravine through which the Conneaut River, or Creek, flows down to Lake Erie, which is picturesque and beautiful.

One of the most attractive dwellings in the place is that of Mr. Hiram Lake, son of Henry Lake, a partner of Solomon and John Spaulding in 1812.

An evening at Mr. Lake's residence was spent in hearing his reminiscences of certain circumstances in connection with the Spauldings—many facts which his father had related to him of the writings of Mr. Spaulding—and particularly how the neighbors gathered to hear him read the novel called "The Manuscript Found," and how the talk of the hour dwelt on the discoveries made by the workmen employed to open the earth-mounds close to Mr. Spaulding's house. The very spot where this house once stood is pointed out—a log cabin, containing some relics of New England comforts, and the best dwelling in the vicinity at the time.

Its owner, it is said, was the most noted and probably the best educated man in that part of the State. There is no trace of this primitive homestead now, or of the earth-mound close to it; but there are many people living in Conneaut who remember both.

Just below this locality, and close to the creek, was the foundry of the Spaulding brothers and Mr. Henry Lake, which was so prosperous until the war of 1812 made its proprietors bankrupt.

There were formerly a number of earth-mounds in the vicinity of Conneaut, all of which have been levelled with the surrounding fields; but numerous evidences of their existence and locality are pointed out at the present time. A few months since some prehistoric relics were unearthed by a ploughman in a corn-field where it is known that an earth-mound had existed, and many persons in and near the village possess pottery, implements of iron, carved beads, or ornaments of personal adornment, that have been exhumed in turning up the soil for agricultural purposes.

Traditions and personal remembrances are numerous among the elder residents of Conneaut of the great Mormon Conference held in that place in 1834. Some traveller, it is said, in that year brought a copy of the "Book of Mormon" to Conneaut soon after it was published, but it does not seem to have created much gossip among the townspeople, until a woman preacher, who had been recently converted to Mormonism, appointed a public meeting, and in her talk made copious extracts from it, which were immediately recognized by many persons present, particularly by John Spaulding (see Appendix, No. 13), who was " amazed and afflicted that his brother's writings should have been perverted for such a wicked purpose."

His grief found vent in a flood of tears, and he arose on the spot and expressed his regretful sentiments. Both Mr. Hiram Lake and Mr. Lorin Gould, whose statements (see Appendix, No. 14) will be found elsewhere, told the author they remembered this occasion, and some incidents in connection with it.

They also said that at the time of this Mormon meeting there was the wildest possible excitement all through that part of the State in regard to the " new faith," as it was called.

It was as a result of these meetings that D. P. Hurlburt, who had resided in or near Conneaut, and whose reputation was not the best for veracity or honesty, and who at the time had joined the Mormons with his wife (the sweet-faced woman the writer saw at Gibsonburg), offered or was selected to visit Mrs. Davison at Munson, Mass., and to request a loan of the Spaulding " Manuscript Found," as it was reported, to compare it with the " Book of Mormon."

It is remembered at Conneaut that he returned with *a* manuscript, or that was so reported. This is presumably the manuscript which E. D. Howe says was lying in his office at Painesville for years, and which the Mormons pretend was compared with " the Golden Bible of Joseph," at a public meeting the Mormons called for the purpose, and found to be entirely wanting in the essentials claimed for it.

It was beyond question, from very strong circumstantial evidence, the *manufactured* manuscript prepared by Hurlburt or his confederates for the occasion. A daughter of Mr. John Spaulding, still living near Conneaut, in a letter to the writer (see Appendix, No. 15) of a recent date, substantiates all that Mr. Lake and Mr. Gould stated at the former gentleman's house.

Of the odd stories told at Conneaut, in 1834, in connection with Solomon Spaulding, was one to the effect that he told his neighbors at the time he entertained them with his romance, that his *"Manuscript Found" was a translation of the "Book of Mormon,"* and he intended to publish a fictitious account of its having been discovered in a "cave in Ohio" as an advertisement, to advance its sale, when his book was printed.

The remarkable features of the Mormon meeting at Conneaut, in 1834, and the conflicts of opinion between the converts to the new doctrines there promulgated, and the affirmations of the old neighbors and relatives of Solomon Spaulding, led to the venture of E. D. Howe in writing the book called "Mormonism Unveiled."

There is a tradition that Mr. Howe was himself half a Mormon when he wrote this volume, and it is believed that his motive in writing it was not a desire to expose an imposture, but to make money.

Another outcome of this meeting at Conneaut, in 1834, was the wild enthusiasm of the people, who travelled from great distances to see the "new prophet," and from it "elders," or preachers, were sent out to those who could not attend.

Stories were circulated at the time that even in the then remote New England States and in the British provinces families were placing their all in wagons—the common method of travelling at that date—and hastening to join the ranks of the " Saints."

How long the Mormons tarried at Conneaut it is now impossible to state. It must have been some weeks, however, as in the interval Hurlburt visited Munson, Mass., and other matters of importance in their history eventuated at this period of their career.

CHAPTER VII.

The Mormons in Missouri.

WHEN Joe Smith found that he could not be a prophet of repute in the State of New York, and after he and Sidney Rigdon had witnessed the favor with which their scheme was received in Ohio, they followed Oliver Cowdrey, whom they had sent on in advance to the State of Missouri to look for a fitting locality for the New Jerusalem, and, as they professed, to evangelize the Indians and Gentiles generally.

Cowdrey's report of Jackson Co., Mo., was so favorable that these two founders of "a religious empire" directed their steps thither, under the most discouraging difficulties of travel, making a portion of the distance of over three hundred miles on foot. On their arrival at Independence they were so enamored of the country that they at once selected it as the place for the New Zion; and, to silence all cavil among his followers, Smith had a "revelation," in the form of a document, which is among the most extraordinary performances of this remarkable man, as this was early in the history of Mormonism, and long before persecutions and dangers had sharpened his faculties by a ripe experience. It commences : "Hearken, oh ye elders of my Church, saith the Lord, your God, who have assembled yourselves together, according to my commandments, in this land which I have appointed and consecrated for the gathering of the Saints. Behold the place which is called Independence is the centre place, and a spot for the Temple is lying westward, upon a lot which is not far from the Court House ; wherefore, it is wisdom that the land should be purchased by the Saints, and also every track lying westward, even unto the line running directly between Jew and Gentile."

. All the ceremony it was possible to secure under the circumstances was given to the occasion. The particular spot chosen as a site for the Temple was named "*Adam-mon diamor*," signifying the " patriarchal blessing."

Here Smith said the Latter-Day Saints would finally gather, Christ would appear in person, and the Mormons would reign a glorious and triumphant people for a thousand years.* With a business-like purpose worthy of the Prophet's most illustrious pupil, Brigham Young, Smith expressed his wishes, appointed a storekeeper and other factotums, including Oliver Cowdrey as assistant editor of a newspaper which was established at Independence, called the *Morning and Evening Star*. Elder W. Phelps, a man who wrote Smith's political papers and distorted several languages to make " *more good* " out of the word " Mormon," was appointed editor-in-chief.

After the " consecration" and these business matters were arranged, the Prophet and Rigdon returned to Kirtland, in order, as they said, " to remain five years and make money."

Meanwhile during these five years the Mormons increased very rapidly in Missouri, settlements being made in Clay, Ray, Jackson and Caldwell counties ; and with their habitual industry and thrift they made homes of comfort, and rapidly gained wealth.

The Kirtland troubles, long threatened, culminated in

---

* Venerable Mormons in Utah have recently been heard to give it as their opinion that they, with other Saints, would return to Zion, Independence, Mo., for the final glorification of the chosen ones.

1838, when Smith and Rigdon again made a journey to Missouri, pursued at first by creditors and afterward guided by a "revelation."

It was on this particular westward march that the Prophet first organized a military command and a body-guard and began to assume the prerogatives of his high military, as well as spiritual, mission. He had two hundred disciplined men-at-arms after he reached the State line of Missouri secretly, his "guard," a fearful band which had been organized as "destroying angels," or "Danites," whose lawless conduct later on precipitated the tragic scenes that were followed by the expulsion of the Mormons from the State. These "Danites" were sworn "to put out of sight" all persons obnoxious to the "Saints;" and even before the Prophet arrived from Kirtland many peaceable residents mysteriously disappeared—"slipped their breath," to use a favorite expression of the band.

From the year 1833 the Mormons had been in trouble in Missouri. While their general cause had advanced, they were correspondingly hated by their neighbors. They were accused of every sort of evil and of secret crime, and yet were admitted to be industrious.

Such was the situation when the Prophet came to rule over his followers in new scenes and under new auspices. A letter was written a short time before his arrival by a man of great natural intelligence, Mr. Ezra Booth, early a local Methodist preacher in Ohio, who was a victim to the Mormon imposture in Missouri.

In a letter to the Rev. Ira Eddy, in which he gives an account of the painful experiences which revealed its iniquities to him, he says: "When I embraced Mormonism I sincerely believed it to be of God. Like a ghost it haunted me day and night, until I was mysteriously hurried, as it were, by a kind of necessity, into the vortex of delusion. At times I was much elated, but generally things in prospect were the greatest stimulus to action. On our arrival in Missouri we discovered that *prophecy* and *vision* had failed, or rather proved false. Mr. Rigdon himself said that 'Joseph's vision was a bad thing.' I do not regret that I made the journey, though I regret the cause of it. Since my return (to Kirtland) I have had several interviews with Smith, Rigdon and Cowdrey, and the various shifts and turns to which they have resorted in order to obviate objections and difficulties proved to my mind additional evidence that Mormonism was nothing else than a deeply-laid plan of craft and deception."

Soon after the Prophet's arrival at Independence (and he was known generally to have become wealthy, and a greater braggart than ever) dark clouds loomed over the horizon of the Mormons. The causes contributing to their expulsion from the State were numerous. The most terrible rumors were afloat respecting the secret deeds of the Danites, and they had acquired so much property that the Missourians resolved that they should have what was termed "the rule of the counties," through their numbers and property.

The Mormons were wont to boast of their political ascendancy, and the dislike which was felt toward them from the first deepened into an intense hatred. Rigdon is said to have still further estranged the "Gentiles" from the Saints by his talk and overt acts at this time, and soon after his arrival charged both Cowdrey and David Whitmer with being connected with some traitors to Mormonism, in counterfeiting, horse-stealing, and villainies of the worst description; and concluded an editorial in the *Morning and Evening Star* against them with this sentence: "Are they not murderers at heart to stir up the Missourians against us by their slanders?"

Smith's power after he was driven out of Ohio seemed for awhile to decline; but the new persecutions in the West came to his aid, and cemented the union of those who were still his friends. A large number had left the ranks, and were anathematized in forcible if not elegant language.

The Mormons began to boast of the "intentions" of their prophet. They called him "the commander-in-chief of the armies of Israel;" the State would soon be in their hands, and finally the whole country in their possession. The facts seemed to justify this braggadocio, as the whole of Jackson County was theirs, and converts were flocking to their ranks in great numbers. A public meeting was, however, convened at Independence by the alarmed and excited "Gentiles," which resulted in the Mormons being driven across the Missouri River, by an infuriated mob, into Clay and Cadwallader counties, where Smith and Rigdon joined them. With this dispersion the other Mormon settlements suddenly developed into places of importance, particularly a town called *"Far West."*

The Saints had received a lesson, but were not wise enough to heed it. Rigdon became very violent, and taught them, by voice and by pen, that they must expect to fight under persecution. In a Fourth of July oration he said: "*We take God and all the holy angels to witness this day, that we warn all men, in the name of Jesus Christ, to come on us no more forever. The set of men who does it makes the attempt at the expense of their lives. It shall be a war of extermination between us, for we will follow them till the last drop of blood is spilled, or else they will have to exterminate us. We will carry the sent of war to their own houses and families, till one party or the other is utterly destroyed.''*

This speech, with various exaggerations, was reported and commented on in every part of the State, and eventuated in the most deadly animosity toward the vainglorious Mormons. While Rigdon thus stirred up the people by talking and writing, Smith was shaping and moulding the rudest materials into a great enthusiastic religious power. Mills, workshops, farms, and industries of many kinds sprang up in the wilderness around their temporary resting-places; and even with all the warnings given and vexations caused them by their enemies of a real or imaginary character, a new impetus was given to their confidence in the Mormon leaders, everything conspiring to make them twofold more the children of the "new faith."

With all these tragic circumstances, there grew into a terrible reality one of those wild and romantic histories which could only have taken shape on a Western frontier, and which was developed by these unusual incidents and by the vanity and egotistical spirit evinced by Mormonism.

To complicate affairs, two Mormons—Thomas B. Hyde and Orson Pratt—"apostles," as they were called, made an affidavit before a justice of the peace in Ray County, to the effect that "the Mormons have a company among them calling themselves 'Danites,' who have taken an oath to support the head of the church in all things, whether right or wrong; that the design of Smith is to take this State, and he professes to his people his intention of taking the United States, and ultimately the whole world; that this is the belief the Prophet inculcates, and every true Mormon believes Smith's prophecies superior to the law of the land."

One of these men further said: "I heard the Prophet say that he would yet tread down his enemies and walk over their dead bodies; that if he was let alone he would be a second Mahomet to this generation, and that he would make it one lake of blood from the Rocky Mountains to the Atlantic Ocean."

Mutual acts of plunder and retaliation between the Saints and Gentiles became frequent and terrible in their consequences, as they naturally would under such peculiar and threatening circumstances; and "trifles light as air" brought them into collision.

The Mormons drove their opponents in many instances from their immediate vicinity, burning their houses and confiscating their property; worse than all, some women and children were driven into the woods, and two children were born of homeless mothers. This was the crowning event that fired the Missourians into a war of extermination against the "interloping Mormons."

A company of militia was called together to keep the peace, who encamped on the borders of a small stream; and the Mormons, supposing it to be a mob ready to destroy their possessions, attacked them, killing and wounding many.

Complaints of the existing seditions were quickly carried to Governor Boggs, who immediately ordered out the State troops, "to enforce order upon all citizens, even if it was found necessary to exterminate the hateful and obnoxious Mormons," who were presumed to be in the wrong and the fomenters of all these unhappy circumstances and terrible discords.

A fearful drama followed under the leadership of "Major-General Clark," U. S. A., who is described as being as rude as the most uncivilized of Mormons, even making brutal addresses to his prisoners while they were calling on the name of "the unknown God." He had "discretionary powers," however, and allowed the enemy to withdraw from the State, and could take their lands to pay the cost of the war. The Mormon property thus confiscated has been estimated to be worth nearly two millions of dollars.

Joseph and Hyram Smith, with Rigdon and other leaders, were arrested and placed in jail. There was a court-martial the same evening, and it was decided to have them shot the next morning ; but in consequence of the protest of General Doniphan, who declared that such an act would be unlawful, the court rescinded its resolution.

Rigdon was discharged, but with their leaders in jail the Mormons submitted to the conditions made, and prepared to withdraw from the State into Illinois, where the Prophet and his fellow-captives joined them after breaking from prison during two days in which their guard was in a drunken slumber.

In an old book at the Astor Library there is a comical representation of the "commander of the armies of Israel" fleeing on horseback from the Missouri jail, with a companion on either side similarly mounted.

Twelve thousand Mormons arrived on the banks of the Mississippi River late in the autumn of 1838, in the most unhappy plight. Their houses had been burned, their fields laid waste, and they were nearly or quite destitute of every personal comfort. Every indignity and personal insult which had been offered to the Missourians by the Mormons was returned with interest, and so terrible were their sufferings, that the hearts of the Illinois citizens were so touched by their distress that they received with hospitality those who had travelled over the bleak prairies amid storms of wind and rain and snow.

The aged, the young, and the sick had been alike houseless and homeless in the most inclement season of the year. Many who had left homes of abundance died from exposure to the pitiless elements. These were the victims of the men who had led them into the snares of a false religion.

A Mormon historian of these " persecutions of the Saints" tells how twenty of them, sleeping in a log cabin by the wayside, in this flight to Illinois, were shot dead through the crevices, and after the massacre was over a boy who had been concealed was dragged out from his hiding-place under a forge and shot, while his murderers danced about him. This historian further writes (after relating a number of such instances of Gentile cruelty): *"We may forgive; but to forget —never !"*

The Illinoisians who opened their doors to the invading Mormons excused their hospitality by saying that matters had been carried too far against them, whatever provocation they had given, and gave them shelter, food, and clothing. A Mormon poet wrote in connection with the times :

"*Missouri,*
Like a whirlwind in her fury,
Drove the Saints and spilled their blood."

Under such trying and tragic events the faith of many of the Mormons succumbed. A most significant fact to a large number was that their Zion had *not* been built at Independence.

They had lost all their property, and even their health had deeply suffered, and were ready to abandon the faith and return forlornly to their former homes in the Eastern States. Some left temporarily, some altogether, and remained in Missouri, wrecked in religious belief and hope of any kind. A large number of these destitute Mormons found their way to Quincy, Ill., where public meetings were held and measures adopted for their benefit; and of these some, on a return of prosperity, joined the Mormons at Nauvoo.

While the Saints were at Independence a "Book of Commandments," for the government of the Church of Christ, organized according to law, on the 6th of April, 1830, was partly written, but not published, as the following extract will show:

A "Book of Commandments," for the government of the Church of Christ, organized according to law, on the 6th of April, 1830. 32mo, pp. 160, boards, Zion, Published by W. W. Phelps & Co., 1833.

This book was never published, nor even completed. Only two copies are known. The sheets were destroyed by a Missouri mob. People who know just enough of Mormonism to call the "Book of Mormon" the "Mormon Bible"—to think they know that it was written by Solomon Spaulding, and stolen from a Pittsburg printing-office by Sidney Rigdon, and handed over by him to Prophet Joe—and who measured the evils of Mormonism only by the number of defections from their own particular sect—and I have never conversed with an anti-Mormon, other than an apostate, whose knowledge or interest extended much farther—will read with distrust or indifference, if they read at all, the assertion which I unhesitatingly make, that this book, if valued by its importance, would bring a larger price than was ever paid for a single volume. People who think they know all about it, suppose the "Book of Mormon" to be to Mormonism what the Bible is to Christianity. Nothing could be farther from the fact. Mr. Stenhouse, who was for many years one of their leading men, and probably the most intelligent man that they ever had among them, once told me that he never read the "Book of Mormon" through in his life, and that he did not believe anybody else ever did.

In a roundabout manner, not a peculiarity of Mormons, but a characteristic of churchmen, the Mormons, in their articles of belief, say, and the elders never tire of repeating, that they believe in the Bible, the "Book of Mormon," and the "Book of Doctrine and Covenants." To know their crooked ways, which, I repeat, are not peculiar to themselves, is to know that they would place the book which they attach the least importance to in the front rank, and that which they regard as most important in the rear. This they would be certain to do, and this they have always done. As the "Book of Commandments" is really the first edition of the "Book of Doctrine and Covenants," one must be made acquainted with the general character and standing of the book before he can understand the special importance attaching to this edition. In short—for I do not propose to write a treatise upon Mormonism, lest from lack of literary ability I should make as miserable a failure as most writers have made from ignorance of the subject—the book is composed of what purport to be "*revelations*" straight from God to Prophet Joe! Professor J. B. Turner, one of the best-informed of the anti-Mormon writers, says of the "Book of Doctrine and Covenants": "It has really exerted a thousand-fold more influence on the doctrines and destinies of the Mormon Church than all other books put together, still it is usually kept in the background, and the 'Book of Mormon' thrown forward as their main authority, next after the Bible." This is perhaps plain enough; but in view of the fact that among all classes of people less is known of Mormonism than of the sea-serpent, I will add, in my own plainer if not stronger words, that the "Book of Doctrine and Covenants" is the whole of Mormonism. Counting deaths and defections, not less than half a million people (mostly fools, as Carlyle said of the population of the British Islands) have been bamboozled, first into a belief that God is the Author of the miserable trash, and, as necessary correlatives, that the Mormons are the Saints, and hell the portion of all others. During forty-five of the fifty years of Mormonism, from the moment the "Book of Doctrine and Covenants" was issued in 1835, there has existed in the "Book of Commandments" proof of the very kind which the circumstances seemed to demand—*i.e.*, proof, plain and convincing, to the meanest understanding, of the fraudulent character of both versions. The proposition could hardly obtain credence, even among the kind of timber from which Mormons are made, that an All-wise Being could, in one hundred and sixty pages 32mo, make so many blunders as have been corrected—if the alterations may be called corrections—in the next following and first known edition of these precious "revelations."

"When Joe was getting up the 'Book of Mormon' he loaned a portion of the manuscript to Martin Harris, the man who was fool enough to pay for printing it. Mrs. Harris got hold of it and secretly burned it. Joe, who, being fearful that Mrs. Harris had not destroyed it, but still had it in her possession, dared not go through with the farce of pretending to re-translate it, lest Mrs. H. should upset his pretensions by printing his first version, which he knew he could not make his second version conform to, left it out altogether, and commenced his book where the lost portion ended ; and so much was forever lost to religion. On that occasion he made a mistake by over-caution. When, under somewhat similar circumstances, he was again called upon to act, he made a still worse mistake by taking the opposite course. One day, while this edition was being printed at what is now Independence, Mo., the anti-Mormon border ruffians pounced upon ' Zion,' as the Mormons called their settlement, and in next to no time their two-story brick printing-office, with all that it contained—building, press, type, sheets, paper and all—were converted into a mass of ruins, and the Saints were running away with nothing but their lives. There can be no doubt that Joe and his lieutenants felt confident that not a copy of the sheets had been preserved. When, in 1835, the book was first given to a wicked world, two years' experience had enabled Joe to make numerous amendments. In some cases he modified or curtailed his revelations ; in some cases they are considerably amplified ; but in all cases the actions are made to meet the requirements of 1835. That Joe was shameless, audacious, brazen-faced, and would not have risked these alterations had he not felt very certain that every printed copy of the original version had been destroyed, is proved to the satisfaction of people of ordinary intelligence by his conduct in relation to the lost translation of the manuscript of the ' Book of Mormon ;' but what renders the conclusion absolutely inevitable is the fact that after the revelations were actually published beyond recall they were never again, even in the slightest degree, subjected to the Almighty revision."

CHAPTER VIII.

The Mormons at Nauvoo—Description of the Temple—The Death of the Prophet.

JOSEPH SMITH was now approaching the zenith of his fame and power. He had arrived in Illinois from his imprisonment in Missouri, so far the darkest period of his history. The injustice with which he and his people (as it was at the time generally considered) had been treated served to awaken pity in their behalf.

The Prophet's prospects at once brightened when Dr. Isaac Gallard, a notorious character, presented a part of a large tract of land to him in Carthage County, with a view of making a market for the remainder.

Immediately Joseph had a "revelation" that this was the "centre spot," and he commanded the Saints to assemble there to build a city, a temple, etc. The city, the angel told him, was to be called "Nauvoo," which, he said, means "the Beautiful." It is located on the east bank of the Mississippi River, forty miles above Quincy, Ill., and twenty miles west of Burlington, Iowa, at a bend of the river, on rising ground, commanding a magnificent view of the "Father of Waters" for many miles.

The land given to Joseph was divided into lots and sold to the Mormons, by which he realized over one million of dollars. The Saints from all quarters responded to the call to hasten to the new city, and it immediately grew into importance.

Fifteen years before Smith had been known as a common vagrant ; now he was known as a mayor, a pontiff, and as a very rich man, the legislature having granted the city a charter with extraordinary privileges, including the authorization of a military body, afterward known as the "Nauvoo Legion," of which he was the lieutenant-general—a corps to which all the male Mormons capable of bearing arms belonged.

Nauvoo became the capital of the world to the Mormons, and attracted general attention. This new "everlasting residence" of the Saints was changed from a desert into an abode of plenty and luxury. Gardens sprang up as if by magic, plethoric with the most beautiful flowers of the New and the Old World, whose seeds had been brought from distant lands as souvenirs to the new "Zion ;" broad streets were laid out, houses erected, and the busy hum of industries was heard in the marts of commerce. Steamboats unloaded their stores, and passengers came and departed for fresh supplies of merchandise ; fields waved with golden harvests, and cattle dotted the neighboring hills. The new settlement was increased by horse-thieves, house-breakers, robbers, and people of the most disreputable character, who joined the community to cloak their villainous deeds in mystery. Speculators, too, came and bought property with the hope of remuneration. Some of these people were baptized, but being unwilling to pay full tithes, were "ousted" from the ranks, which were again quickly filled.

An intelligent officer of the United States Army, who visited Nauvoo in the height of its prosperity, gives an account of the city and its institutions as he saw them at this time : "Yesterday," he says, "was a great day among the Mormons. Their legion, to the number of two thousand men, were paraded by Generals Smith, Bennett, and others, and certainly made a very fine appearance. The evolutions of the troops directed by Major-General Bennett would do credit to any body of armed militia.

"What does all this mean? Why this exact discipline of the Mormon corps? Do they intend to conquer Missouri, Illinois, or Mexico?

"Before many years this legion will be fifty thousand strong—a fearful host, and still augmenting, filled with religious enthusiasm, and led on by ambitious and talented officers, and what may not be effected by them? These Mormons are accumulating like a snow-ball rolling down an inclined plane, which in the end becomes an avalanche. They have appointed Captain Bennett, late of the United States Army, their inspector-general, and he is commissioned as such by Governor Curtin. This gentleman is skilled in gunnery, fortification, ordnance and military engineering generally, and I am told he is now under pay from the tithings of this warlike people. I have seen his plans for fortifying Nauvoo, which are equal to any of Tartan's.

"Only a part of their officers are Mormons, but they act with a common interest, and those who are not Mormons when they come here soon become so, from interest or conviction. The Smiths are not without talent, and are said to be brave as lions. Joseph, the chief, is a noble-looking fellow—a Mahomet, every inch of him.

"The postmaster, Sidney Rigdon, is a lawyer, philosopher, and Saint. Their other generals are men of talent, and some of them men of learning. They are all unquestionably ambitious, and the tendency of their religious creed is to annihilate all other creeds; you may therefore see that the time will come when this gathering host of religious fanatics will *make the country shake to its centre.* A Western empire is certain; ecclesiastical history presents no parallel to this people, inasmuch as they are establishing their religion on a learned footing. A graduate of Trinity College, Dublin, is president of their university.

"The military parade astonished me and filled me with fears for future consequences. The Mormons, it is true, are now peaceable; but the lion is asleep—take care, don't arouse him.

"This place has been settled only three years. It is well laid out, and seems to be well governed. The adjoining country is beautiful—a rolling prairie; Nauvoo contains ten thousand people, and in and near this city are thirty thousand of these warlike fanatics, an incorporated army, to whom the arms of the State have been loaned; and of this army a company has been selected to build the Mormon Temple, the site of which has been selected. I am told that all the converts of Mormonism, here and elsewhere, at this time number one hundred and fifty thousand."

From this statement it is obvious that the Saints were again prosperous some three years after their expulsion from Missouri. Not only was the site of the temple chosen, but a hotel was built, where certain of the leaders were to be entertained, "free of expense, forever."

Conferences were held semi-annually, and missionaries were appointed to Palestine, Africa, and Europe, and to each Congressional district in the United States. The best educated, the most inquiring and restive ones, were sent on these errands in order to give them a chance to let off the steam of discontent. They were sent with all the promptness of military orders, with a three days' notice for an absence of three years from home and family, which were cared for by the presidency and bishops. Three hundred missionaries were appointed at one of these conferences. Previous to starting they received orders from Joseph, who preached a rousing sermon to them that stimulated their pride of conquering difficulties, without scrip or purse ; the main point was that " spiritual wifehood" was to be most pointedly denied ; and that they should teach that one man was to live with one woman " in chaste fidelity." He told them to buckle on the armor, " to confound the wise and unwise," etc., thus enlisting their pride, which was the sure way to make full Mormons of the wavering.

At this time (1842) the Mormons boasted of having a hundred thousand in the faith throughout the States, and their vote was a balancing power. They would go in a body in all political questions. The Prophet commenced to agitate the question of a restitution of the property the Saints had lost in Missouri. He visited Washington, had an interview with President Van Buren, who said to him : " Sir, your cause is just, but I can do nothing for you." In view of the approaching Presidential election of 1844, letters on the subject of the Mormons' alleged wrongs were addressed to prominent candidates, which elicited answers not at all agreeable to the Saints.

In 1843 the Prophet wrote to Henry Clay, who was supposed to have a good chance to be elected to the Presidency, to know what course he would pursue toward the Mormons if he were successful. The correspondence was characteristic of both parties. Smith's letter was to the following effect :

"NAUVOO, ILL., November 4, 1843.
"HON. HENRY CLAY :
"DEAR SIR : As we understand you are a candidate for the Presidency of the next election, and as the Lat-

ter-Day Saints (sometimes called Mormons), who now constitute a numerous class in the school politic of this vast Republic, who have been robbed of an immense amount of property and endured nameless sufferings by the State of Missouri, and from her borders have been driven by force of arms, contrary to our natural covenants, and as in vain we have sought redress by all constitutional, legal, and honorable means in her courts, her executive councils, and her legislative halls, and as we petitioned Congress to take cognizance of our sufferings without effect, we have judged it wisdom to address this communication to you and solicit an immediate, specific, and candid reply to what your rule of action relative to us will be as a people, should fortune favor your accession to the Chief Magistracy.

"Most respectfully, sir, your friend, and the friend of peace and good order and Congressional rights,

"Joseph Smith."

Mr. Clay responded as follows:

"Dear Sir: I have received your letter in behalf of the Church of Jesus Christ, of the Latter-Day Saints, inquiring what would be my rule of action to you as a people should I be elected, etc. Should I be a candidate, I can enter into no engagements, make no promises, give no pledges to any particular portion of the people of the United States. I have viewed with lively interest the progress of the Latter-Day Saints. I have sympathized in their sufferings, under injustice, as it appeared to me. I think, in common with all other religious communities, they ought to enjoy the security and protection of the Constitution and the laws. I am, with great respect,

"Your friend,

"Henry Clay."

Mr. Clay's reply was very unsatisfactory to the Prophet, who wrote him a second letter which received a still more unsatisfactory reply. He wrote an angry rejoinder, calling Mr. Clay "a blackleg in politics." The letter shows the shrewdness and talent of the man. The following is an extract from it :

"The renowned Secretary of State, the ignoble duelist, the gambling Senator and Whig candidate for the Presidency, *Henry Clay*, the wise Kentucky lawyer, advises the Latter-Day Saints to go to Oregon, to obtain justice, and set up a government of their own. Why? Great God, to transport two hundred thousand people through a vast prairie over the Rocky Mountains to Oregon—a distance of nearly two thousand miles—would cost more than four millions; or should they go around Cape Horn in ships to California, the cost would be more than twenty millions; and all this to save the United States from inheriting the disgrace of Missouri for murdering and robbing the Saints with impunity. Benton and Van Buren, who make no secret to say, if they get into power they will carry out (Governor) Boggs's exterminating plan to rid the country of the Latter-Day Saints, are

'Little nipperkins of milk'

compared to

'Clay's great aqua-fortis jars.'"

Then Smith set forth his "views on government," advocated a national bank, denounced punishment for desertion in the army and navy, would pardon every convict in the penitentiaries, curtail government offices and pay, reduce the number of representatives, and would harmonize everything by declaring all men free to try "honesty and care" in their dealings, and become a brotherhood. Joseph was put in nomination for the Presidency, and the Mormons have always declared that if he had lived until the next election he would have obtained that office. He was called "The Lion of the Lord" at this time, from his bold spirit and great bravery and power among his followers. A daughter of Joseph's at this time said to a young woman just arrived at Nauvoo:

"If we all do as father directs us, we shall be able to conquer the whole world. The President of the United States will be glad to black father's boots when the thousand years of our reign upon earth commences, and that time will come before long."

THE MORMON TEMPLE AT NAUVOO.

On April 6th, 1841, the foundation of the remarkable building at Nauvoo, called the Mormon Temple, was laid by General Joseph Smith, who appeared for the purpose at the head of his legion, surrounded by a numerous staff. Soon after the city of Nauvoo had been laid out the selection was made for this crowning triumph of the wealth and perseverance of the Saints, on the brow of a bluff overlooking the lower town on the river and a wide stretch of country on either side.

The design of the temple, Smith said, was given to him by the angel "Maroni," who explained all the details of the building to him. This "Maroni" was the angel who gave him (as he said) the precious box containing the golden plates. However, he employed a Gentile architect, who drafted it by dictation. All the Saints were called upon to contribute to its erection by time and money.

The building, which was of white limestone and

wrought in superior style, was in the centre of a four-acre lot. It was one hundred and twenty-eight feet long by eighty-three feet in width, and sixty feet in height. There were two stories in the clear and two in the recesses over the arches, making four tiers of windows—two Gothic and two round. The two lofty stories had two pulpits, one at each end, to accommodate the Melchisedec and Aaronic priesthood, graded into four rising seats : the first for the president of the elders and his two counsellors ; the second. for the president of the high-priesthood and his two counsellors ; the third for the Melchisedec priesthood and his two counsellors ; and the fourth for the president of the whole church (Smith) and his two counsellors. There was a carved marble font standing or resting on twelve life-sized oxen in marble in the basement, for the "baptism of the living," "for health, for the remission of sin, and for the salvation of the dead." The temple had a single tower one hundred feet in height on the side toward the river. On the front of the building was this inscription :

"The House of the Lord, built by the Church of the Latter-Day Saints. Holiness to the Lord."

This structure resembled no other church edifice, but was remarkably unique and graceful in its proportions, particularly the front of it, with its six fluted columns, its carved Corinthian caps, and broad piazza. The walls were of massive thickness ; the architectural ornaments of the interior were "holy emblems," and the spire was crowned, or tipped, with a gilt angel and his "gospel trump." P. T. Barnum, it is said, had this gilt angel in his New York museum for years after the destruction of the temple. It was the intention of the Mormons to inclose this beautiful temple with a wall ten feet in height and six in thickness.

The other buildings in Nauvoo were the Seventies' Hall, Masonic Temple, and Concert Hall, and the large hotel which the Prophet said was to be the "Mission House of the world," and where he would entertain "emperors, kings, and queens," from the Old World, who would come to him to inquire of the new faith. There was no licensed place to sell liquors, and drunkenness was almost unknown.

Order and thrift were the rule in this growing, prosperous town. Loafers or idle people were in disrepute. If a stranger entered Nauvoo, his habits and calling were at once a matter of watchfulness; and if he was found to be lazy and without employment he was at once "whittled" out of town by the deacons. This whittling process seems to have been a method by which the suspected person was followed by certain officials, who surrounded him or his abode, and in unison whittled at sticks carried for the purpose. At first it might seem to the doomed one a matter of accident, but its continuance from day to day was too much for human endurance, and the undesirable stranger departed, to the satisfaction of his tormentors. The first really traceable indication of the purpose of the Prophet to introduce polygamy was in 1841–42, and then it was so furtively done that the thousands that then believed, and still believe, in the mission of Joseph Smith, as set forth by himself, deny that he *ever* taught such a doctrine. It was brought before the residents of Nauvoo by a quarrel between Major-General Bennett, of the Nauvoo Legion, who (after he had left the Saints) published a book called "Mormonism Exposed," and related his "teaching the Mormon sisters the doctrine of affinity at the command of the Prophet."

There had been whispers of polygamy among the

leaders of Mormonism at Kirtland, and more than whispers of its existence among them in Missouri—Sidney Rigdon, it is said, having suggested it to Smith, who at first was scandalized at the thought of its introduction among his followers, but easily adopted its practice, and had a "revelation" allowing the higher officers of the church to have "as many wives as they could support."

Smith's wife, Emma, the "Lady Elect," made a violent opposition at first to this law, and the consolation given to her was "that a Prophet must obey the Lord, and he would be obedient to the heavenly vision."

It is not now denied that polygamy existed at Nauvoo at first secretly and afterward openly; but everything that could be done was done to mislead the public as to the veritable teachings of the Mormon leaders concerning marriage, from the quarrel of Bennett, in 1842, until the open announcement of the revelation by Brigham Young at Salt Lake City in 1852.

The missionaries were commanded to prevaricate, and even positively deny, that the Mormon Church was other than monogamic.

The sons of the Prophet have denied that their father believed in or practised polygamy; but there is overwhelming proof that Joseph Smith had doubtful relations with many "sisters," and was, as he said, a "law unto himself."

Many Mormons who personally knew the Prophet have affirmed that Joseph said it was necessary to have a "*revelation*" on the subject of marriage "to allay the storm that was brewing among the married women and to satisfy the young women whom it was desirable to convert." Mrs. Smith denounced the "revelation," and talked openly of a separation from the Prophet on that account, but was "softened down" by being told that the angel commanded her "to cleave unto Joseph," and afterward signed a certificate from "persons of families," declaring that they knew of no rule, or system of marriage, save that written by Oliver Cowdrey on marriage, and that Bennett's "secret-wife system is a creature of his own making." An author writes:

"The most forcible arguments that have yet been adduced on Mormon polygamy are furnished by the pens of the three sons of Joseph Smith at the head of a memorial to Congress protesting against Brigham Young's church founded by their father—to wit: 'If this doctrine had been presented to the Mormons with the "first principles" taught by the elders, not one in ten thousand would have accepted it.'"

According to another author: "Few of the Mormon women have ever accepted polygamy from the assent of their judgment, having first been led to consider it by their elders or leaders, as a true doctrine, and afterward having been afraid to question it, their fears counselling submission. Many of them have never been able to give it a careful consideration."

Intestine quarrels on this subject of polygamy and other causes brought on a crisis in affairs at Nauvoo, in 1844. The people in the neighborhood were jealous of the rapidly-growing and flourishing city; they complained that their property disappeared mysteriously, and that law cases tried in Nauvoo courts were always decided against them. No Mormon, they affirmed, was brought to justice. It was widely reported that the Mormons desired to rule the State, and intended to set all laws at defiance. A number of talented and influential persons who had become residents of Nauvoo, finding themselves deluded as to the sanctity of the Prophet and in the advancement of their temporal affairs, deserted his standard, denouncing him for licentiousness, drunkenness, and boastful tyranny.

Smith justified his inebriation by the assertion that it was necessary for him to be seen in that condition to prevent his followers from worshipping him as a God. Women accused him of attempted seduction, and he replied that he made such attempts " to learn if they were virtuous."

The Prophet's newspaper, the *Wasp*, lashed these dissenters with the bitterest sarcasm and hatred, to which they replied in the *Expositor*, one number of which was entirely devoted to a relation of the horrible immoralities of Joseph Smith and his intimate associates.

A city council was called, and eleven members of the twelve voted the *Expositor* a nuisance. Mrs. Foster, wife of Dr. Foster, the editor of this organ, was one of the women who had denounced the Prophet as having made improper proposals to her, and it was said that she wrote the first paper calling attention to the iniquities of the Saints in respect to " spiritual wifery." William Law was the associate editor of the *Expositor*.

Smith and his followers attacked the building where it was printed, destroying the presses and all its contents. Foster and Law fled to Carthage, the county seat, got out warrants against Smith and his brother Hyrum, and sixteen of their intimates. A constable who served these warrants was driven out of Nauvoo. This act fired the smouldering hatred of the Illinoisians into terrible activity, and a dark day was lowering over the fate of the Saints. The county authorities called out the militia to enforce the law.

The charter of Nauvoo had been so cunningly devised that the State authorities were almost excluded from jurisdiction within its limits.

The Mormons hastily armed themselves, and a civil war seemed impending when Governor Ford asked the two Smiths—Joseph and Hyrum—to surrender themselves and take their trial, as the best method of satisfying the existing turbulent parties.

In return, the Smiths sent two men to confer with him, and secretly crossed the Mississippi River into Iowa to watch the course of events, keeping up a correspondence with the council, which, finding their own people incensed by the desertion of their president, military commander, etc., begged the Smiths to obey the summons of the governor, they (the members of the council) and all their friends feeling sure of an acquittal on trial.

Following this advice, they returned to Nauvoo and started for Carthage, but were met by an officer with an order to disband the legion and deliver up the State arms. The Smiths accompanied this officer, who had some troops with him, and the order was duly executed. The two brothers were then conducted to Carthage, with Dr. Richards, John Taylor, and others, were indicted for treason, and lodged in jail.

The dissenting Mormons and all who had suffered injustice and loss of property from the Smiths now swore dire vengeance against the prisoners; but the governor, after discharging the troops, went to Nauvoo and addressed the people, advising them to submit to the laws and conduct themselves as good citizens, promising justice to all parties.

On the 27th of June, 1844, he started to return to Carthage, when he met a messenger who informed him that a horrible massacre of the Smiths had been committed by an infuriated mob.

The governor, fearing a retaliation from the Mormons on the inhabitants of Carthage, advised them to evacuate

Nauvoo, and placed General Deming, with the few troops that could be raised, and himself retired to Quincy to await events. It appears that while the governor was absent from Carthage, and the troops were disbanded, a number of excited and bloodthirsty individuals took matters into their own hands, decided to administer justice after their own fashion, and attacked the jail very early in the morning, breaking down the door of the room where the prisoners were confined.

The Smiths were very brave, and defended themselves as long as their ammunition held out, firing their revolvers in rapid succession. Hyrum was shot first, and then Joseph threw open the window, and in the act of leaping out was killed by the bullets fired by the mob, saying, as he fell, "O Lord, my God!"

Taylor was wounded, and Dr. Richards, in the confusion, managed to escape. This John Taylor, at present at the head of the Mormon Church at Utah, is the one mentioned as being in jail at Carthage with the Smiths, and who came so near sharing their fate.

The murder of their Prophet exasperated the Mormons at Nauvoo, and they determined on a "war to the knife" with all who had participated in that tragedy.

The more sagacious ones, however, perceived that it would be unwise to pursue such a course, and began very skilfully to prevent the entire ruin of their future hopes. They addressed the infuriated citizens, with clubs in their hands, while a great drum was meanwhile beating to arms. It was a fearful struggle. Revenge was deep, and curses were poured out on the Gentiles, and "the time to fight" most of them supposed had arrived; but the leaders made delays, and surrendered their arms.

They talked of a new organization and new leaders, and so the day passed, and wrath was kept for a more propitious season. The following morning the people collected in Temple Square. The apostles promised "the vengeance of heaven" on their enemies when the time was ripe for the vials of wrath to be poured on them, by patience, fire, and sword.

Next, the funeral pageant was of absorbing interest, for the mourning was sore, sad, and deep over "the beloved patriarch and the adored Prophet Joseph."

They were called "martyrs for their faith and triumphant in glory." The bodies of the Smiths were buried in the cellar of Joseph's house, although the ceremony of burying their empty coffins was performed at the grave. Joseph Smith's death by the violence of his enemies was opportune for the support of the system he sought to establish, as he had arrived at a point where the least delay would have made its waves overflow and engulf him.

He had lived long enough for his fame, and died when he could be called a martyr. It has been said of him that "he could begin but not conduct a revolution." He had become too impatient to manage a multitude, and save for his death at the time, and in this violent manner, the internal convulsions in the faith might have extinguished Mormonism.

One version of the return of the Smith brothers from Iowa to surrender themselves to the authorities at Carthage is, that they had started "to seek out a new home" in some isolated place in the Rocky Mountains for the people, of which Joseph saw the necessity, when a letter from his wife, Emma, overtook him, persuading him to come back; and in obeying it he made the fatal mistake which cost his life.

It is now believed on good authority that it was "this specious letter" of his wife's, rather than the governor's wish, which induced him to act against his better judgment, and flee from the Gentiles. She wrote to him reproachfully for his cowardice, denounced him as an impostor, and asked him to give proof of his mission by facing the enemies of the church.

It was the Missourians—who had never forgiven the Mormons—who were mainly instrumental in inciting the mob at Carthage to murder the Smiths. Even their enemies acknowledged that they died manfully. Joseph was heroic in a sense rarely allied to meanness; yet every act of his life and all the circumstances of his death attest the cheat; still he was of no ignoble order.

A few months before the Prophet's death Professor Turner, of Jacksonville, Ill., saw him at Nauvoo, and thus described his personal appearance:

"He is a curious mixture of the clown and the knave; his hands are large and awkward, and he wears a massive gold ring on one of his fingers. He has a downcast look, and nothing of that straightforward appearance that characterizes the honest man. His language is uncouth and ungrammatical."

But this description of the Prophet's appearance is contradicted by other testimony, quite as reliable; and whatever he may have been from the commencement of his pretended mission to the time of his death, the mass of Mormons have been satisfied with him. His personal beauty and magnetism, it is said, controlled those who were about him. He *made* them believe he could work miracles, cast out devils; that angels visited him; that he had revelations, trances, and was the chosen Prophet of the "Latter-Day Saints." In one year he had thirty-seven revelations, which he said were from Jesus Christ. He began all his addresses with "thus saith the Lord."

The New Jerusalem was ever in his mind and conversation; but where it was to be he did not discover. His associations were such as made him acquainted with the weak side of humanity, and he early saw that *numbers* were more convincing to the masses than intellectual attainments in point of religious influence. His "mission" grew with his years and his success, and he had far more power over the destinies of Mormonism than the "Book of Mormon" itself.

During his life he had an unquestioned influence over his wife Emma; she assisted him in every way to delude the credulous and unscrupulous; but a few years after his death she published a statement in the Quincy (Ill.) *Whig* to the effect that she had no belief in Smith's prophetic capacity, and considered his pretended revelations as the emanations of a diseased mind.

The following extract, from a criticism of books on Mormonism, is pertinent to the foregoing chapter. Author unknown. Date, January, 1880:

This ridiculous proposition to establish a Territorial Government within the bounds of a State has underlying it a desperate expedient to save Joe's neck from the halter which it richly deserved. Orrin Porter Rockwell, church murderer, then new to the business, but now the retired hero of a hundred murders, had been sent by Joe over to Missouri to assassinate Governor Boggs. "Port," as he is affectionately called at Salt Lake, shot the governor in the head, but, as he was comparatively inexperienced, did not kill him. On the 5th of June preceding the date of this petition, an indictment against Joe and Port was found in Missouri, and on the 7th Governor Ford issued a warrant for Joe's arrest, and surrendered him to a Missouri officer. He was rescued by the Mormons, taken on a writ of *habeas corpus* before the Nauvoo Municipal Court (!), and, of course, discharged. Governor Ford had been urged to call out the militia to aid in Joe's rendition, and in the petition it is proposed that the Mayor of Nauvoo (Joe) shall have the power "to call to his aid a sufficient number of United States forces, in connection with the Nauvoo Legion, to repel the invasion of mobs, keep the public peace, and protect the innocent from the unhallowed ravages of lawless banditti that escape justice on the Western frontier ; and also to preserve the power and dignity of the Union. And be it further ordained that the officers of the United States Army are hereby required to obey the requisitions of this ordinance." Joe did not get his Territorial Government, but the Illinois election was about to take place, and having three thousand votes to trade on, he was allowed to run at large a few months longer, until he was killed. If he had been taken over to Missouri, and given a fair trial, he might have saved his life by going to State's prison. "Port" was tried, but being advised in better season than Mr. Pickwick, proved " an alibi," and is still an ornament to Salt Lake society and a shining light in the Mormon Church.

CHAPTER IX.

Brigham Young's election to the presidency—The expulsion of the Mormons from Nauvoo in 1846.

AFTER the death of Joseph and Hyrum Smith, the Mormons seem to have been in a state of bewilderment and indecision. It was one of the most critical periods in their history, and the question arose "on whom the mantle of the Prophet should fall." The most influential of the citizens of Nauvoo assembled to debate that question.

Sidney Rigdon had already assumed the *rôle* of chief functionary as of right, and had a "revelation" on this subject. He had strong claims to sustain this assumption of power. He had originated Mormonism, and had very important secrets in his custody; but he miscalculated his influence. He was unpopular, was distrusted, and it was known that Joseph had long kept him at arm's length, fearing to quarrel with him. Rigdon said his new "revelation" commanded the "Saints" to go to Pittsburg, Pa., and this contradicted all that Joseph had received, which indicated that Jackson Co., Missouri, was positively to be their final home.

Ten weeks after the removal of the Prophet, Rigdon was called before the high quorum of the priesthood to answer for his misdeeds. He refused to appear.

Brigham Young was in Boston, Mass., engaged in mission work, when he heard of the death of the Smiths, and hastened to Nauvoo as rapidly as possible after the news reached him, convinced of his right to govern the people. Next to Joseph Smith, Brigham Young was the ablest man in certain ways who has been brought into prominence by the Mormon delusion. The two men had much in common, and each had a keen perception of the character of the other. Brigham was born in Vermont, in 1801, and removed at an early age to Livingston Co., N. Y., where he was a field-laborer. Later he was a house-painter at Canandaigua, N. Y. He joined the Mormons in 1832, at Kirtland, where his natural shrewdness and quickness were immediately recognized.

As one of the "Twelve Apostles" he soon became famous as a successful preacher, and Smith, with prophetic vision, in acknowledging Young's qualities as a ruler, remarked : "If Brigham has a chance he will lead the Mormons to hell." At Nauvoo, however, he saved them from destruction. He saw his opportunity, and had the wit and the nerve to embrace it. His first movement in this emergency was to make a public address accusing Rigdon of "manufacturing revelations," as having a "spirit as corrupt as the devil," and declaring his mind was enveloped in darkness, and that he sowed dissensions in the church.

The following portion of this address is curious as tending to prove Rigdon's complicity in the original fraud by which the "Book of Mormon" was palmed off on the credulous as a divine revelation—to wit :

"Brother Sidney says he will tell our secrets ; but if he tells them, we will tell his. Tit for tat. If there is so much iniquity in our church, he is a black-hearted wretch not to have told it long ago ;" and Young concluded with saying that Rigdon was the prime cause of all the troubles the Saints had had in Missouri and Illinois, and to retain him in the church was to bring utter destruction upon it. A few voices were eloquent in Rigdon's favor—ten in number; but the majority ruled, and Young delivered him over to the "buffetings of the devil for a thousand years in the home of the Lord." His ten friends were also suspended from their fellowship with the church.

Rigdon never sought to re-enter the church, and, what was far more important to the Mormons, he never told their secrets. He left Nauvoo immediately. Three other Mormons desired "the mantle of the Prophet"—Lyman White, William Smith, and Strang—all of whom were excommunicated. Each had his followers. Strang founded a city on the prairies of Wisconsin, where he had a large colony, which ultimately removed to Beaver Island, Lake Michigan, and assumed the title of "king."

Brigham was now triumphant; the same assembly which had rejected Rigdon elected him "First President," and invested him with the "keys." He at once issued a "circular letter" to the Saints, giving his views on the situation. It was calm, hopeful, practical, and got up in a masterly style; but his pacific advice could not heal matters with the "Gentiles," and he gave out that the Mormons must leave Illinois.

The charter of Nauvoo was repealed by the Legislature of the State in 1845. In the midst of these stirring and exciting scenes the Mormons gave a curious exhibition of their faith in Joseph Smith. He had predicted the completion of the temple, and Brigham commanded them to remain in Nauvoo in order to fulfil the "revelation" of the Prophet.

Unheard-of exertions were made to carry out this command, and the temple was finished to its minutest ornamentation. When it was ready the Mormons flocked into the city from every quarter, and there was great rejoicing over the consecration of "*the Pride of the Valley,*" as they called it.

The interior was elaborately decorated with festoons and wreaths of flowers, and symbolic glories "celestial, telestial, and terrestrial;" chants were sung, prayers offered, and lamps and torches lighted to make it resplendent. This done, the walls were dismantled, the ornaments taken down, and the symbols of their faith removed to leave the noble building "to be trodden down and profaned by the Gentiles."

From this time the enemies of the Mormons believed in their promised evacuation of the city. A venerable uncle of Joseph's declared that he had been told in a prophetic vision that "the whole people must retire into the wilderness, to grow into a multitude, aloof from the haunts of civilization."

Brigham Young and the Council took this matter into consideration. The result was, that they decided to move as rapidly as possible across Iowa to the Missouri, into the Indian country near Council Bluffs. It is stated that hostilities had been mutually suspended between the Mormons and their enemies, the State Government having promised its protection to the "Saints" until they could dispose of their property. The exodus had been delayed to finish the temple, and the mobocratic spirit of the Illinoisians and Missourians was again aroused.

THE EXODUS FROM NAUVOO.

In the winter of 1846 the Mormons commenced to leave the city. An indescribable pageant of ox-carts and mule teams, loaded with women, children, and all sorts of furniture, passed out from Nauvoo to the miry tracks of the prairies; but the spirits of all, save the sick and the helpless, were unbroken. Brigham superintended every detail of this evacuation of Nauvoo. He arranged that the population should leave in companies as carefully selected and as well ordered as the situation allowed. In spite of this preparation there was a report that the Mormons really intended to remain, as their progress was so tardy to the impatient Illinoisians; and in violation of all promises and State faith they called out the militia and drove the defenceless residents from their homes at the point of the bayonet, after bombarding the city for three days and nights.

This was in September of 1846. The militia seems to have been a rabble of two thousand men, who gathered to fight less than three thousand of the old Nauvoo Legion. While this barbaric war was being conducted against those who had been left in the city (the most helpless and defenceless) Brigham was leading his companies across the prairies to Council Bluffs, Iowa, which had been selected as a temporary halting-place, where the Mormons could recuperate their energies and prepare for a more extended pilgrimage.

Men and women had been sent forward, through Brigham's foresight, to plant crops by the wayside for those who should follow to gather; but there was terrible suffering and much sickness among these bands, who toiled onward, obedient to their leader's dictation.

The following description of the city of Nauvoo, immediately after the Mormons were driven from it by their foes, was written by Colonel Kane, of the United States Army (a brother of Kane the Arctic explorer), who afterward made the journey from Council Bluffs to Utah in company with the Mormons, and wrote an account of it. From this time Colonel Kane's sympathies were deeply enlisted in behalf of the Mormons, as will be further seen.

"Ascending the upper Mississippi in the autumn (1846), when its waters were low, I was obliged to travel by land past the region of the rapids. I had left the steamer at Keokuk, at the foot of the lower fall, and hired a carriage to where the deep water of the river returns. I was descending the last hillside upon my journey, when a charming landscape broke upon my view. Half encircled by a bend in the river, a beautiful city lay glittering in the morning sun. Its bright new buildings were set in cool green gardens, ranging up around a stately, dome-shaped hill, which was crowned by a noble marble edifice, whose high, tapering spire was radiant with white and gold.

"The city appeared to cover several miles, and behind it in the background there rolled off a fair country, checkered by the careful lines of industry, enterprise, and educated wealth; everywhere the scene was one of singular and most striking beauty.

"It was natural to visit this interesting region. I was rowed across the river, landing at the chief wharf of the city. No one met me there. I looked and saw no one. I could hear no one. It was quiet everywhere, save for the buzzing of the flies and the water-ripples on the shallow of the beach. The town lay in a dream, under some deadening spell of loneliness, from which I almost feared to waken it, for plainly it had not slept long. There was no grass growing up in the paved ways; rain had not entirely washed out the prints of dusty footsteps; yet I went about unchecked into empty workshops, rope-walks, and smithies. The spinner's wheel was idle, shavings were on the carpenter's work-bench, fresh bark was in the tanner's vat, light wood stood piled against the baker's oven. No work-people looked to learn my errand. I went into gardens, clinking the latch loudly after me, to pull the marigolds, heartsease, and lady-slippers; drank from a well with a noisy chain, but no one called out to me from the windows or dog came forward to bark an alarm. The house-doors were all unfastened, and when at last I timidly entered them, I found dead ashes white upon the hearths, and awoke irreverent echoes by walking over the naked floors. On the outside of the town was the city graveyard, but there was no record of a plague. Some of the stones were newly set, and their dates recent. Beyond the graveyard, out in the fields, I saw where the fruited boughs of a young orchard had been torn down, and noticed the still smouldering remains of a barbecue fire, which had been made from the fence-rails that surrounded it. It was the latest sign of life there; fields upon fields of yellow grain lay rotting around.

"Only two portions of the city seemed to suggest the import of this mysterious solitude. In the southern suburb the houses looking out upon the country showed, by their splintered woodwork and walls battered to their foundations, that they had lately been the mark of a destructive cannonading. In and around the splendid temple, which had been the chief object of my admiration, armed men were barracked with their stacks of musketry and pieces of heavy ordnance. These challenged me, and wondered I had had the temerity to cross the river without a written order from their leader. They told me the story of the dead city; that it had been a great manufacturing and commercial mart, sheltering over twenty thousand persons; that they had waged war for several years with its inhabitants, and had only lately been successful in driving them away at the point of the sword. They boasted of their powers in the three days' battle, and of their exploits ; told how they killed a boy of fifteen and his father, who had just become residents, and whom they admitted were without reproach. They conducted me to the sculptured walls of the curious temple, where they said the banished inhabitants had been accustomed to celebrate the mystic rites of an unhallowed worship, and pointed out certain features of the building which they had sedulously destroyed as having been peculiar objects of a former superstitious regard. There was a deep well in one of the chambers, which they said had been constructed with some dreadful design ; and they told me romantic stories of a great marble basin supported by twelve oxen the size of life. They said 'here parents went into the water for their lost children, and children for their parents ;' 'widows for their spouses, and young persons for their lovers ;' and thus 'the great vase' was associated to them with tender memories, and was the object of all others in the building of the most idolatrous affection. They permitted me to ascend to the steeple to see where it had been struck by lightning the Sunday previous, and to look out east and west on wasted farms, like the one mentioned, extending until they were lost in the distance.

"It was nightfall when I crossed the river on my return. The water was rough, so I made for a point higher up, landing where a faint glimmering light invited me to steer. Here among the rushes, sheltered only by the darkness, were several hundred human creatures in an uneasy slumber on the ground. My movements roused them. Dreadful indeed were the sufferings of these forsaken beings, bowed and cramped by the cold and sunburn alternating, as each weary day and night dragged on. Almost all of them were the crippled victims of disease. They were there because they had no homes, nor hospital, nor poorhouse, nor friend to offer them any. They were all alike bivouacked in tatters. These were Mormons turned out of Nauvoo, too poor, too ill, to follow their more fortunate companions, who were *en route* for Council Bluffs. There were six hundred and forty persons thus lying on the Iowa flats opposite Nauvoo, and the last who were turned out of it."

Mrs. Emma Smith, the true wife of the first Mormon Prophet, with her children and several of the older members of the numerous Smith family who had followed the fortunes of Joseph to Nauvoo, did not leave the neighborhood of the city to go west with the other Mormons under the leadership of Brigham Young. Mrs. Smith afterward married Major L. C. Bidamon, and died a few years ago.

The temple, after being partially destroyed by the militia in 1846, was burned in 1848. Two years later it was partly rebuilt by the French Icorrians (brought to Nauvoo by Monsieur Cabet, the Socialist) for their own use; but a terrible tornado in 1850 threw most of the splendid edifice to the ground.

The rise, progress, and destruction of Nauvoo occupied seven years. Its history is as wonderful as that of any city ever built, and many of its mysteries have yet to be told.

CHAPTER X.*

The journey through the wilderness—The arrival of the Saints in Utah—The early political situation of the Mormons in "the Land of the Honey Bee"—The Mountain Meadow butchery—The influence of the Mormons over the Indians.

WE have seen how Brigham Young hastened from Boston to Nauvoo, "convinced of his right to lead the people," and that the Mormons willingly yielded to his conviction, and obeyed him implicitly. He was at this time under forty years of age. He is said to have had a most prepossessing countenance, a very frank and pleasing address, and to have had the art of inspiring enthusiasm without allowing it to influence his own motives or actions.

We have also seen that, owing to his persuasive eloquence, Rigdon had been sent adrift, and that he had commanded that the temple should be completed, as he said, to fulfil Joseph Smith's "revelation" to that effect, but probably to make plans for the future welfare of the Saints. Seeing that their position was fraught with dangers of both a seen and unseen character, he determined that it must be changed—in short, that his followers must seek "pastures new," find fresh surroundings and possibilities somewhere. Meanwhile he announced to his people that they must be ready to

---

* In continuation of the history of the wanderings of the Saints from Kirtland to Deseret, and the events following in their career up to the present time, the most reliable authorities upon this subject have been carefully consulted.

sacrifice their all whenever he called upon them to do so. They wept and hesitated ; but his authority prevented further expressions of regret, as they were bound to him by oaths which they shuddered to remember, and which yet made them love him all the more as their president, brother, and spiritual adviser. Agents were sent by him to explore the Western Territories. Their glowing accounts of Utah, both for its great natural resources and beauty, induced him to select that locality as the future residence of the Mormons. Besides, Utah at the time belonged to Mexico ; it was beyond the control of the detested Stars and Stripes and the uncomfortable people who had thrice expelled " the chosen ones" from their resting-places. He made his purpose known to those nearest to him in office, but the common herd were merely informed that their destination was to be somewhere in the Rocky Mountains, and that they were to move on in that direction as far as Council Bluffs that season. This new exodus began in February, 1846, the bleakest and coldest month of the year in that section of the country. Here Brigham Young proved himself a general, as well as commander. He directed everything, and as the long trains of wagons, filled with the Saints and such of their household effects as they could carry, passed by him and crossed the " Father of Waters," he comforted and inspired and counselled the weeping emigrants. Certain men were left behind at his desire to sell the property of the church, and then shake off the very dust of that unfortunate locality.

This journey proved to be one of intense suffering. Many of the wretched wanderers fell ill and perished by the way, and the survivors gladly received the command to make Council Bluffs a temporary abode for rest and recuperation. The church was reorganized on the arrival of the advanced company of the Saints, as they had moved in sections and not in one solid body, probably so as not to disturb the inhabitants of the sparsely populated country with their numbers. Some of the historians of Mormonism have asserted that when the Mormons left Nauvoo they intended to go no farther than Council Bluffs; but there is very strong evidence that Brigham Young had fully laid his plans to make Utah his future scene of action and rule before he crossed the Mississippi. So far on the route, he must make plans for the completion of the journey. The obstacles in the way of this intention would have intimidated a less courageous man. There was still over one thousand miles to traverse through an almost unknown country. If it was difficult to transport armed troops through the wilderness, what skill and energy must it not have required to send a nearly unprovided-for, feeble, and impoverished company of men, women, and little children such a distance! But his wisdom and forethought controlled the whole matter.

An event in our national history, the war between the United States and Mexico, was imminent. He had had inklings of it; he hoped for it, and was prepared to take advantage of it. His followers could wait a little longer before making, as he believed, their last "hegira" to a land flowing with milk and honey. The government had offered large bounty money to all who would enlist in the army.

The Mormons took advantage of this offer, and, concealing their real design under a sham patriotism, sent an agent to Washington asking that they should be permitted to form an organization to fight the common enemy. The government approved, or, at all events, allowed this scheme to be carried out, and in this way money was furnished which assisted the emigrants to cross the plains toward Utah. July 24th, 1847, one hundred and forty-three men, pioneers, entered Salt Lake Valley accompanied by Brigham Young. Five days later a portion of the "Mormon Battalion" enlisted under the call for troops for Mexico—about one hundred and fifty men—under Captain Brown, who had arrived escorting a company of emigrants, gathered from various quarters in the East and the Old World. The men belonging to these two companies, at Young's command, had left their families at Council Bluffs.

From Fremont's reports of Utah, we learn that Salt Lake City was at this time already laid out. The men, under Captain Brown's command, were sent on to join General Scott's army, while the others commenced improvements for domestic comfort, farming operations in the vicinity, etc., and preparing for the residence of the Saints, who were still at Council Bluffs in sickness, poverty, and discontent. Getting matters into material shape, Brigham returned to Iowa, where his presence seemed to inspire the waiting Mormons.

In the spring of 1848 the Mormons, a company of nineteen hundred men, women, and children, started from Council Bluffs for Salt Lake. Colonel Kane's description of this journey has all the interest of a romance. The distance was enormous, the perils of the way great, and the zeal of the travellers and their courage under difficulties, sufficient to try the stoutest hearts, were only equalled by their faith. "It was a pilgrimage which has not been paralleled in the history of mankind since Moses led the Israelites from Egypt," wrote the enthusiastic Kane. They had sickness, weariness, skirmishes with the Indians, and they also had their pleasures and rewards in this extraordinary journey of several months. They were surprised by beautiful scenery, and they languished over dreary wastes. Brigham told them stories, encouraged dancing to make them merry, and had theatrical performances to distract their attention. It was their custom, whenever the camp rested for a few days together, to make great arbors, or "bowries," as they were called, for meetings of devotion, conference, and when the ground was trodden firm as places for conviviality. Colonel Kane's account of a Mormon ball in the wilderness is graphic. "If anything told the Mormons had been bred to other lives, it was the appearance of the women as they assembled here," he wrote. Before their flight they had sold their trinkets to raise ready money. The men wore waistcoats with useless watch-pockets, and the ears of the women bore the loop-marks of rejected pendants. Otherwise they lacked nothing becoming decorous maidens and matrons. The gravest and most trouble-worn of the company seemed the most anxious to throw off the burden of heavy thoughts. To the combination of violins, sleigh-bells, horns, and tambourines did they trip "the light fantastic toe." French fours, Copenhagen jigs, Virginia reels, and other figures were executed with the spirit of people too happy to be slow, or bashful, or constrained, from an early hour until the sun had gone down behind the sharp sky line of the mountains. Children were born, and numbers died and were buried on the route, but they pressed on, under their leader's direction, for the new home beyond the States and their enemies, arriving at Deseret, "*the Land of the Honey-Bee,*" in the autumn of 1848. And now lands were surveyed and placed under careful cultivation, and Salt Lake City was made habitable; and then followed an era of enterprise and success that was as wonderful as it was unprecedented and contradictory. Settlements were established in every direction, the soil was subdued and irrigated for cultivation, and the people built the city and the temple, and established mills, and workshops, and numerous industries, under the personal directions of the ever-watchful bishops. Missionary corps were newly organized for foreign lands, and an Immigration Fund established, which soon resulted in a swarming influx to Utah from all parts of Europe.

This "Immigration Fund" supplied the new converts —mainly from the working classes—from the time they left their homes until they reached some little farm in Utah, to which each person or family was assigned, and was under a regularly-organized police government, by which the percentage of casualties and cost of transportation were greatly lessened. *The same system of bringing Mormon emigrants to Utah is in use at the present time.*

As early as March, 1849, a convention, or "conference," was held at Salt Lake City for the organization of a State, which was accomplished under the name of "*Deseret.*"

Congress refused to accept the constitution which was adopted, but elected the country into a Territory in the following September, and President Fillmore appointed Brigham Young its governor.

But troubles still followed the career of the Mormons. The judges appointed by the President for the new territory were driven out of Deseret by the "Prophet" governor. Colonel Steptoe, of the United States Army, was sent by the President to occupy Brigham's place. He arrived in Utah with his command in August, 1854, but he found the Mormons so numerous and so belligerent, and his military escort was so small, that he deemed it prudent not to assume the functions of his office; and after wintering there went to California with his troops.

The effect of this retirement of the troops was most unfortunate. From that day the Mormon "Prophet" successfully defied the government and outwitted the Federal authorities.

After Colonel Steptoe's departure, Brigham said, in a sermon to his people: "*I am and will be governor, and no power can hinder it until the Lord Almighty says: 'Brigham, you need not be governor any longer.'*" Everything from that time seemed to consolidate his power.

In February, 1856, Judge Drummond, of the United States District Court, was driven from his bench by an armed Mormon mob, and he was forced to adjourn his court, and all the United States Army officers, except the Indian agents, were obliged, by the terrible condition of affairs, to leave the country.

The Mormons endeavored to justify their treatment of the Federal officers by alleging that many of them were disreputable and profligate — statements that have a foundation in truth. In 1857 Alfred Cumming, of Missouri, was appointed Governor of Utah by President Buchanan. At the same time Judge Eckels, of Indiana, was made Chief-Justice of the territory. Colonel S. A. Johnson, with a body of twenty-five hundred United States troops, was sent to protect them and enforce the laws. The Mormons were greatly excited over the approach of the troops, and Brigham Young, in his capacity as governor, issued a proclamation denouncing the army as a mob, forbidding it to enter the territory, and called upon the people of Utah to arms to repel its advance. It was September when the army reached the confines of Utah, and, owing to delays, was overtaken by the snows of winter. A party of mounted Mormons, on October 5th, destroyed several supply trains, captured eight hundred oxen, and drove them into Salt Lake City. The army went into winter quarters at Fort Bridger, where it suffered greatly. Their expedition had been fitted out with great care, and cost our government $14,000,000. October 27th Governor Cumming issued his war proclamation, declaring the Territory to be in a state of rebellion. Colonel Kane, who had been with the Mormons during their last exodus, and seems to have been at this time very much their friend and confidant (if not convert), arrived at Salt Lake in 1858 with letters from President Buchanan, and succeeded in bringing the hostile "Saints" and the governor sent to subdue them into relations of harmony.

He was quickly followed by two peace commissioners " offering pardon to all Mormons who would submit to Federal authority." This "offer of pardon" was carried by Governor Powell, of Kentucky, and Major McCullough, of Texas. The conditions were accepted by the heads of the church. With a becoming consideration for this subdued people, the army was stationed forty miles from Salt Lake City, where it remained until the spring of 1860, and was then withdrawn.

The Mormons were now exultant and hopeful. They trusted in their prophet, and echoed his boastful assertions that "nothing could harm them." He had exhibited a rare union of reckless daring with the subtlest prudence, recognizing a point beyond which he could not go, which Joseph always failed to do ; and though lacking the lion-like personal courage of the first Prophet, he was more than his equal in moral heroism, and the mysterious control he exercised over his people.

During the war for the suppression of the great rebellion the Mormons were in a measure forgotten and overlooked; but since that time public attention, through the facilities of travel, has been continuously turned in that direction. The Pacific Railway has brought Utah in close relations with the Eastern States. The isolation of the "Saints" is again disturbed by tourists, many of them distinguished travellers, who have investigated the exceptional social system of this people through the forbearance of their leaders.

On the 5th of October, 1869, Vice-President Colfax, at the time a visitor at Salt Lake City, was invited to make a speech from the portico of the Townsend House. He embraced the opportunity to tell the Mormons his opinion of polygamy in a bold and fearless way. "It seemed to break the spell of the Prophet's authority," and the wildest excitement ensued among his people. The Schismatics, under the leadership of one Harrison, established a paper called the *Mormon Tribune*, and organized a liberal movement. They and all the disaffected were cut off from the church.

On the other hand, Brigham and the leading magnates stood their ground firmly. John Taylor (the present high priest, ruler, and president of the Mormons), the leading mind and the best writer among them, answered Mr. Colfax by a letter in the New York *Tribune* of November 19th, 1869, in which he very cleverly disputed all his arguments and most of the assertions he had made at Salt Lake City.

The *Tribune* of the Schismatics was hopefully received by certain people in Utah, as it professed to aim to break down bigotry and fanaticism, to foster ideas in harmony with the age, and to be in direct opposition to polygamy; but the attempt to bring Mormonism into agreement and adjustment with the accepted standards of the civilized world as to right and wrong soon grew to be an absurdity.

New "revelations" were announced by these opposers of the Prophet, but their publication made no difference in the general estimate of the situation of affairs. In 1870 Miss Anna Dickinson made the following statements concerning Brigham Young, in her popular lecture entitled "Whited Sepulchres:"

All this vast machinery is controlled by a single mind; he is the fourth largest depositor in the Bank of England; he controls the largest emigration fund in the world, whose emissaries appeal to the poor, and homeless, and destitute, and ignorant, and misguided of all lands, with the offer of a home, and a free passage to it, etc. Yet he it was who, through his trained assassins disguised as Indians, committed the Mountain Meadow massacre, and by whose order William Hickman committed over four hundred murders in Utah.

Brigham Young was treated with the consideration of a "political offender," and while the people of the United States organized powerful agencies for the conversion of the heathen abroad, it is justly said we neglect to interpose an enlightened Christianity in behalf of the victims of Mormonism.

Of the many items of interest concerning the second "Prophet," the following is given by an English writer on Mormonism:

Brigham Young was sent with others to England to preach the Gospel. They landed at Liverpool, April 6th, 1840, partook of the sacrament, and commenced preaching. They were penniless, and dependent on their enemies for support—which at first was small—and Brigham suffered much and often. He superintended affairs, issued an edition of the 'Book of Mormon,' inaugurated the publication of the 'Millennial Star,' and on April 30th, 1841, shipped seven hundred and sixty-nine converts to Nauvoo, sailing himself with them, and leaving many Mormon organizations and churches well established behind him.

This was but one of his many "missions," all of which seem to have been successful.

The anniversary of the day on which Brigham Young (with the heads of the church) arrived at Salt Lake City is still observed and celebrated; hence the 24th of July is the great national day with the Mormons, instead of the 4th of July.

The second Prophet inaugurated a military corps known as "Minute Men," which was quite distinct from the "Danites." It was a well-drilled company of armed men, taking the character of a militia held in reserve for general defence. The Danites were also well organized, in a military point of view, with habits of undying watchfulness and hardy enterprise, acquired by a long experience of continued conflict with the Gentiles. Ever on their guard, skilled in all the arts of wood-craft, able to read as on a printed page upon the desert—by which many of their homes were surrounded—those signs which to inexperienced eyes would pass unnoticed, familiar with the laws of life and climate which characterize their country, and thus enabled to turn all to their own advantage as against strangers, and, more than all, familiar with the wild passes and deep mountain gorges through which all approach at that time could be made, they seem to have been in possession of many elements of strength to use for their own ends and in self-defence. Some of the most horrible deeds of violence against the enemies of Mormonism in Illinois, Missouri, and Utah have been committed by this "band." It is denied by the Saints at the present time that such an organization now exists, if it ever existed; but the truth in this matter is too fully established to admit of a doubt as to the past, and there is every reason to believe that any unusual hostility shown to the Mormons by individuals or the Government would prove that the "Danites" are not all dead.

Mormonism in Utah has always been associated with the *Mountain Meadow Massacre*, the most shocking event in its history. The following brief account of this horror has been taken from the most reliable sources extant.

In the year 1857 there were two trains of emigrants crossing the plains, with the intention of going to Southern California—one from Missouri and one from Arkansas. The former was made up of men who called themselves "Missouri Wild Cats;" the other a company of highly respectable persons, who had many indications of wealth and ease, that were seeking a new home. They travelled leisurely through the week and rested on Sundays. There were men, women, and children of every age among them, and many families related to each other by the ties of consanguinity and marriage. They were generally Methodists, and had morning and evening prayers.

The "Wild Cats" contracted a high respect for them, and came as near them in travelling as the methods of the camp at night would allow. Like all other pilgrims of the time toward "the golden Pacific coast," the emigrants counted upon recruiting at Salt Lake City, while camping by the side of the river Jordan. Ordinarily the Mormons were glad to see the arrival of Gentile emigrants *en route* for the far West, as it gave occasion for trade and barter; but certain events had changed the spirit of the people. Federal troops were then advancing toward Zion, and the Saints were preparing for a defence of their homes. The Missouri company, it has been asserted, boasted on the way that they had helped to drive the Mormons from their State, and that they intended to further assist the approaching United States troops to " wipe out the Mormons."

The alleged animus against the other company was that Orley P. Pratt, the Mormon apostle, missionary, etc., had been recently shot in Arkansas by Hector McLean for an attempt to steal his children and send them to their mother in Utah, who years before had been converted to the Mormon faith in California, and had subsequently become one of the wives of Pratt. McLean was not arrested for this act, as Mormonism and the apostles were unpopular. Brigham Young, as Governor of Utah and a sworn officer of the United States, was in honor bound to protect these two companies of emigrants that were resting by the Jordan. Those from Arkansas were told to move on, and they took up their line of travel for Los Angeles. From this time they were made to suffer discomforts of many kinds by the way; the Mormons denied them provisions of every kind and food for their cattle. The Indians were their only friends, and sold them all the corn they had to spare. They halted at Cedar City one day, and then started on that fatal trip which soon came to a conclusion that has shocked the whole civilized world. The fourth day after the emigrants left Cedar City, a regiment of Mormon militia, under the command of Major John D. Lee, left that place in pursuit of them. This militia had the "make up" of a military force in the field, with the exception of artillery. Lee invited the Piede Indians to accompany him, and with these auxiliaries he had a force that could not be resisted by the poor hungry emigrants.

At Mountain Meadows the victims were overtaken. They had "rolled out" from camp ignorant of the danger which awaited them; and when fairly *en route* the Indians commenced firing upon them. The emigrants were taken completely by surprise. They had no idea that the military expedition had been sent against them until they saw and felt it. They were not confused, however, but immediately corralled their wagons and prepared for defence, but were, alas! too far from water. For four days they fought the soldiers and Indians heroically. At the end of the second day Major Lee sent for re-enforcements, which arrived on the morning of the fourth day's fight. During the third day's battle it became a necessity with the emigrants to get water. It was in plain sight, but covered with the rifles of the troops. Hoping that the Mormons might have some pity on them, they dressed two little girls in white and sent them with a bucket in the direction of the spring. The soldiers shot them down! The morning of the fourth day Lee told the men under his command that his orders from headquarters were "*to kill the entire company except the children.*" He sent a flag of truce to them, offering to them, if they would lay down their arms, to protect them. What could the men do but believe in this promise? They marched out of their little fort, laid down their arms, and marched up to the spring where Lee stood, and placed themselves under his protection. The line of march was then taken up, and after the distance of half a mile had been traversed Lee gave the command to halt; then immediately the command to shoot them down. A long wail of agony from the surviving women and little ones who had followed their fathers, husbands, and brothers is beyond the powers of description. All the men had been slain. Another scene followed too revolting to be told, wherein these Mormon demons were allowed to commit the last outrage on these poor women. They were then killed, and the whole company stripped of their clothing and left without burial. Seventeen children were saved, and afterward distributed in Mormon families.*

In 1859 General Carlton raised a cairn of stones over the bleached skeletons of the emigrants. On one of the stones he caused to be written : "*Here lie the bones of*

---

* An Englishman, who, while still very young, married a Mormon woman, but was not himself a convert to the faith, has related to his son the incidents of a journey he made from Utah to California the year after the horrible butchery of the emigrants at Mountain Meadow. He saw the skeletons of some of the victims, and a fine gold watch which had been found close to this locality, and from certain marks was known to have belonged to some one of them. Farther on in this journey he visited a village where some children of the emigrants were housed by different Mormon families. Only one of them was old enough to remember and tell of the story of the massacre. The fate of that child is uncertain, but the others were sent to their relatives in the East for adoption. One of that fated band who were *en route* for California escaped, and, as Mr. —— relates, reached a settlement beyond Utah, where he believed he was in safety ; but the Indian savages employed by the Mormons in the fiendish work hunted him down, caught him unaware, and actually filled his body with arrows.

An English lady who has visited Utah during her travels in America is responsible for the following story. She says it was related to her by a missionary teacher to whom the experience occurred, in Utah. The lady teacher asked a neighbor, a carpenter, to make some repairs to the schoolhouse. The work was accomplished at noon-time, while the children were away, and the man said one day : " I believe you are a Christian, and I want to ask if you think I can be forgiven for helping in the Mountain Meadow Massacre ? I want to tell you ; it is on my mind all the time ; but if you betray me my life will be of no account." The teacher said she would not betray his confidence, and she believed, whatever his sins might be, they would be forgiven if he repented of them.

The carpenter then told her how a lovely, golden-haired little girl was sent to a spring for water that dreadful day, and that he was one of those commanded to shoot her down. That her look of entreaty was forever before his eyes—and then the strong man wept at the remembrance, while making this confession, of a barbarity that he dared not refuse to accomplish.

one hundred and twenty men, women, and children from Arkansas, murdered on the 10th day of September, 1857." Upon a cross-beam he caused to be painted: "*Vengeance is mine, saith the Lord, and I will repay it.*"

Brigham Young ordered this monument to be destroyed, and said the inscription should have read: "Vengeance is mine, saith the Lord, *and I have repaid it.*" John D. Lee was tried and executed by our Government for his part in the Mountain Meadow butchery. He was but the instrument of Brigham Young's hatred to McLean and the Gentiles generally, and was bound to carry out the malignant wishes of his leader, however willing or unwilling he may have been to do so. To Mormons freedom of thought is as impossible, it is said, as to idiots and to slaves. Elder W. C. Penrose, a church magnate, and editor, at the present time, of the Deseret *News*, the official church paper, has recently been giving, on successive Sunday evenings in Salt Lake City, some carefully-prepared lectures on "Blood Atonement" and "Mountain Meadow Massacre"—themes upon which hitherto a discreet silence has been kept, or, if alluded to, have been called "absurd Gentile lies" and "mere bugaboos." "His line of defence (writes a correspondent of a Boston paper) concerning the ruthless slaughter of the emigrants, is that they did evil things against the Indians of Southern Utah, and that three or four wicked bishops in those parts concluded not to let them escape from the Territory alive, but wrote to Brigham Young for advice, and then helped the redskins to cut their throats before the messenger returned. The Mormon monarch knew nothing of the shocking performance until some weeks later, and for thirteen years was duped into the belief that only Indians were concerned in it.

Alas for Penrose! the facts are against his theory. There is not a shadow of doubt that Brigham knew the whole story, and that for nineteen years he did his best to conceal the facts and shield the criminals from justice." It is said that he gave Lee several new wives as a reward for conducting the massacre. The policy of the Mormons in regard to the Indians, whom they call "Lamenites," from the first has been to conciliate them in every way; that every tribe should be visited by their missionaries, to instruct them in their faith, and by intermarriage and every other means to bring them under Mormon control. This influence has been used to prejudice the red men against the United States Government and to stir up the tribes to open hostilities toward unprotected settlements; and in cases of collision between the Mormons and United States troops to assist their professed friends, the Saints. The Danites and the Indians have been allies in ambush fights and murders of travellers through the Territories; and in many horrible deeds of violence, where innocent men, women, and children on the frontiers have been slain by the red men, the incentive for vengeance has been given by Mormon agents. Men wise in the affairs of our nation and in the policy of the Mormon Church have predicted that if Uncle Sam ever rigidly attempts to abolish polygamy and to force the Saints into an outward show of morality, there will be serious trouble; that a civil war will eventuate, in which the "Lamenites" and the Mormons will act as a unit against the Gentiles. The Indians are commonly called "the Battle-axes of the Lord" throughout the Territory. They are a most degraded people, the Mormon missionaries having done little or nothing toward their civilization. Some of the terrible deeds attributed to the Lamenites have been committed by Mormons painted and dressed as Indians, as the following extract will prove:

> "I am in possession of the evidence that bands of these Salt Lake Mormons, armed, dressed, and painted—having the appearance of Indians—are stationed on the way to California and Oregon, for the purpose of robbing the emigrants. Many murders and robberies have already been committed by these demons in human shape, which have been published to the world and attributed to the Indians. . . .* WILLIAM SMITH."

William was the Prophet's brother, and wrote the above nearly eight years before the "Mountain Meadow Massacre."

---

* "Melchizedek and Aaronic Herald." By Isaac Sheen. Vol. I., No. 8. Covington, Ky., February, 1849.

CHAPTER XI.*

Polygamy in Utah—The Granting of Woman's Suffrage in 1871—The Edmunds Bill—Sketch of Brigham Young.

The sons of Joseph Smith, the first Mormon Prophet, have denied that their father practised or approved of polygamy at any time in his career; but the evidence against such assertion is so strong and multiplied that we cannot fail to accept it. The best authorities upon this subject state that it was both preached and practised by Smith and his followers at Nauvoo, much to the horror and disgust of his first wife. Indeed, it was one of the sins of the Mormons at Nauvoo which their neighbors held in the greatest dislike, and which made up the sum total of a depravity which they determined to be rid of at any sacrifice. It was Brigham Young's policy immediately after the settlement of the Saints in Zion to have a "revelation" concerning polygamy, or "celestial marriage," for his people. He told them the "peculiar institution" should have the fulness of its glory in Utah, "where the faithful can sit under their own vine and fig-tree, none daring to make them afraid." Marriage was no longer a civil contract; it was to be a sacrament of the church and a sacred tenet of the faith. Nevertheless, Utah belonged to the United States, and it was

---

* Frequent quotations are made in this chapter from Mrs. Joseph Cook's "Face to Face with Mormonism," read before the Woman's Home Missionary meeting in Boston, March 27th, 1884, and Miss Kate Field's lecture entitled the "Mormon Monster," delivered in Boston, in the autumn of 1884.

uncertain what Congress might wish to do with such a direct innovation upon Christianity. His mind grasped the conclusion that there was power in numbers. It would be difficult to deal with a whole people for an infraction of the law; he would make an ostentatious show of a plurality of wives, which should be a virtue and not an indiscretion. He made constant arguments in favor of polygamy in the Tabernacle in winter, and in the open-air places of worship in summer. He said the world was rapidly hastening to a close, and there were multitudes of spirits in the other world waiting for honorable bodies, in which they could dwell in the flesh. The Gentiles were corrupt, and the ethereal spirits were waiting anxiously for the favors of the Mormons. This argument was considered lucid; it appealed to the grandest sentiment of humanity—self-abnegation. The women would be selfish if they could not endure the wandering affections of their lords and masters. It was their duty to make a self-sacrifice! The greatest of all the human family had given His life to redeem; why could they not help to save? From that time the women of Utah have not only made the sacrifice of the most vital principle of their souls, but have willingly or unwillingly submitted to a life of daily affliction for the sake of an article of faith.

An authority upon Mormonism has written: "Whoever has read debasement in the women of Utah has done them injustice. Some there be who are devoid of refined sentiment and the nobler instincts of their sex, but no women in history ever deserved more respect and sympathy than the true women among the Mormons." They are taught to believe that polygamy is a divine institution, required in these latter days to regenerate and sanctify a world steeped in wickedness. They have endured the most heartrending sorrows, while the men have been told that he is noblest who values the companionship of the soul the least, that his wife is but the mother of his children. Thus the poor Mormon women are often placed upon the level of the most inferior animals. One of the noted of the apostles said: "We think no more of taking another woman than we do of buying another cow." The women of Utah have ever lived in constant dread of the time when their husbands would be obliged by church command to become practical polygamists. They have had a fearful struggle between obedience to the supposed laws of the Deity, as taught by the Mormon priesthood, and the wishes of their own natures. However pure, however true these poor women may be when converted to Mormonism, is it remarkable that, under the influences by which they are surrounded, they become *living martyrs?* What days of silent grief and misery they must endure! The story of such women can never be told. The Mormon men have claimed that the women "get used to plural marriage, and are happy in it." It is a libel upon the nature of woman to believe this statement for a moment. No woman ever desired to share her husband with another woman, and no husband could ever please two wives. Polygamy has enslaved the Mormon men, while it has martyrized the Mormon women. Brigham Young openly avowed that when Joseph Smith gave him "the order" for the first time that it was a great trial to his soul. The locks of an apostle turned white in a single night, it is said, when he was "commanded" to take another wife. In the earlier days of Mormon life in the mountains the elders made no concealment of their courtships. The maiden in her teens would be escorted by the already married intended husband of twice or thrice her years to places of public festivity, with all the attention of a romantic and love-stricken youth. When the day of marriage arrived, the bridegroom and his wife, and the bride with the relatives and invited guests, assembled in some place appointed for the ceremony. A scribe proceeded to carefully record the names, ages, native towns, States, and country of the parties to be married. · Brigham Young, who was the president, seer, Prophet, revelator, etc., and alone held the "keys" of this solemn ordinance, called upon the bridegroom and his wife and the bride to stand before him, the wife on the left hand of her husband, the bride to stand on her left. The wife was then called upon to place the hand of the bride in that of her husband, if she was willing to give the woman to her husband "to be his lawful wedded wife for time and all eternity." The president concluded the ceremony by saying:

"In the name of the Lord Jesus Christ, and by the authority of the Holy Priesthood, I pronounce you legally and lawfully husband and wife for time and for all eternity; and I seal upon you the blessings of the holy resurrection, with power to come forth in the morning of the first resurrection clothed with glory, immortality, and eternal lives; and I seal upon you the blessings of thrones, and dominions, and principalities, and powers, and exaltations, together with the blessings of Abraham, Isaac, and Jacob; and say unto you, Be fruitful, and multiply, and replenish the earth, that you may have joy and rejoicing in your posterity, in the day of the Lord Jesus Christ. All these blessings, together with all other blessings pertaining to the new and everlasting covenant, I seal upon your heads, through your faithfulness unto the end, by the authority

of the Holy Priesthood, in the name of the Father, and of the Son, and of the Holy Ghost. Amen."

The scribe then entered on the general record the date and place of the marriage, with the names of witnesses.

This was the fashion of "*sealing*" by President Young in "the good old days," when the ceremony was performed with as much ostentation as the parties could afford, openly, and without the slightest attempt at concealment. Plural marriages have latterly been made in a much quieter manner, but with the same form. Brigham drove a thriving trade both in marrying and divorcing the Saints. He said these services "supplied his wives with pocket money." With all the commanding influence of his position he could not silence the bickering and unhappiness in his own household, until he threatened to divorce all his wives, and told them that if they despised the order of heaven he would pray that they would be cursed by the Almighty. After such violence they "schooled themselves into silence and submission." In 1873 T. B. H. Stenhouse (twenty years a Mormon elder and missionary, and later an apostate), in his "Rocky Mountain Saints," wrote of polygamy as follows : "Thirty years of its practice under the most favorable circumstances have stamped it as a withering curse." The doctrine of plural marriages is not made prominent when Mormon missionaries seek to make converts in foreign lands. When the trains loaded with emigrants reach Salt Lake City the apostles and dignitaries of the church gather to receive them, and select fairer and more youthful inmates for their harems. A young girl from Sweden, not more than eighteen years of age, was thus selected by one of the twelve apostles—a man of sixty. She acknowledged that the union with so high a dignitary of the church would confer great honor upon her, but confessed that a young countryman of hers had won her affections during the voyage, and that she was to be married to him the following day. She supposed this statement would be sufficient, but was told that she must not resist the wishes of one of the anointed in Israel. The expectant bridegroom was interviewed by a bishop, but with no better success. Such contumacy was surprising. The will of one of the twelve must not be gainsaid. That night the girl was forced into his harem. The lover was found the next morning in a glen of the Wahsatach Mountains, alive, but mutilated.

All Mormons are not polygamists, but the priesthood urges the practice of polygamy on their followers, particularly upon young men of talent, influence, and independence of character. It keeps them in the church; for if such an one were to apostatize, a Mormon jury would require very slight evidence to find him guilty of bigamy. The idea of taking a second wife to a man who is happily married is at first extremely distasteful if he is at all sensitive; but a woman who was for thirty-five years in the Mormon Church says " no matter what a man may be, if he receives Mormonism *as a whole*, and governs himself by its teachings, he becomes hopelessly bad." Wife-whipping is not uncommon in Utah. It is a saying there that a man who is good at managing his cattle will be able to manage his women. The question has often been asked what induces women to go into "plurality" when they are acquainted with its horrors. It is to them a duty to be performed, no matter what the sacrifice may cost them —in short, it is their religion. They affirm that there is no salvation without it. They confess to their Gentile friends that they never see a day's happiness after their husbands take the second wife, but they yield to that sound Mormon doctrine that " the first duty of a woman is submission, the second silence." The following story is from the lips of the first wife of Orley Pratt, one of the most intellectually gifted of the Mormon leaders. At the time of its relation she was sixty years of age and in delicate health. Mrs. Pratt is said to have " a refined manner and unusual strength of character." Mrs. Pratt and her husband were married young, and for love. They became Mormons when there was very little said of polygamy among them or it was a prominent feature of their faith. They had three sons, of whom they were proud, and they were happy in each other. Orley Pratt developed great powers of oratory, which made him acceptable as a preacher at home and missionary abroad. In these days Brigham Young found fault with him for being such a strict monogamist. It was a bad example for the young men. This went on for three years, a season of anguish to both husband and wife, particularly to her, as she saw that the president's insidious influence was gaining ground with him. He told her it was his duty to yield to the teachings of Christ. At last he yielded, although reluctantly. The second wife did not come into their family, and Mrs. Pratt says her husband was as wretched as herself; but this feeling wore away with him, and then she had only begun to drink of the bitter cup. A third, fourth, and fifth wife was added, but were not admitted into the house of the first wife, where her children were growing up. Mrs. Pratt began to see the effect of this unnatural mode of life upon her husband. His affections seemed blunted. He was indifferent to her and her children. In the earlier stages of this man's polygamous career he spent most of his time with the wife of his youth, visiting his other wives at rare intervals. As a crowning insult to her, he informed her that henceforth he should divide his time equally between his different households. With the true spirit of a woman, Mrs. Pratt then said to him that she would never again receive him as her husband, as he had lost his place in her heart. He did not believe her—it was only a woman's threat. She remained true to her word. She so trained her sons to hate the system that had made her life wretched, that they became pronounced Mormon apostates, although they endured repeated persecutions from Brigham Young.

If a polygamous Mormon is wealthy each wife can have a separate establishment. Sometimes cottages are seen side by side, where there is a wife in each cottage. One of the apostles kept nine wives in a large house, each wife having her own apartments. When an impecunious Mormon takes several wives, he expects them not only to support themselves, but sometimes to take care of him as well. Poverty with polygamy renders these people positively brutish. A Christian minister, who is thoroughly acquainted with the Mormons, says: " Nowhere in the United States is there more squalid poverty in proportion to the population, or a greater lack of the comforts of life among the lower classes, than in Utah." This will apply to the Territory at large rather than to Salt Lake City, where poor people have as many comforts as the impecunious enjoy in other large cities. It is an established fact that Mormonism degrades all the finer feelings of the soul, and that old age is not honored among them. If there is an aged wife in a household, she is the common drudge. Sometimes she is sent adrift to take care of herself. The missionaries of Christian churches in Utah report that they have their hands full in caring for the sick, the aged, the destitute, and the helpless, who are brought there by the Mormon missionaries, and then left to shift for themselves.

Mormon polygamy has an infamous pre-eminence over that of the Turks in the intermarriage of near relations. It is not uncommon for a man to marry sisters, or mother and one or more daughters, as they agree better than strangers. In the southern settlements of Utah are found all the most revolting features of Mormonism. In the *Fortnightly* for October, 1881, a Federal judge, who has resided near Salt Lake City for years, testifies that there is no law on the statute-book of the Territory against incest. The claim that polygamy produces finer offspring than monogamy has been proved to be an insolent fallacy. "The looseness of divorce among the Saints has never had a parallel among the most depraved of Gentiles," says a recent observer of Mormon methods in Salt Lake City. Brigham Young granted divorces to his people, while admitting they were not worth the paper they were written upon. He did not hesitate to untie as many elders in Israel as could pay for the luxury.

The granting of woman's suffrage by Brigham Young, in 1871, was a *coup d'état* for the purpose of strengthening Mormonism and circumventing "the enemy"—in other words, the Gentiles. But in a Territory where polygamy is proclaimed to be "divine," and that has no laws against bigamy, adultery, and kindred crimes, there can be no just appreciation of woman. Female suffrage under such conditions is a mockery and delusion. Polygamy, although "the corner-stone of the Mormon Church," is not inserted in its thirteen printed articles of faith. It would alarm those turning their eyes toward "the land of promise." The elastic conscience of John Taylor, the present "Prophet, seer, and revelator" to "the chosen people," is exemplified by his emphatic denial of polygamy, in 1850, when he "rejoiced in multitudinous households."

The refrain of a "song of Zion" runs

> "Then, oh, let us say—
> God bless the wife that strives
> And aids her husband all she can
> To obtain a dozen wives."

The meaning of the spiritual wife doctrine is that man without woman, and woman without man, cannot be saved. The more wives a man has the fuller will be his glory in the next world. It is the policy of wealthy Mormons to treat visitors to Salt Lake City with effusive hospitality; hence these careless tourists who are willing to accept such courtesies remark: "These Mormons don't seem so bad, after all. At all events, they are very polite." English travellers are singularly lenient to this relic of barbarism in our American civilization. A member of Parliament gave a decidedly rose-colored view of Salt Lake City in the January, 1884, number of the *Nineteenth Century*. He wonders at the antipathy toward the Mormons manifested by Americans in the Eastern States, and considers it due to the exalted idea respecting women entertained by Americans generally, which explains their aversion to the Mormons as identified with polygamy. This gentleman undoubtedly received attentions from the wealthiest of the Mormons, and had only seen the fair exterior of this apple of Sodom. An Anti-Polygamy Society has long been established in Salt Lake City, and a heroic fight against Mormonism is being made by a Gentile daily called the *Salt Lake Tribune*. There are twelve thousand polygamists in Utah, and its obnoxious doctrines are more openly and defiantly preached than ever. Under the statutes there has been one conviction for polygamy within twenty years.

March 2d, 1882, the "Edmunds Bill" passed both Houses of Congress, after weary delays and much opposition. It reads as follows:

[PUBLIC—No. 30.]

AN ACT to amend section fifty-three hundred and fifty-two of the Revised Statutes of the United States, in reference to bigamy, and for other purposes.

Be it enacted by the Senate and House of Representatives of the United States of America in Congress assembled, That section fifty-three hundred and fifty-two of the Revised Statutes of the United States be, and the same is hereby, amended so as to read as follows, namely:

"Every person who has a husband or wife living who, in a Territory or other place over which the United States have exclusive jurisdiction, hereafter marries another, whether married or single, and any man who hereafter simultaneously, or on the same day, marries more than one woman, in a Territory or other place over which the United States have exclusive jurisdiction, is guilty of polygamy, and shall be punished by a fine of not more than five hundred dollars and by imprisonment for a term of not more than five years; but this section shall not extend to any person by reason of any former marriage whose husband or wife by such marriage shall have been absent for five successive years, and is not known to such person to be living, and is believed by such person to be dead, nor to any person by reason of any former marriage which shall have been dissolved by a valid decree of a competent court, nor to any person by reason of any former marriage which shall have been pronounced void by a valid decree of a competent court, on the ground of nullity of the marriage contract."

SEC. 2. That the foregoing provisions shall not affect the prosecution or punishment of any offence already committed against the section amended by the first section of this act.

SEC. 3. That if any male person, in a Territory or other place over which the United States have exclusive jurisdiction, hereafter cohabits with more than one woman, he shall be deemed guilty of a misdemeanor, and on conviction thereof shall be punished by a fine of not more than three hundred dollars, or by imprisonment for not more than six months, or by both said punishments, in the discretion of the court.

Sec. 4. That counts for any or all of the offences named in sections one and three of this act may be joined in the same information or indictment.

Sec. 5. That in any prosecution for bigamy, polygamy, or unlawful cohabitation, under any statute of the United States, it shall be sufficient cause of challenge to any person drawn or summoned as a juryman or talesman, first, that he is or has been living in the practice of bigamy, polygamy, or unlawful cohabitation with more than one woman, or that he is or has been guilty of an offence punishable by either of the foregoing sections, or by section fifty-three hundred and fifty-two of the Revised Statutes of the United States, or the act of July first, eighteen hundred and sixty-two, entitled "An act to punish and prevent the practice of polygamy in the Territories of the United States and other places, and disapproving and annulling certain acts of the Legislative Assembly of the Territory of Utah," or, second, that he believes it right for a man to have more than one living and undivorced wife at the same time, or to live in the practice of cohabiting with more than one woman; and any person appearing or offered as a juror or talesman, and challenged on either of the foregoing grounds, may be questioned on his oath as to the existence of any such cause of challenge, and other evidence may be introduced bearing upon the question raised by such challenge; and this question shall be tried by the court. But as to the first ground of challenge before mentioned, the person challenged shall not be bound to answer if he shall say upon his oath that he declines on the ground that his answer may tend to criminate himself; and if he shall answer as to said first ground, his answer shall not be given in evidence in any criminal prosecution against him for any offence named in sections one or three of this act; but if he declines to answer on any ground, he shall be rejected as incompetent.

Sec. 6. That the President is hereby authorized to grant amnesty to such classes of offenders guilty of bigamy, polygamy, or unlawful cohabitation, before the passage of this act, on such conditions and under such limitations as he shall think proper; but no such amnesty shall have effect unless the conditions thereof shall be complied with.

Sec. 7. That the issue of bigamous or polygamous marriages, known as Mormon marriages, in cases in which such marriages have been solemnized according to the ceremonies of the Mormon sect, in any Territory of the United States, and such issue shall have been born before the first day of January, Anno Domini eighteen hundred and eighty-three, are hereby legitimated.

SEC. 8. That no polygamist, bigamist, or any person cohabiting with more than one woman, and no woman cohabiting with any of the persons described as aforesaid in this section, in any Territory or other place over which the United States have exclusive jurisdiction, shall be entitled to vote at any election held in any such Territory or other place, or be eligible for election or appointment to or be entitled to hold any office or place of public trust, honor, or emolument in, under, or for any such Territory or place, or under the United States.

SEC. 9. That all the registration and election offices of every description in the Territory of Utah are hereby declared vacant, and each and every duty relating to the registration of voters, the conduct of elections, the receiving or rejection of votes, and the canvassing and returning of the same, and the issuing of certificates or other evidence of election in said Territory, shall, until other provision be made by the Legislative Assembly of said Territory as is hereinafter by this section provided, be performed under the existing laws of the United States and of said Territory by proper persons, who shall be appointed to execute such offices and perform such duties by a board of five persons, to be appointed by the President, by and with the advice and consent of the Senate, not more than three of whom shall be members of one political party ; and a majority of whom shall be a quorum. The members of said board so appointed by the President shall each receive a salary at the rate of three thousand dollars per annum, and shall continue in office until the Legislative Assembly of said Territory shall make provision for filling said offices as herein authorized. The secretary of the Territory shall be the secretary of said board, and keep a journal of its proceedings, and attest the action of said board under this section. The canvass and return of all the votes at elections in said Territory for members of the Legislative Assembly thereof shall also be returned to said board, which shall canvass all such returns and issue certificates of election to those persons who, being eligible for such election, shall appear to have been lawfully elected, which certificates shall be the only evidence of the right of such persons to sit in such assembly : *Provided,* That said board of five persons shall not exclude any person otherwise eligible to vote from the polls on account of any opinion such person may entertain on the subject of bigamy or polygamy nor shall they refuse to count any such vote on account of the opinion of the person casting it on the subject of bigamy or polygamy ; but each house of such assembly, after its organization, shall have power to decide upon the elections and qualifications of its members. And at, or after the first meeting of said Legislative Assembly whose members shall have been elected and returned according to the provisions of this act, said Legislative Assembly may make such laws, conformable to the organic act of said Territory and not inconsistent with other laws of the United States, as it shall deem proper concerning the filling of the offices in said Territory declared vacant by this act.

Approved, March 22, 1882.

[*Printer's No.*, 8925.]

48th CONGRESS,
1st *Session*.

S. 1283.

IN THE HOUSE OF REPRESENTATIVES.

JUNE 19, 1884.

Ordered to be printed.

AN ACT to amend an act entitled " An act to amend section fifty-three hundred and fifty-two of the Revised Statutes of the United States, in reference to bigamy, and for other purposes," approved March twenty-second, eighteen hundred and eighty-two.

Be it enacted by the Senate and House of Representatives of the United States of America in Congress assembled, That in any proceeding and examination before a grand jury, a judge, justice, or a United States commissioner, or a court in any prosecution for bigamy, polygamy, or unlawful cohabitation, under any statute of the United States, the lawful husband or wife of the person accused shall be a competent witness, and may be called and may be compelled to testify in such proceeding, examination, or prosecution without the consent of the husband or wife, as the case may be ; but such witness shall not be permitted to testify as to any confidential statement or communication made by either husband or wife to each other during the existence of the marriage relation.

SEC. 2. That in any prosecution for bigamy, polygamy, or unlawful cohabitation, under any statute of the United States, whether before a United States commissioner, justice, judge, a grand jury, or any court, an attachment for any witness may be issued by the court, judge, or commissioner, without a previous subpœna, compelling the immediate attendance of such witness, when it shall appear to the commissioner, justice, judge, or court, as the case may be, that there is reasonable ground to believe that such witness will unlawfully fail to obey a subpœna issued and served in the usual course in such cases; and in such case the usual witness fees shall be paid to such witness so attached: *Provided*, That no person shall be held in custody under any attachment issued as provided by this section for a longer time than ten days; and the person attached may at any time secure his or her discharge from custody by executing a recognizance, with sufficient sureties, conditioned for the appearance of such person at the proper time as a witness in the cause or proceeding wherein the attachment may be issued

Sec. 3. That any prosecution under any statute of the United States for bigamy, polygamy, or unlawful cohabitation may be commenced at any time within five years next after the commission of the offence; but this provision shall not be construed to apply to any offence already barred by any existing statute of limitation.

Sec. 4. That every ceremony of marriage, or in the nature of a marriage ceremony, of any kind, in any of the Territories of the United States, whether either or both or more of the parties to such ceremony be lawfully competent to be the subjects of such marriage or ceremony or not, shall be certified in writing by a certificate stating the fact and nature of such ceremony, the full names of each of the parties concerned, and the full name of every officer, priest, and person, by whatever style or designation called or known, in any way taking part in the performance of such ceremony, which certificate shall be drawn up and signed by the parties to such ceremony, and by every officer, priest, and person taking part in the performance of such ceremony, and shall be by the officer, priest, or other person solemnizing such marriage or ceremony filed in the office of the probate court, or, if there be none, in the office of the court having probate powers in the county or district in which such ceremony shall take place, for record, and shall be immediately recorded.

Such certificate shall be prima facie evidence of the facts required by this act to be stated therein, in any proceeding, civil or criminal, in which the matter shall be drawn in question. Any person who shall violate any of the provisions of this section shall be deemed guilty of a misdemeanor, and shall, on conviction thereof, be punished by a fine of not more than one thousand dollars, or by imprisonment not longer than two years, or by both said punishments, in the discretion of the court.

Sec. 5. That every certificate, record, and entry of any kind concerning any ceremony of marriage, or in the nature of a marriage ceremony of any kind, made or kept by any officer, clergyman, priest, or person performing civil or ecclesiastical functions, whether lawful or not, in any Territory of the United States, and any record thereof in any office or place, shall be subject to inspection at all reasonable times by any judge, magistrate, or officer of justice appointed under the authority of the United States, and shall, on request, be produced and shown to such judge, magistrate, or officer by any person in whose possession or control the same may be. Every person who shall violate the provisions of this section shall be deemed guilty of a misdemeanor, and shall, on conviction thereof, be punished by a fine of not more than one thousand dollars, or by imprisonment not longer than two years, or by both said punishments, in the discretion of the court. And it shall be lawful for any United States commissioner, justice, judge, or court before whom any proceeding shall be pending in which such certificate, record, or entry may be material, by proper warrant, to cause such certificate, record, or entry, and the book, document, or paper containing the same, to be taken and brought before him or it for the purposes of such proceeding.

Sec. 6. That nothing in this act shall be held to prevent the proof of marriages, whether lawful or unlawful, by any evidence now legally admissible for that purpose.

Sec. 7. That it shall not be lawful for any female to vote at any election hereafter held in the Territory of Utah for any public purpose whatever, and no such vote shall be received or counted or given effect in any manner whatever; and any and every act of the governor and Legislative Assembly of the Territory of Utah providing for or allowing the registration or voting by females is hereby annulled.

Sec. 8. That all laws of the Legislative Assembly of the Territory of Utah which provide for numbering or identifying the votes of the electors at any election in said Territory are hereby disapproved and annulled; but the foregoing provision shall not preclude the lawful registration of votes, or any other provisions for securing fair elections which do not involve the disclosure of the candidates for whom any particular elector shall have voted.

Sec. 9. That the laws enacted by the Legislative Assembly of the Territory of Utah conferring jurisdiction upon probate courts, or the judges thereof, or any of them, in said Territory, other than in respect of the estates of deceased persons and in respect of the guardianship of the persons and property of infants, and in respect of the persons and property of persons not of sound mind, are hereby disapproved and annulled; and no probate court or judge of probate shall exercise any jurisdiction other than in respect of the matters aforesaid; and every such jurisdiction so by force of this act withdrawn from the said probate courts or judges shall be had and exercised by the district courts of said Territory, respectively.

SEC. 10. That the laws enacted by the Legislative Assembly of the Territory of Utah which provide for or recognize the capacity of illegitimate children to inherit or to be entitled to any distributive share in the estate of the father of such illegitimate child are hereby disapproved and annulled; and no illegitimate child shall hereafter be entitled to inherit from his or her father or to receive any distributive share in the estate of his or her father: *Provided*, That this section shall not apply to any illegitimate child born previous to the passage of this act.

SEC. 11. That all laws of the Legislative Assembly of the Territory of Utah which provide that prosecution for adultery can only be commenced on the complaint of the husband or wife are hereby disapproved and annulled; and all prosecutions for adultery may hereafter be instituted in the same way that prosecutions for other crimes are.

SEC. 12. That the acts of the Legislative Assembly of Utah incorporating, continuing, or providing for the corporation known as the Church of Jesus Christ of Latter-Day Saints, and the ordinance of the so-called General Assembly of the State of Deseret incorporating the Church of Jesus Christ of Latter-Day Saints, so far as the same may now have legal force and validity, are hereby disapproved and annulled, so far as the same may preclude the appointment by the United States of certain trustees of said corporation as is hereinafter provided. The President of the United States, by and with the advice and consent of the Senate, shall appoint fourteen trustees of the said corporation, who shall have and exercise all the powers and functions of trustees and assistant trustees provided for in the laws creating, amending, or continuing the said corporation, which trustees so appointed shall hold their respective offices for the term of two years; and the trustees of said corporation shall annually or oftener make a full report to the Secretary of the Interior embracing all the property, business affairs, and operations of the said corporation; and the Legislative Assembly of the Territory of Utah shall not have power to change the laws respecting said corporation without the approval of Congress. Said trustees shall each give bond, payable to the United States, with good and sufficient security, for the faithful discharge of the duties incumbent upon him as trustee, in such sum as may be prescribed by the Secretary of the Interior.

SEC. 13. That it shall be the duty of the Attorney-General of the United States to institute and prosecute proceedings to forfeit and escheat to the United States the property of corporations obtained or held in violation of section three of the act of Congress approved the first day of July, eighteen hundred and sixty-two, entitled " An act to punish and prevent the practice of polygamy in the Territories of the United States and other places, and disapproving and annulling certain acts of the Legislative Assembly of the Territory of Utah," or in violation of section eighteen hundred and ninety of the Revised Statutes of the United States ; and all such property so forfeited and escheated to the United States shall be disposed of by the Secretary of the Interior, and the proceeds thereof applied to the use and benefit of the common schools in the Territory in which such property may be : *Provided*, That no building shall be forfeited which is held and occupied exclusively for purposes of religious worship.

SEC. 14. That in any proceeding for the enforcement of the provisions of law against corporations or associations acquiring or holding property in any Territory of the United States in excess of the amount limited by law, the court before which such proceeding may be instituted shall have power in a summary way to compel the production of all books, records, papers, and documents of or belonging to any trustee or person holding or controlling or managing property in which such corporation may have any right, title, or interest whatever.

SEC. 15. That all laws of the Legislative Assembly of the Territory of Utah, or of the so-called government of the State of Deseret, creating, organizing, amending, or continuing the corporation or association called the Perpetual Emigrating Fund Company are hereby disapproved and annulled ; and it shall not be lawful for the Legislative Assembly of the Territory of Utah to create, organize, or in any manner recognize any corporation or association for the purpose of or operating to accomplish the bringing of persons into the said Territory for any purpose whatsoever.

SEC. 16. That it shall be the duty of the Attorney-General of the United States to cause such proceedings to be taken in the Supreme Court of the Territory of Utah as shall be proper to dissolve the said corporation and pay the debts and to dispose of the property and assets thereof according to law. Said property and assets, in excess of the debts and the amount of any lawful claims established by the court against the same, shall escheat to the United States, and shall be taken, invested, and disposed of by the Secretary of the Interior, under the direction of the President of the United States, for the benefit of common schools in said Territory.

Sec. 17. That the existing election districts and apportionments of representation concerning the members of the Legislative Assembly of the Territory of Utah are hereby abolished ; and it shall be the duty of the governor, Territorial Secretary, and the United States judges in said Territory forthwith to redistrict said Territory, and apportion representation in the same in such manner as to provide, as nearly as may be, for an equal representation of the people (excepting Indians not taxed), being citizens of the United States, according to numbers, in said Legislative Assembly, and to the number of members of the counsel and House of Representatives, respectively, as now established by law ; and a record of the establishment of such new districts and the apportionment of representation thereto shall be made in the office of the secretary of said Territory, and such establishment and representation shall continue until Congress shall otherwise provide ; and no persons other than citizens of the United States otherwise qualified shall be entitled to vote at any election in said Territory.

Sec. 18. That the provisions of section nine of said act approved March twenty-second, eighteen hundred and eighty-two, in regard to registration and election offices, and the registration of voters, and the conduct of elections, and the powers and duties of the board therein mentioned, shall continue and remain operative until the provision and laws therein referred to be made and enacted by the Legislative Assembly of said Territory of Utah, shall have been made and enacted by said assembly and shall have been approved by Congress.

Sec. 19. That whoever commits adultery shall be punished by imprisonment in the penitentiary not exceeding three years ; and when the act is committed between a married woman and a man who is unmarried, both parties to such act shall be deemed guilty of adultery ; and when such act is committed between a married man and a woman who is unmarried, the man shall be deemed guilty of adultery.

Sec. 20. That if an unmarried man or woman commits fornication, each of them shall be punished by imprisonment not exceeding six months, or by fine not exceeding one hundred dollars.

Sec. 21. That commissioners appointed by the Supreme Court and district courts in the Territory of Utah shall possess and may exercise all the powers and jurisdiction that are or may be possessed or exercised by justices of the peace in said Territory under the laws thereof, and the same powers conferred by law on commissioners appointed by circuit courts of the United States.

SEC. 22. That the marshal of said Territory of Utah, and his deputies, shall possess and may exercise all the powers in executing the laws of the United States possessed and exercised by sheriffs and their deputies as peace officers; and each of them shall cause all offenders against the law, in his view, to enter into recognizance to keep the peace and to appear at the next term of the court having jurisdiction of the case, and to commit to jail in case of failure to give such recognizance. They shall quell and suppress assaults and batteries, riots, routs, affrays, and insurrections, and shall apprehend and commit to jail all felons.

SEC. 23. That the office of Territorial superintendent of district schools created by the laws of Utah is hereby declared vacant; and it shall be the duty of the Supreme Court of said Territory to appoint a Territorial superintendent of district schools, who shall possess and exercise all the powers and duties imposed by the laws of said Territory upon the Territorial superintendent of district schools, and who shall receive the same salary and compensation, which shall be paid out of the treasury of said Territory; and the laws of the Territory of Utah providing for the method of election and appointment of such Territorial superintendent of district schools are hereby suspended until the further action of Congress shall be had in respect thereto. The said superintendent shall have power to prohibit the use in any district school of any book of a sectarian character or otherwise unsuitable. Said superintendent shall collect and classify statistics and other information respecting the district schools in said Territory, showing their progress, the whole number of children of school age, the number who attend school in each year in the respective counties and average length of time of their attendance, the number of teachers and the compensation paid to the same, the number of teachers who are Mormons, the number who are so-called Gentiles, the number of children of Mormon parents and the number of children of so-called Gentile parents, and their respective average attendance at school. All of which statistics and information shall be annually reported to Congress, through the governor of said Territory and the Department of the Interior.

SEC. 24. (a) A widow shall be endowed of the third part of all the lands whereof her husband was seized of an estate of inheritance at any time during the marriage.

(b) The widow of any alien who at the time of his death shall be entitled by law to hold any real estate, if she be an inhabitant of the Territory at the time of such death, shall be entitled to dower of such estate in the same manner as if such alien had been a native citizen.

(c) If a husband seized of an estate of inheritance in lands exchanges them for other lands, his widow shall not have dower of both, but shall make her election to be endowed of the lands given or of those taken in exchange; and if such election be not evinced by the commencement of proceedings to recover her dower of the lands given in exchange within one year after the death of her husband, she shall be deemed to have elected to take her dower of the lands received in exchange.

(d) When a person seized of an estate of inheritance in lands shall have executed a mortgage on such estate before marriage, his widow shall nevertheless be entitled to dower out of the lands mortgaged as against every person except the mortgagee and those claiming under him.

(e) Where a husband shall purchase lands during coverture, and shall at the same time mortgage his estate in such lands to secure the payment of the purchase-money, his widow shall not be entitled to dower out of such lands, as against the mortgagee or those claiming under him, although she shall not have united such mortgage; but she shall be entitled to her dower as against all other persons.

(f) Where in such case the mortgagee, or those claiming under him, shall, after the death of the husband of such widow, cause the land mortgaged to be sold, either under a power of sale contained in the mortgage or by virtue of the decree of a court of equity, and if any surplus shall remain after payment of the moneys due on such mortgage and the costs and charges of the sale, such widow shall nevertheless be entitled to the interest or income of the one third part of such surplus, for her life, as her dower.

(g) A widow shall not be endowed of lands conveyed to her husband by way of mortgage unless he acquire an absolute estate therein during the marriage period.

(h) In case of divorce dissolving the marriage contract for the misconduct of the wife, she shall not be endowed.

Passed the Senate June 18, 1884.

Attest: ANSON G. McCOOK, Secretary.

Brigham Young died August 29th, 1877. He was a remarkable man in many ways, although illiterate. He flattered himself that he would live to the age of Moses, as he was of a long-lived family; but physically he was not strong. He was born in Whittingham, Vermont, in 1801, of poor but respectable parents. While very young his family removed to central New York, and at a suitable age he became a painter and glazier by trade at Canandaigua, and later in New York City. It was his boast in his days of power, when saying that the meek and poor were to inherit the kingdom of heaven, that he had been "only eleven and a half days at school." In 1832, when he joined the Mormons at Kirtland, Ohio, "the gift of tongues" seemed to "fall on him." He affected to believe that Joseph Smith held "the keys of Salvation;" that he was God's servant; that he did not belong to the people, but to the Lord, and was doing the work of the Lord; and if he should lead them astray, it was because they ought to be led astray. If they were chastised or destroyed it was to accomplish some righteous purpose.

Such a blind and unreasoning faith in Joseph, with the abject slavery of mind and will it involves, it is evident was the key to Brigham Young's after life. No one had the right to sit in judgment upon Joseph's actions; no one should question his successor's motives or performance. Joseph, it is said, had a secret fear of Brigham's power, and sent him on long missions for reasons of a prudential character. During these journeys, and the intercourse he had with the world, his wits were sharpened, and his natural powers of intellect were quickened by keen observation. He established the first Mormon mission in England at Liverpool. He was naturally a leader, and the Mormons yielded to his magnetic sway when he succeeded the prophet at Nauvoo. After the establishment of the Saints at Zion he is said to have had slight acquaintance with the outside world for several years, and was seldom seen by his people at large save on Sundays. He was always occupied with affairs, and nothing in public or private life of the slightest moment escaped his knowledge. His residence in Salt Lake City, called the "Lion House" from the figure of a crouching lion over the portico, is a group of houses of unequal dimensions, that has neither architectural beauty nor grace. There are twenty rooms on the "living floor," with sleeping rooms above, and weaving rooms, laundry, dining-room, etc., on the lower floor. Here most of his nineteen wives and children resided. The largest of the buildings he called the "Bee Hive House." It was his official residence. Here he had his *chambre à coucher;* here his buttons and stockings were adjusted to his satisfaction. After business hours it was difficult to determine where he would be, as he was "master of his own actions." The legal Mrs. Young lived at the White House, a modest dwelling at a little distance from the Lion House. Three favorites had each a separate establishment. All the wives were working women save Amelia, Emmeline, and Mrs. Cobb Young, the last favorite and "best beloved." He wanted no "ornaments" about him, and despised fashion and conventionalities. When the first millinery shop was established in Salt Lake City, he said it was as "terrible" to him "as an army with banners." His wives had none of the Christian marital relations with him. They met in the dining-room or in the parlor at evening prayer, when the household collected at the ringing of a bell; but the greater part seldom saw him elsewhere. They had no romance in their lives, only hard work and the sacrifice to their faith. The penalty of a scandal to a Mormon woman is death, and few women have the bravery to hazard it;

so Brigham's wives endured the situation. His attentions to his wives in public were calculated. His first wife and a favorite sat on a sofa with him at all festivities. The other wives found places as they pleased, although he usually danced with five or six of them after he had done the duty dance with Amelia, Emmeline, or "the best beloved." He danced well for a man of his years, and enjoyed a break-down at the close of the evening. He was habitually an early-riser, and transacted a great deal of business before breakfast. At nine o'clock he began the routine of the day in his office, with the assistance of a private secretary. He schooled himself to settle any point in once thinking of it deliberately, then gave his decision, and never wished to hear of it again. From ten to eleven he gave audience to apostles, bishops, leading citizens, and strangers ; and not infrequently to "Sisters" who had complaints to make of their husbands. Brigham had complete control over his people. He knew everything. He claimed that the Saints could do nothing without his knowledge and approval, "even to the ribbons a woman should wear." He assumed the most vital interests in every man's affairs. The only rank in Zion is the priesthood, but the "royal blood of Young overtops them all," he said. His journeys through the territory were processions of state. Banners were paraded before him bearing "Hail to Zion's Chief," "God Bless Brigham Young," and other sentiments of welcome and adulation. He took his favorite wife with him in these triumphal visits. As a preacher he was forcible and vigorous, but his language was a mixture of profanity, vulgarity, bad grammar, "cheap rant, and poor cant." He was ever listened to attentively, as his hearers expected he would "say something" they were anxious to learn. The actual wealth of this prophet will never be known. He had vast tracts of land in Utah, interests in various railways, mines, and manufactories, was the third largest depositor in the Bank of England, and had other moneys "salted away" for necessities. As he had control of the tithing, and possessed unlimited credit, he could add "house to house" and "field to field." He could have left imperishable records for the care of the sick and needy behind him; but he never founded a hospital or institution worthy of mention. There never were people more willing to obey than the Mormons during his administration. He could have swayed them as he pleased; and if he had been a good man he had a rare opportunity for proving it. In the later years of his life an English tourist described Brigham Young as being above the middle height, portly in person, and as having a sensual expression of countenance. He had the look of a determined man and the character of an obstinate one, and, as an enthusiastic admirer once said of him, "If he makes up his mind to do a thing, all hell can't stop him." The Prophet's dress was of gray homespun cloth, with which he wore a black satin vest and cravat, with a broad, unstarched collar turned over it. He was a paragon of neatness. He slept alone; his life was ascetic; his favorite food baked potatoes, with buttermilk, and his drink water. His followers deemed him "an angel of light; his enemies a goblin damned." His two most conspicuous qualities were his selfishness and his imposture. No mortal can estimate the dreadful influence of Brigham Young's thirty-years' rule upon the Mormons.* He set them examples of robbery, perjury, open murder, and secret assassination. He often preached the neces-

---

* Appendix No. 25.

sity of murder (blood atonement) in order to save souls. In 1857 Ann Eliza, his fifteenth wife, left him, and petitioned the United States Court for a divorce, which was denied on the ground that the marriage was polygamous, and therefore null and void. In 1871 Brigham was indicted for polygamy, but no conviction was reached through the lax enforcement of the law by the United States officials then in power. Besides his other offices, he was "Grand Archer of the Order of Danites."

He left seventy-five children, all amply provided for. According to some authorities, he had thirty-six wives. Dora Young, one of his numerous daughters, apostatized, and declared that the first thing that opened her eyes to the atrocities of Mormonism was her father's wholesale perjuries. With the bravery of spirit in which this remarkable man encountered every circumstance in his eventful career, Brigham Young arranged his temporal affairs before making his exit from life. He ordered where and how he should be buried. Evidently he feared that some of his many victims would endeavor to procure his body after death, either through motives of revenge or the desire for profit, and his wishes were carefully executed. His grave is in an otherwise unused yard in the rear of one of his houses of residence. An iron railing surrounds a flat gray stone slab, which bears no inscription. The slab is said to weigh several tons, and covers the vault wherein the remains of the second Prophet rest, in a stone sarcophagus surrounded by several outer casings that are cemented with extraordinary care. After his burial there was a report that he was still living, which probably arose from the fact that the most ignorant and deluded of the Mormons were unwilling to believe that Brigham Young was mortal. There are still people among the Saints who aver that their great Prophet is alive and dwelling somewhere in obscurity from motives that he deems wise and prudential, and that when the time arrives for him to reappear he will return to them with renewed power and glory.

His demise to the better educated of his followers, to his partners in fraud and delusion, was an evident relief. During his life they were merely his puppets, which he swayed at his will. They accepted his policy in all directions, but could carry it out in agreement with their own ideas.

This man will always stand out as a unique character in history. His mental abilities were greater than those of Joseph Smith, but his personal powers of attractiveness were far less. Some one has written of him as follows: "Brigham Young is very human. He can button himself up to an unwelcome visitor in a style that a stranger is not likely to forget; but when he is in excellent humor he is a perfect Chesterfield." He bewailed the fact that there was silver and gold in the hills of Utah; he forbade his people from searching for it, and the first prospectors who went to Utah to look for it he ordered should be assassinated. He said: "If men grow rich they will want fine houses and horses; their women will want fine clothes, and it will be the destruction of our holy religion."

He called himself "*the lion of the Lord*," and he made freedom of thought as impossible to the Mormons as to idiots or slaves. In common with the elders and other Mormons, Brigham was fond of talking of the mysteries of his religion. Whether it is ever permitted to the unsanctified to gain an insight into these "mysteries" or no, this much is certain—the facts which are hidden by the sayings and writings of the Mormons are ofttimes more interesting than any, if any, which they have yet disclosed.

CHAPTER XII.

John Taylor elected as successor to the second Prophet—The trial of Rudger Clawson for bigamy—Salt Lake City—Its beautiful location—The Tabernacle and public buildings—Mormon conferences—The freedom of the ballot in Utah—The present generation of Mormons—The Territory of Utah—Predictions regarding the future of Mormonism—Far-seeing Mormons preparing a rendezvous for the victims of the Edmunds law.

WHEN Brigham Young died, in August, 1877, it was generally believed throughout the civilized world that the disintegration of Mormonism would follow that event. With the removal of his iron and arbitrary rule, it was supposed that there would be an independence of feeling among the Saints that had not previously existed, and that as railways were constructed, mines developed, and industries established, together with the influx of a Gentile population, the founding of Christian schools, and various institutions under the patronage of Christian missions, the whole scheme of "exclusive salvation" would gradually become extinct. The fallacy of such an opinion is shown by the situation of affairs in Utah at the present time. Brigham Young, Jr., failing to secure his father's office, John Taylor was elected as the successor of the second Prophet. The office fell to Taylor, but upon the shoulders of George Q. Cannon the mantle of authority really descended.

Both men have played conspicuous *rôles* in the history of Mormonism. Both are of English birth, and emigrated to this country when very young. John Taylor is adroit, shrewd, subtle ; is well educated, is a vigorous writer, and possesses the rarest tact, or he never could have steered his way through the stormy seas of Mormon experiences successfully, or adapted himself to the changeful and tyrannical rule of Brigham Young. He was a favorite with Joseph Smith, and was with him and his brother Hyrum in the jail at Carthage, Ill., at the time they were killed by an infuriated mob. He was then called the "Apostle Taylor," and, it is said, "comforted" the brothers while they were in durance vile. As he was a man of marked ability, and made himself useful in many ways in Utah, he was intrusted with important missions by Brigham Young to distant countries, and possibly to keep him from the realization of ambitious schemes at home, as many other men of talent were sent by the shrewd Prophet. In the year 1852 Taylor founded a Mormon school in Paris called "L'Etoile du Deseret," and has translated the "Book of Mormon" into French and German. He has also written several books for the enlightenment of the Mormons in spiritual matters. Of these is a work he calls "The Government of God," which has been translated into several languages. President Taylor is now considerably over seventy years of age, and has been a resident of the United States for fifty years. He is tall and distinguished in his personal appearance, and has the winning arts which culture and travel frequently give to a man of wit. His residence in Salt Lake City is called "the Gardo," a handsome house that Brigham built for his favorite Amelia, and after the Prophet's death was purchased as the future home for Mormon presidents. It is, in fact, the "White House" to the people, who look upon Taylor as their real president and political as well as spiritual ruler. He has four wives, and while on a mission in the Isle of Jersey a few years ago made proposals of polygamous marriage to a pretty maiden whom he converted to Mormonism. Through the preaching of Young, Taylor, and Cannon, and other noted men of the faith, there are seventeen places for Mormon meetings in London alone, and a large number of Mormon missionaries scattered over Great Britain. George Q. Cannon has been a resident of the United States for forty years. For several years he was attorney for the Mormons at Washington, and although he has four wives and four broods of children, occupied a seat as delegate in Congress. Some one has said of him: "He is the sweetest and most plausible sophist on earth." When Brigham Young named him for the place he said: "I will thrust polygamy down the throats of Congressmen." Mr. Cannon's Congressional record proved that his leader's opinion of him was amply justified, and that the affairs of his people were adroitly managed by his wily stratagems and the influence of his honeyed speech.

Mr. Cannon has recently been appointed legal controller and counsellor of Mormon affairs by President Taylor. He is the premier of the Mormon estate, the head centre of all matters concerning his people. From his office at St. George he issues the commands, openly or secretly, which are to direct his people. His expressed opinion on any given subject is an *Ultima Thule* to the followers of Joseph, which they dare not dispute. In a defence of Mormonism Mr. Cannon has written: "Utah has been the Cinderella of the family of States; give her a fair opportunity, and see if she will not rank with all that is admirable and attractive with her more favored sisters."

With the death of Brigham Young the American leadership of the Mormons was at an end, as nearly all of their more influential men are of foreign birth. If a Mormon is asked of his belief, he will show a card, prepared for such inquiry, on which are printed the thirteen most important articles of his faith; but there is nothing of polygamy included in these articles. Their belief, as professed and practised, are two different things. While Mormonism preaches that polygamy is the one divine institution required in these latter days to regenerate and sanctify a world steeped in ignorance, their articles of faith, as shown to Gentiles, do not even mention it. Mrs. Paddock, the author of "The Fate of Madame La Tour"—a powerful story of Mormon life—and also a keen observer of passing events in Utah, has recently written to a friend in the East: "There have been few material changes in the condition of affairs in the Territory, with the exception of those resulting from the enforcement of the Edmunds law. Polygamists have been disfranchised and rendered ineligible to office, but practically the old men, the Mormon leaders who have controlled the affairs of Utah for thirty years, have simply abdicated in favor of their sons. Consequently the Territory is still under Mormon rule, and the priesthood have it still in their power to inflict severe punishment upon those who apostate from the Mormon faith. This power is exercised even outside of Utah toward apostates. Please understand that polygamy is not dying out. It is strengthening itself, enlarging its borders, and claiming fresh victims. What was done openly in this direction a few years ago is now done in secret, but the effect is as bad, or worse. Young girls with babes in their arms are taught to endure anything rather than give the names of the fathers of their children—the men to whom they have been 'sealed.' It is the man's safety that is secured by such means, and his interests are to be considered in advance of everything else. But Mormon ingenuity has devised still another method by which men may escape legal penalties. According to the present interpretation of the law, it is the *marriage ceremony* that constitutes the crime of bigamy; and if this is dispensed with, prosecution for bigamy cannot follow."

An intelligent woman, at present a member of the Presbyterian Church, who was formerly a Mormon, lived with Bishop Johnson ten years (according to her own testimony) as a plural wife before she was sealed to him; and says it is a common thing in the settlements for men to take plural wives *without any ceremony whatever*. The condition of the women who live in polygamy is not the saddest feature of the system. It is the children who suffer for the sins of their parents; who, in consequence of the life lived by their mother, are born deformed in body as well as in soul.

"A few years ago an educated, intelligent gentleman, a journalist, came here from Europe, bringing his young wife with him. How such people came to be entangled in the meshes of Mormonism was a marvel; but both appeared to be sincere believers in the Latter-Day Gospel. Soon a strong pressure was brought to bear upon the husband to induce him to contract a second marriage. The wife, finding opposition in vain, at length gave her consent, and the bride was brought home. A few months afterward the first wife gave birth to a child. The poor babe, doomed to bear the sins of others, never smiled, and never cried aloud, but always, night and day, it wept silently. Even in sleep great tears forced themselves from beneath its closed eyelids, and rolled over its cheeks, while its face bore the expression, not of infantile grief, but of the terrible anguish that the mother had endured in secret. After a few weeks it began to pine away, and at length, without any visible ailment, sank into its grave.

"'My baby died of a broken heart,' said the wretched mother. 'Every hour of its little life it shed the tears that I repressed before its birth, and the agony that I hid in my heart killed it at last.'" *

---

* From "Face to Face with Mormonism," by Mrs. Joseph Cook.

Every Mormon has a vote to be cast as John Taylor commands; and while the leaders of the Saints observe the forms of republican polity, their despotism is as absolute in its control as any on earth. Behind the Mormon creed there is a deadly menace to free government few suspect. Between their creed and the Government of the United States, the latter is of no account. To circumvent the laws and defeat justice is the aim of every Mormon who is a true convert to the faith.

President Arthur has won the respect of the law-abiding citizens of Utah by his recent reappointment of Governor Eli H. Murray, and placing Judge Zane, of Illinois, at the head of the Supreme Court. Judge Zane's first act was to try a polygamist, get him convicted, refuse bail, and send him to the penitentiary. This polygamy case of Rudger Clawson, the son of Bishop Clawson, has attracted attention throughout the country. The witnesses in Clawson's defence were among the most influential of the Saints. Of them was John Taylor, who is said to have surprised his followers by his testimony. As it bears upon polygamy, it will be given in part as it was reported in the *Salt Lake Tribune* of Saturday, October 18th, 1884, with the speech of Mr. Varian, the indictment, Judge Zane's charge to the jury, and the "sentence." He testified:

"I am president of the Church of Jesus Christ of Latter-Day Saints; don't know how long I have been president; the records would show; am acquainted to some extent with the doctrines of the church; am acquainted with the marriage sacrament; there is an Endowment House in this city; marriages by members of the Mormon Church are celebrated at the Endowment House or elsewhere; couldn't say where else; there is a doctrine of the church of plural marriage most certainly; the church does not require that when members of the faith enter into plural marriage, they must go through the Endowment House; as far as I know, most of the marriages are not performed in the Endowment House ; I know of plural marriages being performed outside of the Endowment House ; can't say who the parties married were ; I have no recollection of any plural marriage taking place outside of one of the places designated ; there is no place set apart specifically for performing plural marriages ; there is a place set apart for marriage ceremonies ; one place is the Endowment House and the other at our temples ; the Logan Temple was dedicated this past summer in May ; prior to that there was but one Endowment House in the Territory ; it was in this city ; there was a temple at St. George ; there were no others ; prior to May last there were no other places set apart for the performance of marriage ceremonies than St. George and this city ; St. George is in Washington County ; the church recognizes other places where plural marriages may be performed outside of endowment houses and temples, under certain circumstances ; can't say what those circumstances are ; if a man and woman were living in this city who desired to enter plural marriage, they would not necessarily have to be married in the Endowment House ; if they desired to marry outside of the city, they would have to have a dispensation for the performance of the act, but not for a specific place ; I give the authority to marry in all cases ; persons that I might appoint might also confer that authority ; I have conferred that authority in the past three years on Joseph F. Smith, George Q. Cannon, and others ; I don't remember what others at present ; this authority would be a general one till rescinded ; I cannot give the names of the priests authorized to perform these plural marriages within the past three years ; can't give any of them ; I could give you hundreds of names of parties in this Territory who have the authority ; there are no records kept of these appointments ; I don't know who all these parties are ; there are parties whom I do not know whether they are authorized or not ; I cannot give you the names of parties who were authorized to perform the marriage ceremonies in the Endowment House in 1883 ; I might ascertain the names, if there is a record of marriages kept ; if I wanted to find out where the records were I might be able to find them ; I don't think I will be good enough to look for the records for you ; I don't know anything about the record ; I can't tell you who the custodian of the records is ; I don't think I ever saw the marriage record ; I have never given any direction as to the custody of the record ; can't say that I ever made inquiry as to the whereabouts of the record ; have never been told who the custodian of the record was ; don't know whether in 1883 Angus Cannon or Elias Smith were custodians of the record ; I do not know whether there is any regulation of the church in regard to the records; no one who has not had the authority conferred on him can celebrate marriage; a number of others besides myself can confer this authority; I am the only one having the authority; I can't give you the names of parties in this city authorized to perform plural marriage; the ceremony of marriage is secret as to some; with the exception of those present taking part in the ceremony and the contracting parties, it is not necessarily a secret ceremony; there might be a great many others in whom the church had confidence, who would have a right to attend; the parties present at such a marriage are not sworn to secrecy, not that I know of."

"What is the ceremony of plural marriage?"

"I decline to answer the question."

Mr. Varian, in his speech in behalf of the prosecution, made a number of telling points relating to the Mormon hierarchy. In substance he said:

"That the Government had again been brought face to face with the Mormon Church. There had been many violations of the law of 1862, but there had been few prosecutions. The reasons for this were apparent to men who resided in the community. For years the dominant church had arrayed itself in one particular against the law of the land, holding that the Constitution of this country guaranteed religious liberty to every man. This church has not only set itself against the laws, but against the decisions of the Federal courts, claiming to be governed by a higher law than human law; forgetting that it had its very existence from the Government; that the very land upon which were built its temples and its tabernacles; that the very fields from which it drew its tithing fund; that the very expenses which enables it to carry on its local government, in great part, at least, had fallen from the munificent hand of the Government.

"It was at first claimed that polygamy was a tenet of the faith, and upon that ground claimed protection for their religious belief under the Constitution. On that issue it went to the country, and the courts and the United States Supreme Court in the Miles case said unmistakably that no such article of faith could claim protection under the Constitution of the country.

"Recollecting that the practice of polygamy was said to be enjoined by God, it would appear that if obedience was required to the law of God, that the same obedience would require a submission to the consequences. If martyrdom was to be invoked, martyrdom ought to be endured. It was not the history of martyrs, when called upon to suffer for their faith or belief, to seek to defeat the administration of law by acts of concealment, by denial and evasion, and by equivocation and fraud. The spectacle presented here was that of an organized community, an organized religious society, teaching from its pulpit and press that polygamy was right and commanded of God ; that the Supreme Court of the United States was not the final arbiter of the laws of the country, notwithstanding the Constitution has said that it shall be.

"In this case the prosecution had called many witnesses, it might seem to the jury unnecessarily. But there was a reason for it. The heads of the church, those prominent in authority, the bishops and elders, as well as the immediate relatives on all sides of the defendant, had been brought in for the purpose of exhibiting to the court something of the difficulty and the reason of its existence, in carrying on a prosecution in this community against a member of this church. The prosecution wanted to show to the jury directly if they could, indirectly if they could not, that although it was enjoined upon this people publicly at their meetings and in their tabernacles to live their religion, yet that command was only to be carried out in secrecy, that it was to be enshrouded in the darkness of night, that no one connected with the ceremony must know of his neighbor, that no one connected with the ceremony must allow his right hand to know what his left hand did.

"No one from President Taylor down has been able to tell anything about a record being kept of marriages performed in the church. Such an utter absence of memory, such an utter mental void, such absolute forgetfulness was perhaps never before exhibited in a court of justice. 'I do not remember,' 'I do not recollect,' 'I think there must be such a record, but I do not know where it is,' 'I do not dare to inform myself,' 'I will not be good enough to inform myself'—these and similar expressions fell from the mouths of the witnesses ; and he submitted to the jury that, as they looked over the case and reviewed it in their minds, all this must plainly show to them that there was an organized effort, an organized system directed in its objects to frustrate and defeat the administration of justice. There was a forgetfulness which was guilty in its origin and conception, and a man could as easily commit perjury by saying he did not remember or he did not recollect, as he could by affirming a negative to a fact. In a celebrated trial in England a witness baffled all the efforts of Lord Brougham to elicit the facts in the case by simply responding to all questions, 'I don't remember,' and for years after the words ' I don't remember' passed in the households of England as a synonym for fraud and perjury.

"The prosecution had been charged with excessive zealousness. He failed to see it in this case, but took the opportunity of saying, in behalf of the office he represented, that they purposed manifesting in all these cases all the zeal that the cases would warrant, until they could establish the law here as it was written on the statute books.

"This case against the defendant stood before the jury on two charges—one that of unlawful marriage and the other that of unlawful cohabitation. He directed the attention of the jury to the first of the two charges, stating that such a charge could be substantiated as well by circumstantial as by direct evidence. No witness saw the marriage performed, there was no record produced because none was kept, and nothing but circumstances and admissions could establish the guilt of the defendant. It was not to be supposed that defendant in entering into this illegal relationship would publish it to the world. The admissions of defendant make the strongest kind of evidence, and when corroborated, as they are in this case, are entitled to great weight.

"It is not disputed that defendant married Florence Dinwoodey for a first wife in August, 1882, and it is alleged that he married Lydia Spencer some time during the following year. Defendant was a member of the Mormon Church in good fellowship, his father was and is a bishop, and his family are all followers of the faith. The first that is known of defendant's connection with Lydia Spencer is her coming to Spencer Clawson's store, where defendant was employed. She moves to a house on Third South Street, and lives there in a bedroom and kitchen alone. Defendant is seen going and leaving there a great number of times. Connect the visits of defendant to Lydia Spencer in the Tenth Ward, his visits with her to the theatre and Tabernacle, his drawing water for her in midday a number of times, her moving to defendant's house in the Eighteenth Ward, her dining and living there as a wife would, her joining the Eighteenth Ward Mutual Improvement Association under the name of Lillie Clawson the night defendant did, and a chain of circumstances is linked together, whose strength cannot be disputed. Then after defendant was indicted Lydia Spencer moves to Mrs. Smith's house on West Temple Street, where defendant visited her a number of times, and had access by a back door. Lydia Spencer, who, above all persons on earth, ought to have an interest in the matter in protecting her fair name, has disappeared so utterly that no one appears to know where she has gone. She has gone where the woodbine twineth, but will 'bob up serenely' when the jury has brought in its verdict and the case is concluded. Even her own mother does not appear to know where she is or when she will return. The mother of defendant's first wife has also mysteriously disappeared. Mrs. Margaret Clawson, the mother of defendant, has also dropped out of existence in a miraculous manner, she who is interested above all others in maintaining her son's fair name. These are all small circumstances, but they are sufficient to cast upon the defendant the burden of explaining them away.

"Now, as to the admissions of defendant. You saw Mr. Caine on the stand. He could have no motive to attack the people of his faith or his ancestry. His father to-day represents this people in Congress. He is positive that defendant admitted to him that Lydia Spencer was his second wife. Three witnesses are brought forward to contradict Mr. Caine, and these are the only three witnesses for the defence. Instead of the defence bringing witnesses to contradict the marriage, they bring forward three men to impeach Caine's testimony. These witnesses were all witnesses for the prosecution, and were asked whether they had ever heard the matter of defendant's marriage to Lydia Spencer mentioned in defendant's presence, and they all answered no. The witness Lund remembered no conversation about defendant acknowledging Lydia Spencer as his second wife, and yet when he was put on the stand as a witness for the defence, he remembers clearly a conversation on the subject had in April, 1883.

"His memory was refreshed by reading Mr. Caine's testimony the day before he testified the first time, and yet when he testified the first time he remembered nothing about it. This witness slunk out of the court-room when he had finished testifying, as though the burden of his infamy would crush him to the ground.

"The next witness brought to impeach Mr. Caine was Orson Rodgers, and he was another of the gibbering idiots who knew nothing. R. V. Decker was the third and last witness brought to impeach Mr. Caine. I ask you whether this evidence for the defence did not strengthen Mr. Caine's testimony?

"When these circumstances are woven together they make a case concerning which there can be no reasonable doubt. It was to the speaker's mind a rather solemn occasion than otherwise, for never before had the exact condition of affairs here been brought home so forcibly to his mind. I now direct your attention to the question of jurisdiction—that is, as to whether the second marriage was performed within the jurisdiction of this court. If the marriage had not taken place in the counties over which this court had jurisdiction, the defendant might easily have proved this by the testimony of persons other than himself. A *prima facie* case having been made out by the prosecution, and there being no explanation by the defence, the jury is to presume that the marriage took place within the jurisdiction. Defendant was employed at the Z. C. M. I. prior to December, 1882, and being a private corresponding clerk, it is testified to that he was there continuously. After January, 1883, the testimony shows that the defendant was not absent from town one day up to the time of his indictment. It was about January, 1883, that Lydia Spencer's connection with defendant is first shown. As book-keeper of Spencer Clawson, the entries on the book show conclusively that he was within this jurisdiction for the past two years. The jury would be warranted in presuming from the circumstances the fact that defendant was not absent from the jurisdiction, and that the second marriage took place within it.

"The defendant is a young man, standing upon the threshold of life. If he went into the marriage relation under the laws of the church, he knew what would follow the results of his act. Had he reflected, he would have seen that civilization was coming westward and that the time was coming when the law would rise up in its majesty and be vindicated. He would have known that when the conscience of the American people was pricked, as it was when slavery was dominant, that this government would rise up in its glory and crush out all opposition to its laws. Had he reflected, he must have known that the laws of this country are supreme, and that all church laws in conflict with it must sooner or later become nugatory and of no effect. The defendant must suffer for the consequences of his own act."

VERBATIM REPORT.

By the Court. Mr. Clawson, will you stand up?

The defendant rises to his feet.

By the Court. You were indicted in this court upon an indictment charging that you have been guilty of polygamy on the dates charged thereon, by marrying Lydia Spencer, while your former wife, Florence Ann Clawson, was still living. In the second count of that indictment you were charged with unlawfully cohabiting with two women, Florence Ann Clawson and Lydia Spencer. To that indictment you entered a plea of not guilty, and a jury was sworn to try the issue; and after hearing the evidence, and the arguments of counsel, you were found guilty upon both charges.

Have you any further legal cause to show why judgment should not be pronounced against you?

By the Defendant. Your Honor, since the jury that recently sat on my case have seen proper to find a verdict of guilty, I have only this to say, why judgment should not be pronounced against me. I may much regret that the laws of my country should come in contact with the laws of God ; but whenever they do I shall invariably choose the latter. If I did not so express myself I should feel myself unworthy of the cause that I represent.

The Constitution of the United States expressly states that Congress shall make no law respecting the establishment of religion, or prohibiting the free exercise thereof. It cannot be denied that marriage, when attended and sanctioned by religious rites and ceremonies, is the establishment of religion.

The law of 1862 and the Edmunds Bill were expressly designed to operate against marriage, as practised and believed in by the Latter-Day Saints. They are, therefore, unconstitutional, and cannot command the same respect that a constitutional law would. That is all I desire to say, your Honor.

By the Court. The Constitution of the United States, as construed by the Supreme Court and by the authors of that instrument, does not protect any person in the practice of polygamy. While all men have a right to worship God according to the dictates of their own consciences, and to entertain any religious belief that their conscience, reason, and judgment dictate, they have not the right to engage in a practice which the American people, through the laws of their country, declare to be unlawful and injurious to society.

There have been among barbarous and superstitious people various conditions of men and women, with respect to each other ; and different classes of unions have been recognized. Promiscuity, the intercourse of the sexes without any definite relations ; polyandry, one wife and many husbands, or more than one husband ; and polygamy, one husband and many wives, or more than one wife ; and also monogamy, one wife and one husband. This last union has emerged with civilization from barbarism and superstition, and it is the institution of marriage that exists throughout the whole civilized world. It is the institution which that infinite source that manifests all things has manifested as the natural and true union to exist between men and women in civilized society. This marriage elevates women to an equality with men, so far as their different organizations will permit ; it recognizes the great principle which lies at the foundation of all justice and all equity—equality. No just government on earth can stand which permits any violation of this great principle of equality, upon which all just laws must rest at last. This union elevates woman, places her upon the high plane beside man, and in its light I believe that man and woman will ascend to the glorious future, will climb the hills of progress, through all time, side by side.

This belief that polygamy is right the civilized world recognizes as a mere superstition; it is one of those superstitions which, honestly believed in in the past, have done infinite injury—one of those religious superstitions whose pathway has been lit by the fagot, and red with the blood of innocent people. The American people, through their laws, have pronounced polygamy a crime, and the court must execute that law. In fixing this punishment the statute gives the court a wide discretion. It provides, among other things, that a person found guilty of polygamy shall be punished by a fine of not more than five hundred dollars and by imprisonment for a term of not more than five years; and for the crime described in the second court upon which you were found guilty, it provides that a person shall be punished by a fine of not more than three hundred dollars or by imprisonment for not more than six months, or by both said punishments, in the discretion of the court. From these provisions it is apparent that the great object of the law was to protect the institution of marriage as recognized by law, the marriage of one woman to one man. And the court, in fixing the punishment, must not only take into consideration the consequences of the sentence to you and to your family, but to society.

The great object of punishment applied to crimes is to deter other people from committing like offences, and protect society from the evils resulting from the crime; and with that in view the court must fix the punishment, where it has the discretion. The court, however, looks at the circumstances, and where the crime is aggravated the punishment is usually greater, and should be more severe; and where there are palliating circumstances the punishment should be less. In your case there is one circumstance, probably, that should be taken into consideration. You have been taught, as it seems, and I presume it to be true, by your ancestors, or by those from whom you received religious instructions, that polygamy was right; and those who taught you are, probably, to some extent almost as much to blame as you, although they could not be punished, because they have committed no overt act that could be proved; no such act as they could be punished for. That, of course, should be taken into account. But you are an intelligent man, over thirty years of age, I believe. '

Clawson. No, sir.

Court. I am mistaken, then. I understood some witness to so testify. What is your age?

Clawson. Twenty-seven.

Court. I was mistaken then. I probably misunderstood the witness. You probably were between twenty-four and twenty-five when the offence was committed?

Clawson. As charged.

Court. As charged in the indictment.

Clawson. Yes, sir.

Court. You unquestionably knew of the existence of this law?

Clawson. Yes, sir.

The Court Continued. And understood it, and you deliberately violated it. You violated it also with the understanding, as you say, that you had a right to do it, because there was a higher law, as you claimed, by which you govern your conduct. That being so, it makes the case aggravated.

You deliberately violated a law of your country, knowing the consequences and the effects. And there is another thing to be taken into consideration in fixing this punishment, the object being to prevent the crime. As you state, and, as I presume from the evidence in the case it is true, there is a class—a large class—of persons in this district, in this Territory, and probably many in others, who claim that it is right to violate the law. The object of the law is to prevent it, and it is the duty of the court to so fix the punishment as that it will be most likely to prevent other persons from committing like offences against society.

The institution of marriage is one of the most important to society of any that exist. When free love, polygamy, or any other system shall be substituted for the monogamic marriage, then this great social fabric, which is now protected by law, will probably be crumbling about us; and chastity, virtue, and decency will fall with it, in my judgment. And that seems to be the judgment of the American people and of the whole civilized world; because, I believe, polygamy is not lawful in any civilized government on the globe. For the purpose of protecting society, therefore, and protecting this institution, which is of such great interest and importance to society, the court must fix the punishment so that it will be likely to prevent its recurrence.

The law provides, in the case of polygamy, for a fine not to exceed five hundred dollars, and for imprisonment not exceeding five years. I confess that I should have been inclined to have fixed this punishment at less than I shall, were it not for the fact that you openly declare that you believe it is right to violate this law. I shall therefore fix your punishment in the case of polygamy on the first count at a fine of five hundred dollars, and imprisonment for the term of three years and six months, and on the last count, for unlawful cohabitation, I will fix your fine at three hundred dollars and your imprisonment at six months. Judgment will be entered by the clerk accordingly. I wish to add one more remark to the judgment, which is that the imprisonment on the last count of the indictment will begin at the termination of the imprisonment of the first.

Judge Zane read the following charge to the jury in the Rudger Clawson case:

GENTLEMEN OF THE JURY: The court charges you that the laws of the United States of America in force in this Territory, declare that every person who has a wife living and marries another is guilty of polygamy; and that the first count of the indictment upon which the defendant stands charged states that on the first day of August, 1882, he married Florence Ann Dinwoodey, with whom he is still living as his wife, and from whom he has not been divorced; and that afterward and on the 1st day of July, 1883, he married Lydia Spencer in this, the Third Judicial District of the Territory of Utah. To this count the defendant has pleaded not guilty. The court further charges you that the law presumes the defendant innocent until he is proven guilty beyond a reasonable doubt. It is not necessary that the evidence should show that the marriages charged actually occurred on the days therein named. There is no dispute in the evidence with respect to the marriage of the defendant to Florence Ann Dinwoodey, and the real contention is as to the charge that he married Lydia Spencer, and that such marriage was in this judicial district. To prove this marriage, admissions of the defendant and circumstances are relied upon. The court further charges you that admissions and declarations of the defendant hastily made are entitled to but little weight; but when deliberately made and precisely identified, they should receive great weight. You should not look at the circumstances in evidence separately, but should consider them with respect to the fact to be proven, and with respect to each other, and should endeavor to discern their connections, their coincidences, and their disagreements, if such they may present, and so considering them together, give them such weight as in your best judgment they may be entitled to. If you can reconcile the evidence before you upon any reasonable hypothesis consistent with the innocence of the defendant, it is your duty to do so.

With respect to the second count of the indictment, the court instructs you to find the defendant not guilty on that count. The court further charges you that a reasonable doubt is one based upon reason, and such doubt must be reasonable in view of all the evidence. And if, after an impartial and careful consideration of all the evidence in this case, you can candidly say that you are not satisfied of the existence of any fact essential to the defendant's guilt you have a reasonable doubt, and in that case you should find the defendant not guilty upon the first count of the indictment also. But if after a candid and careful consideration of all the evidence you have such an abiding conviction of the defendant's guilt that you would be willing to act upon it in the more weighty matters relating to your own affairs, you have no reasonable doubt. And if you should be so satisfied of the defendant's guilt you should find him guilty.

Gentlemen, you are the sole judges of the credibility of the witnesses, of the weight of the evidence, and of the facts. You should diligently investigate and carefully consider all the evidence before you together, and give it such weight as you may believe it entitled to when so considered. But if you shall believe that any witness or witnesses have wilfully sworn falsely to any fact material in this case, you are at liberty to wholly disregard the testimony of such witness or witnesses, except so far as they may be corroborated by other trustworthy evidence.

The court charges you with respect to the form of your verdict, that if you find the defendant guilty of polygamy, as charged in the first count of the indictment, the form of your verdict will be, "The jury find the defendant guilty on the first count of the indictment."

If you find the defendant not guilty on the first count of the indictment, the form of your verdict will be, "The jury find the defendant not guilty."

THE FORMAL SENTENCE.

The following sentence was then entered of record by the clerk of the court:

United States v. Rudger Clawson. Polygamy and unlawful cohabitation.

This being the time fixed by the court for passing its sentence herein, and the defendant, with his counsel, Bennett, Harkness &

Kirkpatrick, being present and having filed no motion for a new trial, and declining to move for a new trial, and the defendant being requested to state if there be any reason why the sentence of the court should not be passed upon him, and no cause being shown for stay of sentence, it is by the court ordered, adjudged, and decreed that you, Rudger Clawson, on the first count of the indictment and the conviction had for polygamy, do forfeit and pay to the United States the sum of five hundred dollars, and that you be confined and imprisoned in the Utah Penitentiary upon said first count for the term of three years and six months.

And it is further adjudged and decreed that, pursuant to the conviction had under the second count of the indictment against you, the defendant, Rudger Clawson, for the crime of unlawful cohabitation, that you do forfeit and pay to the said United States the further sum of three hundred dollars ; and further, that you, the said defendant, be confined and imprisoned in the Utah Penitentiary the further time of six months.

And it is further adjudged and decreed that you, the said Rudger Clawson, be detained and confined, by the officer in charge of said penitentiary, until the above imposed fines be paid and satisfied.

With such evidence concerning the Clawson trial it would suggest that the beginning of the end of Mormon hierarchy had arrived ; but as evidence to the contrary it is stated, on reliable authority, that the Mormons in Idaho at a recent election were ordered by George Q. Cannon to vote for a certain candidate for Congress. Mr. Cannon did not leave his office, but his order was faithfully carried out. The Mormons in Idaho voted as a unit for his man.

The converts to Mormonism throughout the world at the present time number about 200,000. Of the 150,000 people in Utah are 120,000 Mormons, and of these 12,000 are polygamists. A distinguished son of Mormon parentage, but who is not himself a believer, makes the statement that a Mormon's practice of polygamy depends on his ability to support plurality of wives. Long ago the hive swarmed, and to-day hold the balance of power in Idaho and Arizona, and are rapidly peopling Washington, Montana, and Wyoming Territories, as well as Colorado and New Mexico. While this people profess to observe the forms of a republican government, the despotism of its leaders is as absolute in its control at the present time as it has ever been, and is greater than any other despotism on earth. That such an institution has been able to maintain itself in the very heart of a free country, and to steadily increase in power and wealth, is one of the problems of the age. Polygamy is considered by many persons to be the most objectionable feature of Mormonism, forgetting that its creed is a deadly menace to free government, and that it preaches a celestial kingdom of God, and the kingdom of God on earth, the latter meaning that the whole earth is to be subjugated to Mormon rule. The only allegiance given by the Saints is to their church and chiefs. Between their creed and the Government of the United States the latter is nothing. The Mormonism of to-day has been described as " a combination of a limited number of knaves pretending to have a sanction for their rule from the Most High to exercise boundless dominion over a multitude of dupes, who submit to their despotism as to the commands of God. Suppose, says the same author, that a set of low, shrewd, sleek, uneducated Yankees, escaped from the jails of the region in which they were born, and dismissed with scorn by the inhabitants of the Western States to which they may have emigrated, should gratify their peculiar tastes and inclinations by instituting a new religion which should justify their crimes, and that they should entice a great number of unchristianized and uncivilized fools and fanatics to submit to their dictation ; suppose all these seemingly improbable facts, and you have Mormonism in its central idea. It can have no development which is not essentially brutish, vulgarity being at the very heart of its animal creed and constitution, however much these may have been varnished over by superficial tourists, who merely observe them from the outside." There are more polygamists now than ever, and the obnoxious doctrines are more openly and defiantly preached. But one conviction has been had for polygamy under the statutes in twenty years. In a word, the Mormons of to-day are cursing the Stars and Stripes. They are obedient to John Taylor, as they were to Joseph Smith; they break the laws and defy the government, accepting polygamy as a revelation from a just God. It is known that the people of this faith are ready for any anticipated emergency. Most of them, if not all, keep fire-arms in their dwellings, in the use of which they are trained experts. Some of the observers of the situation in Utah predict a civil war without our government defends its authority and punishes treason as it deserves, while others affirm that the Mormon leaders are too sagacious to allow their affairs to lead to such an issue.

The converts to Mormonism are either cranks or persons of slight education, who listen to the stories of "a land flowing with milk and honey," to which they must flee for salvation, with delight. The missionaries are not, many of them, educated men, but are familiar with the Bible from end to end. Brigham Young said that he did not require college graduates, but could take a youth who had cut wood and killed bears among the hills and send him on a mission, and he would come back a man. No one can refuse a mission, although it has frequently been a place of exile for the too inquiring, too ambitious, and too knowing. Dissipated young men have been sent off, and returned quite reformed. The indifferent and doubting have also been sent, and came home extreme fanatics in their belief. The Mormon missionary starts out without purse or scrip. He is forced to be on his good behavior, as he is a professional beggar, and breaks bread with the stranger. He thus gains an admittance into households, and works upon the susceptibilities of women, wherein lies a more assured success than if he lodged in hotels. But without visible means they live well, and dress well, and travel luxuriously. They have never been known to starve. Of the three hundred of them now out, one hundred are preaching in the Southern States, where in recent years they have made many converts. The other two hundred Mormon missionaries are scattering the seeds of their horrible doctrines over the broad world. A convert in his first year's residence must give one tenth of his time, one tenth of what he raises, and one tenth of his possessions on his arrival, even if he have no money. This payment of tithes is an onerous burden to the Mormons, who, in spite of all reports, are taxed to an exasperating degree. They cannot evade this tithing, yet the roads and bridges are not in good order, and there is not a hospital in Utah. The only decent school building in the territory is the University of Deseret. The Gentiles are taxed to support Mormon schools, which their children do not attend, where the hymns and prayers are Mormon, as well as the teachers. Brigham Young denounced colleges, yet sent one of his sons to Cornell University, one to the University of Michigan, and another to West Point. The latter, when asked if his oath of allegiance to the government brought him in conflict with the commands of John Taylor, which he would obey, without hesitation answered he would obey John Taylor.

Salt Lake City has a population of from twenty to

twenty-five thousand. It is situated on the east bank of the Jordan, a short river which connects Lake Utah with the great Salt Lake, eleven miles distant. The location is at once beautiful and picturesque, with the grand snow-capped Wahsatch Mountains on the east, the valley of the Jordan on the south and west, while in the distance are other ranges of mountains. It is the metropolis of Utah, "the chief city of Zion," "the habitation of the Saints," "the grand centre of the kingdom of God," "the city of prediction, beautiful for situation, and the joy of the whole earth." The streets are one hundred and thirty-seven feet wide, and the blocks forty rods square. Water is conveyed along the streets for irrigation and other purposes, and the shade and fruit trees render it conspicuous from the country at large. The site covers nine thousand acres, not more than one fourth of which is occupied. Fort Douglas is situated on one of the heights overlooking the city, where several regiments of United States troops are stationed, under command of Federal officers. The climate is clear and dry, rain seldom falls, and the air is delightfully cool and invigorating. Its railway facilities with the East give the residents the comforts and luxuries of modern civilization, and yet it is unlike all other cities, with its half-finished temple, which has already cost two millions of dollars, its Tabernacle for summer worship—there is no method of heating it—its Endowment House, Tithing Office, and its other places for Mormon services and residence. One hundred thousand dollars is annually collected from tithes. The city is lighted by gas, and has six miles of street railway. It is a very gay city, as the Mormons are not only fond of public amusements, but of all manner of social festivities and dancing. Their public balls sometimes last from twelve to fourteen hours. The women are given to fine dress and the fripperies of fashion, and are as fond of the elegant accessories which make life pleasant as their Gentile sisters. Their advance in such indulgences has been remarkable since Brigham harangued against the follies of women.

There is a Territorial Library, a City and a Masonic Library; a museum of the productions and curiosities of the region; three daily and weekly newspapers, a weekly in the Scandinavian tongue, and some minor periodicals. The City Hall cost $70,000. The Tabernacle has a costly organ, which is the second largest in the United States, and it will seat eight thousand persons.* There are Mason and Odd Fellows' halls, theatres, several hotels, Episcopalian, Methodist, Presbyterian, and Catholic churches, and a Jewish synagogue. The immense co-operative store is a Mormon institution.

The Endowment House has its peculiar rites. Here the Mormons are "sealed for time and eternity" in "celestial marriage," and here one day in the week there is an all-day performance, when "each Mormon is invested with the Adamic costume (a garment made all in one piece, high-necked and with long sleeves), and receives grips, tokens, and new names. If living and dying he wears this garment, and does not forget the grips and the name, he is sure of heaven whatever may befall him. A sacred drama forms a part of the ceremonies. The man who plays the part of the devil therein is also janitor of the Tabernacle, passes the bread and

---

* Oscar Wilde, in describing the Tabernacle, remarked that at a distance it resembles a copper kettle turned upside down. The huge domes rest on columns between which are doors, in its whole circumference, that in warm weather can all be opened. The building is only used in summer, and is sometimes called "The Bowerie" for that reason.

wine at the celebration of the Lord's Supper, and leads an orchestra in the church theatre." The Endowment House rites are a kind of bastard Masonry instituted by Joseph Smith at Nauvoo. There is the Aaronic grip, and the grip of Melchisedec. There is the oath of vengeance against the United States Government for the death of Joseph Smith and his brother Hiram (or Hyrum, as it is usually spelled), and the oath of implicit obedience to the priesthood. It is impossible with these oaths that loyalty to the government should exist. A remarkable resemblance has been pointed out between the ceremonies in the *Eleusinia*, a festival among the Cretans, and the mysteries of the Endowment House, as they are represented by some of the historians of Mormonism.

Ecclesiastically the city is divided into twenty wards, over which is a bishop and two councillors. These are men who "do as they are told, and see that the Saints pay their tithing regularly." In each ward the bishop holds a meeting every Sunday night. Under this divisional supervision the city, if twenty times larger, would be under the same complete control. At home and abroad a Mormon is never free from the vigilant watch of church officers. A Presbyterian clergyman of Salt Lake City has recently asserted before an Eastern audience that it is this priestly despotism which is the central and great evil of the Mormon system. Polygamy—bad as it is in his estimation—is sweet in comparison with this constant and deadly tyranny. All understand it. None can escape from it save through apostasy or death. The Tabernacle, according to Stenhouse, should be visited on a Sunday afternoon. The "spirit" is hardly warmed up in the morning services. The organ is better played, the choir sing better. The choir occupy seats around the great organ, directly in front of which sits the president and his two councillors. In front of them is a long bench for the twelve apostles, and before these are the bishops and other officers. Several barrels of water are placed in front of the assembled church dignitaries, and after it has been blessed is handed about in tin cans to every person in the congregation. A sip of the water and a morsel of bread constitutes the ceremony of partaking the sacrament, according to Mormon rites. Hymns are sung, a prayer is made by some bishop, apostle, or elder, which is followed by a sermon either by the president or an apostle, after which the congregation sings a doxology and is dismissed with a brief blessing. The sermons are talks on practical matters, and the Saints are expected to attend to these "droppings of the sanctuary." The architectural design of the Tabernacle is hideous. From east to west it is one hundred and fifty feet, and from north to south one hundred and twenty. There is not a column to obstruct the vision. Its acoustic properties are remarkably good. Christian churches, schools, and associations have been firmly founded in Zion. For many years there was no place where anything but Mormonism could be heard, and the stranger was entirely cut off from all religious communion. But all this is past; and while "the Gentile and Mormon elements of the community can no more mix than oil and water," each have their places of worship. From the beginning of Mormonism the Saints have held conferences, great yearly or half-yearly meetings, lasting several days. They are usually held in Salt Lake City, and are seasons of especial enjoyment to the pilgrims who journey from afar and near to these festivals of the elect. They have a certain resemblance to the camp-meetings of the Methodists, but were probably instituted in imitation of the old Jewish custom of assembling the Israelites in the chief city from the remotest parts of Palestine, at stated intervals, for worship. Mr. P. W. Penrose, a well-known Mormon leader, has recently denied that " blood atonement " * has ever been practised among the Saints, but adds, " in the good time coming it will be." A more disinterested observer, after a residence of several months in Salt Lake City last year, writes: " As to the ' blood atonement ' which Mormons generally deny, you may be sure it is still practised." The shedding of innocent blood has been one of the mysterious horrors of Mormonism from its inauguration, and there is no more reason to suppose it has been suppressed than its other abominable practices, which are falsely denied. It is only more adroitly managed under Taylor's rule than it was under the dominion of Brigham Young.

The boasted freedom of the ballot in Utah is a farce, as every ballot is numbered, and the number is placed against the name of the voter; and in this way those who vote contrary to the published ticket are known to the priesthood. In other parts of the Union the numbering of the tickets might be of no moment; but in Utah, where the slightest opposition is branded as rebellion, and is treated accordingly, it is of the last importance, as it practically precludes all free voting. The present generation of Mormons is in many respects in violent contrast to " the very prophets of in-

---

* The Blood Atonement of the Mormons is the severing of the windpipe—a gash across the throat—to let the soul out of the body, and thus save it from destruction.

dustry" who preceded it. By all accounts the young men are idle and immoral. The relaxing climate and the influence of their surroundings has something to do with their condition. They are advised to stay at home. An elder said in the Tabernacle last summer: "We do not want our young men to leave Utah; if they have talent of any kind, let them cultivate it here." As there are no factories in Utah, and comparatively few openings for young men, many of them are obliged to work on the railways and in the mines of Utah for a livelihood. Some of the wealthier Mormons send their sons and daughters to Eastern schools for educational advantages not to be obtained in Zion, in spite of the protest against it.

One of the most influential of the youthful Mormons is John Young, one of the sons of Brigham, who is a polygamist of the worst kind, having married, it is said, and deserted several women. He is described as being handsome, rich, and well educated.

Mormon children are baptized at the age of eight years. They are then members of the church. The baptism for the dead is one of the most cherished of their ordinances, and in this way they can save their ancestors from everlasting punishment, and bring their souls within Zion. This benevolence is extended beyond the confines of relationship, and is given to the heroes and heroines of history. "In fact," says a facetious recorder of events in Salt Lake City, "no one is safe from the clutches of Mormonism after death. You may be made a Mormon without desiring it for all eternity." A wealthy Mormon in the summer of 1884, during a visit in Boston, employed a young woman to look up his genealogy. In this way he learned the names of some two hundred of his Gentile ancestors, for all of whom he had the rites of baptism performed.*

If Salt Lake Valley were to become the home of a really free people, it would become one of the glories of the American Union. It is about thirty miles long. The view of it from Salt Lake City is enchanting. It is a picture, of farm, lake, and mountains clothed in prevailing tints of gray, with patches of verdure that is seldom seen in any country. The atmosphere is very clear.

The Territory of Utah lies mostly in the great Wahsatch Basin, between the Rocky Mountains and the Sierra Nevada. It is bounded on the north by Idaho and Wyoming territories, east by Colorado, south by Arizona, and west by Nevada. It is three hundred and fifty miles long and three hundred miles in width, and has eighty-four thousand square miles. The Wahsatch range of mountains, which forms the eastern wall of the basin, traverses the territory from north to south, and with the Unitah Mountains at the north-east, and the Iron Mountains in the south-east, the rivers have no outlet, and fall into the great Salt Lake and other lakes of the basin. All these rivers have cut their way through

---

* An apostate Mormon, in speaking of the Baptism for the Dead, which is a vital doctrine of the Latter-Day Saints, told the following story :

"An old man, long a convert to Mormonism, residing in the southern part of Utah, last summer made a pilgrimage to Georgetown, thirty miles distant, where the Saints were in conference, for the purpose of saving nearly one hundred of his ancestors from everlasting destruction by being baptized for them. He made the journey in an ox cart with his two sons. The baptism was by immersion in a river, and the old man was "dipped" as many times as he could stand the operation, each dip representing an entrance into the Mormon paradise for some one of the otherwise lost hundred of his forefathers. Then his sons in turn were baptized until the object of their visit was accomplished."

the easily corroded rocks, and form cañons varying in depth from two to five thousand feet; and after reaching a lower plain spread out into broad streams. The eastern section of Utah, although from six to seven thousand feet above the level of the sea, is fertile, and largely productive. Western Utah is also elevated, the summits of the Wahsatch rising from the plain from forty-two hundred to six thousand feet in height, attaining a further elevation from the valley of six thousand to seven thousand feet in height. Saline and fresh lakes are numerous. Great Salt Lake is one hundred miles in length, fifty in width, and sixty feet deep, holding in solution twenty per cent of salt. The river Jordan connects it with Lake Utah, which is twenty-four miles long by twelve in width. Much of the scenery of Utah is magnificent and of the most varied description. Echo and Weber cañons are a perpetual series of surprises, as well as Parley's Park, Ogden, and Cottonwood cañons, which are all sublimely beautiful. Landscape painters consider American Fork Cañon the finest cañon in our country. The north-western portion of the territory, the elevated plateau, is a barren alkaline desert, yielding but little beside the sage bush, but under irrigation is made to yield large crops. The Mormons are not confined to Utah alone, but possess some of the best portions of Arizona, Wyoming, New Mexico, Idaho, and Colorado. The land of these territories is worthless without irrigation, and the Mormon Church has entire control of the irrigating canals. In this way they can secure themselves from Gentile intrusion, and they can subdue rebellious spirits among themselves; for the moment a man rebels the water is shut off from his land, and he is literally starved into submission, or obliged to leave the territory.

The government surveys commenced in 1855, and a land office was opened in Salt Lake City in 1868. In the year 1873 Stenhouse made the statement that surveys had extended over 4,016,825 acres, of which 92,637 acres were embraced in vacated Indian reservations. These surveys included Colorado. From that date declaratory statements under the Pre-emption Act of September 4th, 1841, had been filed for 400,000 acres. Of that extent of land 68,315 acres had been paid for with cash, mainly at the minimum price of $1.25 per acre. In addition, 20,480 acres had been located with military bounty land warrants, and 23,200 acres with agricultural scrip. Homestead entries covering 167,250 acres have been made under the act of May 29th, 1862. Estimating that there are 2,000,000 acres, or the one twenty-seventh part of the territory susceptible of cultivation, there yet remain 1,500,000 acres unappropriated for future settlement. The emigrants to Utah and the territories contiguous to it are given small farms of 160 acres government lands, which they are entitled to after becoming citizens of the United States. The Mormon settlements extend to the full limits of the territory in every direction, following the natural sweep of the valleys at the base of the mountains, from north to south. It was Brigham's policy to occupy the best lands as quickly as possible. For this and other ulterior purposes he was gracious to his dusky neighbors—the Utes, and other tribes of Indians.

Until the completion of the Union and Pacific Railroad the vast mineral wealth of Utah was untouched, the Mormon leaders being utterly opposed to exploiting the mines, knowing well that their development would bring in a non-Mormon and anti-Polygamous population. Since the building of the Union Pacific and the extension branches, north and south, Utah has produced fifty millions of dollars in silver and lead, and its other mineral wealth, except coal and salt, is yet undeveloped.

With such natural resources, what might not Utah become if Mormonism were "stamped out of it" by our government, to which, it is plain, it has become a problem difficult to solve. "Nothing can change the old Mormons. They are a hardy race, indifferent to hardships and privation; but despite the blinding influence of this system, under which, the hearts of so many women have been broken and are breaking, there is a restlessness among the young which is growing with an increasing sense of shame and wrong. The thing to do is to strike at the animalism which underlies the whole system, while carefully guarding all personal property and rights of those who have sinned through ignorance, to make further plural marriages impossible, and never relax until polygamy and the rule of the Mormon Church in temporal affairs is forever abandoned. If it is postponed fifteen years, it will take a civil war to overcome this open enemy of republican government."*

If Mormonism is allowed to go on for a few years longer, its rulers will dictate the elections in all the regions between the Rocky Mountains and the Pacific Ocean except California and Oregon—a region as great as all the United States, east of the Mississippi River. The renewing influences of active emigration is still going on. Within eight months of last year three thousand Mormon proselytes arrived in New York. To these converts from the peasant classes of Great Britain, Norway, and Sweden, the most flattering promises have been made of land and wealth. The Mormon leaders want

---

* C. C. Godwin, *North American Review*, 1881.

the strong young men to cultivate the land and to work in the mines—increase the property which will accrue to the church from the tithing system. One is struck with the dull expression on the faces of these peasants from the Old World. More women than men emigrate from foreign parts to Utah. The fate of these women who come thus to a Christian country can easily be imagined.

A special despatch to the Boston *Herald* from Salt Lake City, dated January 10th, 1885, states that some "high Mormons have recently returned from Mexico. They had reached the stronghold of the untamable Yayni savages, and made a conditional treaty with them. Within a few days John Taylor, Counsellor Smith, Bishop Sharp, and others have left Zion, and are known to be *en route* to Mexico ; and it is believed they have gone to the capital to treat with the Mexican Government for lands and a charter like the Nauvoo charter. It is thought that the plan is to make a rendezvous for Mormons liable to persecution under the Edmunds law, and also to form a nucleus for a future empire in their favor. The Yaynis are terrible Indians who have never been subdued, the people of the northern Mexican States fearing them exceedingly."

The prediction that the Saints would eventually make Mexico their final resting-place is not new. Time alone will show the destiny of these people.

In closing this brief history of Mormonism, we may state what the most recent students of its methods have learned in a few words, as follows : Mormonism was evolved from the crafty brain of Sidney Rigdon, who found a fitting and willing assistant in Joseph Smith. Between them they formulated the only religion that has been originated in America, from a romance written by a clergyman born in New England.

It does not seem probable that the Spaulding manuscript is still in existence. There are old men and women living who may know its fate. They may carry the burden of their sworn secret regarding it to the grave; but whether the manuscript which was so shamefully stolen was or was not destroyed, or whether it was ever returned to its rightful owners, the great scheme of the "Latter-Day Saints," with its perfidies and crimes, cannot easily be expurgated from our national history.

It may be likened to some baleful plant that has been allowed to spring up and grow into a fruition of poisonous influences, and which cannot be exterminated save by one process—a general and thorough uprooting.

It has been the darling ambition of the Mormons since their settlement in Utah to have the Territory admitted into the Union of States; but to-day they seem as far from the realization of their anticipations in this respect as they were three decades ago, when they called their new home "Deseret."

CHAPTER XIII.

The "doctrines" of Mormonism—Analysis of the Mormon faith—Hierarchical organization—The "Book of Mormon"—Church polity—The faith of the Latter-Day Saints—Their modes of worship.

DOCTRINE.

THE Mormons are almost incredibly materialistic in their doctrines. Their idea of the Godhead is taken from Buddhistic principles. While they profess to believe in the Trinity, they say that God was once a man, who has advanced in intelligence and power; that now He may be called perfect; that He has still the form and figure of a man; He has even legs, from His appearance to Abraham, though He has the advantage over His creature that He can move up and down the earth without moving them.

Christ is the offspring of the "material" union, on the plains of Palestine, of God and the Virgin Mary—the latter being duly married after betrothal by the Angel Gabriel. Yet He is believed to have had a previous existence, and to have made the universe out of "unformed chaotic matter as old as God," and His worship is enjoined as Lord of all. The Paraclete is also material. There is, however, an older Trinity, that of Elohim, Jehovah, and Michael, which is Adam. Adam is declared to be the "god" of Jesus Christ, Jesus Christ the "god" of Joseph Smith, and Joseph Smith the "god" of this generation. Any Mormon by faith, obedience, and holiness may rise into a Deity, and peopling, and ruling a world forever.

The second article of Mormon faith affirms that men will be punished for their own sins, and not for Adam's transgressions.

The third article states that through the atonement of Christ all mankind can be saved by obedience to the laws and ordinances of the (Mormon) gospel.

The fourth article affirms the ordinances to be : 1st, faith in the Lord Jesus Christ ; 2d, repentance ; 3d, baptism (which takes place at eight years of age ; they also baptize for the dead) ; 4th, imposition of hands by the gift of the Holy Spirit ; 5th, the Lord's Supper administered kneeling (in which water is used instead of wine in the sacrament, which is taken every week).

The sixth article is, that the same organization exists now that existed in the Primitive church.

The seventh, that miraculous gifts—discerning of spirits, prophecy, revelations, visions, healing, tongues, etc.—have not ceased.

The eighth, that the word of God is recorded in the "Book of Mormon," the Bible, and all other good books.

The ninth article expresses the belief in all God has revealed, is revealing, or will reveal.

The tenth article affirms the literal gathering of Israel, the restoration of the ten tribes (the American Indians), the establishment of the new Zion on the Western Continent, the millennial reign of Christ on earth, and the transformation of earth into Paradise.

The eleventh article maintains the literal resurrection of the body to flesh and bones, but not blood, " the principle of mortality " (according to Smith).

The twelfth asserts the absolute liberty of private judgment in matters of religion.

The thirteenth declares it to be the duty of the Saints to be "subject to the powers that be," whether monarchical or republican.

The fourteenth is, "We believe in being honest, chaste, temperate, benevolent, virtuous, and upright ; in doing good to all men, and that an idle or lazy person cannot be a Christian, or have salvation." *

ANALYSIS OF MORMONISM.

The "Book of Mormon" is a plagiarism of "Manuscript Found," written by Solomon Spaulding. The Mormon religion is a parody on the old Hebrew faith, in common with Methodism, Millerism, Catholicism, Mohammedanism, spiced with doctrines of the Baptist, Presbyterian, and Episcopal Churches, as well as with the peculiar religious ideas of the Quakers and Shakers. The constant effort to imitate Hebraic customs and laws all through Mormonism is wearisome, nothing being formulated without some allusion to Biblical history.

Its originators and leaders have, many of them, been men of great natural intelligence, force, and persuasive eloquence. It is eminently a proselyting religion, and its greatest numbers of converts have come from the old world.

The commonly accepted idea of Mormonism is, that it is an institution based upon polygamy ; but it was years after Mormonism was established before this system was more than whispered among the "Latter-Day Saints ;" and if this enormous blot were wiped out from their his-

---

* The articles of faith have been reduced to thirteen in number in the more recent history of Mormonism, but which of the number has been expunged the writer cannot learn.

tory and their faith, the essential attributes of Mormonism would remain. As an organization, Mormonism is complete. It reaches every condition and position in life, and controls every action from the cradle to the grave, being a combination of military rule and Jesuitical penetration and perseverance.

The rapid increase of Mormonism is due, in part, to its main recognition of the truths of the Bible, its congeniality to every shade of erratic religious character; to the lofty pretensions of its priesthood, and the knowledge that, without previous study, a blacksmith may become a bishop or an apostle.

For the superstitious it has miracles, ecstasies, visions, and revelations, astonishing legends respecting the early inhabitants of America and the wonderful story of Christ's coming to this country after His resurrection.

For the lovers of prophecy there is promised the New Jerusalem, an actual reign of the Saints, and an equality with the Redeemer.

Another attraction is its congeniality with the wild views of religion as produced by the preaching of certain schismatical bodies, and its holding itself up as the only sanctuary to which men may flee for the solution of their doubts and the hope of an eternal harmony; with the fact that there is no strict standard of morals in connection with Mormonism, and its being an open asylum for the refuse of all other persuasions—the excommunicated, the despised, or endangered.

The gross see charms in its sensual paradise, and listen eagerly to the announcement that a conversation with their spiritual ruler or a journey on a mission, while facing a frowning world, will immediately clear them from all their iniquities.

Sidney Rigdon said: " 'The Book of Mormon' is to

govern the Millennial Church;" but whatever may have been its uses to the "Saints" in the beginning of their career, it has had little to do with their practices for many years, save as a text-book.

The great success of the Mormon missionaries, both here and in foreign countries, has been gained through their promises to the ignorant, the superstitious, and the poor of a home and certain support.

Labor has always been dignified among the Mormons, every man, woman, and child, from the highest to the lowest, having his or her task to perform.

Natural quickness of mind and shrewdness have ever been valued by them, but culture has never been indispensable for promotion. Faith and blind obedience have been requisite, but education, although prized, has not been material to the ambitious Mormon.

As a people, the Mormons are chargeable with the gravest crimes; but these have been perpetrated by the few, while many of them have been and are devoted to what they believe to be the truth; contrasts are drawn by their preachers between "the unworldly lives of the Saints and the evil practices of the Gentiles," and pertinent examples are given of aberrations from rectitude of men intrusted with the making of our laws, or those who minister at the altars of divine worship, until they regard themselves as clothed with the resplendent robes of righteousness.

In ten years from the origin of Mormonism its devotees numbered thousands, and Joseph Smith announced that it was to be the religious faith of the Western Continent. To-day Mormonism numbers its hundreds of thousands, its organizations extend over every part of the globe, and the most careless observer of the times must realize that this institution has become one of the gravest and most difficult religious, social, and political problems of the day.

The Mormons have made four "Hegiras" since they left Palmyra. There are indications that at no distant day they must enter upon a fifth pilgrimage ; the question is, what portion of the earth will next be selected as their "Zion"?

HIERARCHICAL ORGANIZATION.

Mormonism is a pure theocracy ; its priesthood, who rule in matters temporal and ecclesiastical, are divided into various orders. The highest is the First Presidency, elected by the whole body of the church, and possessing supreme authority. The second office in point of dignity is that of Patriarch, whose chief duty is to administer blessings.

The third in order is The Twelve, who ordain all other officers, priests, teachers, and deacons ; they baptize, administer the sacraments, and take the lead in meetings.

Next comes the Seventies, who are under the direction of the Twelve Apostles, and are the great propagandists, missionaries, and preachers. The fifth order is that of High Priests, whose duty lies in officiating in all the offices of the church, when no higher authority is present.

After these come the Bishops, who are overseers of the church in secular matters, the support of "literary concerns," house-visiting, and the settlement of private grievances.

The seventh in order are the Elders, who conduct meetings, and have a general surveillance over the priests. The lowest orders are Teachers and Deacons, who simply assist the other orders.

The whole priesthood is divided into two classes—the

Melchisedec and Aaronic. To the first belong the offices of apostle, seventy, patriarch, high-priest, and elder; to the second those of bishop, priest, teacher, and deacon. The latter can only be held by "literal" descendants of Aaron, who are pointed out by special revelation.

THE "BOOK OF MORMON."

The "Book of Mormon" is a collection of sixteen separate or distinct books, professing to be written at different periods by different prophets. Its style is in imitation of the Bible, incorporating three hundred passages from it without acknowledgment, but often quoted by the Mormons as specimens of their book, and Hebrew, Greek, Biblical, and Latin names are introduced.

The first book professes to be written by Nephi, a Jew, the son of Lehi, who dwelt at Jerusalem in the days of King Jedekiah, 600 B.C. In obedience to a command of the Lord, who appeared to him in a dream, he went into the wilderness of Arabia and dwelt there a long time with his family. At length, under divine instruction, he, with his family, set out in search of a promised land, and after travelling nearly eastward for eight years they reached the ocean. Here they built a ship, and, guided by a compass, sailed to America.

The "Book of Mormon" itself gives no indication of the part of the Continent on which they landed; but through subsequent Mormon revelations, it is declared to have been Chili.

Of this company who arrived in America were Lehi and his wife and four sons—Taman, Lemuel, Sam and Nephi, and their four wives; and Toran, a servant, and his wife—in all eight adult men and eight women. Two infant sons were born to Lehi on the journey through the wilderness—Jacob and Joseph. In America they found beasts of every kind in the forests, including the cow, the ox, the ass, the horse, and the goat. Lehi died immediately after his arrival in America, and discussions speedily arose between Nephi and his elder brothers, Laman and Lemuel; and separating from them Nephi moved into the wilderness accompanied by Sam and Toran and their families, the boys, Jacob and Joseph, and such of the women and children as agreed with them. Laman and Lemuel and their families, as a punishment for rebellion against Nephi, whom the Lord had appointed to be their ruler, were cursed by the Lord, and they and all their posterity were condemned to have dark skins and to become an idle people, full of mischief and subtlety, which sought out the wilderness for beasts of prey. This is the origin of the American Indians, whom the Mormons profess to believe are of the Jewish race. Nephi died fifty years after his arrival in America, and his people continued to be called Nephites and to be governed by kings bearing the name of Nephi for many generations.

The record of their history was continued on golden plates by Jacob, the brother of Nephi, Enos, the son of Jacob, Jarom, the son of Enos, Arum, the son of Joram, and finally by Mormon, whose name is given to a single book as well as to a whole volume, and who, many hundred years after Christ, transmitted to his son Moroni the plates containing the writings of the authors mentioned, as well as those of Mosiah, Teniff, Alma, Helamon, Nephi the second, and Nephi the third.

These books are narratives of transactions in North and South America, chiefly of wars between the Nephites and Lamanites, or red men, and of revolutions in the land Tarahenila, a country near the Isthmus of Darien, where there was a great city. A supernatural light, which lasted three days and three nights, informed the inhabitants of America of the birth of Christ, and later a terrible earthquake announced the crucifixion of Christ at Jerusalem; and three days after the Lord Himself appeared, descending out of heaven into the chief city of the Nephites, in the sight of the people, to whom He exhibited His wounded side and the prints of the nails in His hands and feet.

He remained with them forty days, teaching them the principles of Christianity, and founding that faith. These Christians of the new world, unlike those of the old world, immediately adopted the Christian era for their chronological computations, and in agreement with the record in the four following centuries, the wars between them and the heathen Lamanites continued to rage with great destruction to the Christians, whose populous and civilized cities, extending throughout North America, were gradually captured and destroyed.

In the year 384 the Christians made a final stand at Cummorah in western New York, where in a great battle two hundred and thirty thousand of them were slain; Moroni, one of the survivors, after wandering as a fugitive until A.D. 420, sealed up the golden plates on which all these events and circumstances were written, and hid them in the hill, where they were found by Joseph Smith.

One of the books of the collection gives an account of an earlier settlement of America than that of Lehi, by a colony from the Tower of Babel, soon after the deluge, which was led by Jared, and which in time became a great nation, but which was destroyed for their sins before the arrival of the colony from Jerusalem.

The "Book of Mormon" appeared first in Palmyra,

in 1830, in England in 1841, in Paris in 1852. Versions have been printed in German, Italian, Danish, Welsh, and Hawaiian. There is a copy in the British Museum, in the Astor Library in New York, and other noted public libraries throughout the United States.

CHURCH POLITY.

The acknowledged president of the church of the Latter-Day Saints holds the keys of the kingdom—"that is, heaven." Without his permission none can be saved. He is an acknowledged "revelator," and is acknowledged by the church to be the supreme pontiff of the world, with both temporal and spiritual jurisdiction, and as such is entitled to the implicit personal and unquestioned obedience of all Mormons.

The next order of the church is the Twelve Apostles, usually called the "Twelve." The members of this order are subject to do duty as missionaries.

The following in order, in point of dignity, is the president of the Seventies, and each seventy has a president. These presidents form an administrative council over the subject of missions and preaching and all matters connected with the propagandism of the church, subject to the approval of the head of the church.

There is another body, called a Quorum of Seventy, having in theory seventy members. They form the bone and muscle of missionary labor, and have no reference to rank in the church as apostle or a High Priest, as either may be a member of a quorum. These are the outside working bees of the central hive, and go into all the world to preach the gospel without purse or scrip, returning frequently loaded with money, and escorting many converts.

Each Mormon preserves its secret archives, a complete record of the genealogy of each of its members, as also of the official acts of each. This organization has a certain resemblance to the celebrated order of Jesuits. The first in rank in this order is the high-priest, second the apostles, third the elders, and last and lowest the simple priest.

All true male Mormons are priests; it is necessary for their salvation. Women are sealed (married) to some priest, either for time "or eternity;" in the latter case they are not required to reside together, the ceremony being a saving grace merely, they having no souls of their own, and amounting to nothing of themselves alone.

The Mormons' use of the terms "exaltation" and "salvation" are thus defined: "A male Mormon, outside of the priesthood, may be saved by favor of the President, as also may a Gentile to be used as a servant." "Exaltation" means having a kingdom in the next world, emoluments, and power, with numbers of wives and servants in his possession in this belonging to him in the other.

For a woman to marry an apostle or high-priest is a great honor, while to be the wife of the Prophet or First Presidency is the highest possible dignity to which a woman can aspire. Coercion is seldom used to effect marriages; but a woman must marry some one, and "the man of her choice" is not at liberty to refuse her, the women as frequently making the first proposition of this kind, in agreement with Mormon etiquette.

A Mormon with but one wife would hardly be admitted to "good society," and few men have the moral courage to appear in public with less than two. Men of "position" appear on state occasions with numerous wives—the more the better. All Gentiles are to be the servants of the "Saints" in the world to come and after the second coming of Christ, which is expected soon.

The city of Salt Lake is divided into twenty-four wards, each of which has a governing officer called a bishop, who is also an informer to the high powers. They hear and determine upon civil or religious complaints, and inquire into the temporal and spiritual condition of each member of their ward in domiciliary visits each week; and all persons found to be disaffected as to word or doctrine are reported to the First President.

All "Gentiles" are watched and reported of in the same manner. The bishops also collect the tithing. The intermediate tribunal between the bishops and First President is the High Council, composed of fifteen men chosen among the high-priests, twelve of whom act as jurors, who decide the case in hand by vote, the remaining three acting as judges, passing sentence, fixing damages, costs, etc. An appeal can be made from this council to the First President; but from him there is no appeal.

Each bishop has assistant teachers, who catechise the children and people, and report all heresies. The different orders of the priesthood, and the quorum of the Seventies, are not elective, but permanent orders of the church; but all the other officers are elective, from the First President down to the teachers, twice a year—in April and in October. These elections are made by the whole body of the people, and are called "conferences," during which anybody is at liberty to prefer charges against any officer, from the highest to the lowest. There are other organized bodies within the Mormon Church polity, which are of a secret character, such as the band of Danites and the Endowment Rooms.

The highest test of faith as a body is the placing of

the entire church property in the hands of the first officers.

The cheerful payment of the "tithing" is regarded as a test of orthodoxy, and consists in the giving by every male member of every tenth day of his time in labor upon the public works (or the pay of a substitute for the same) and a tenth of his income.

THE FAITH OF THE LATTER-DAY SAINTS.

We believe in God, the eternal Father, and His Son, Jesus Christ, and in the Holy Ghost.

We believe that men will be punished for their own sins, and not for Adam's transgressions.

We believe that, through the atonement of Christ, all mankind may be saved by obedience to the laws and ordinances of the gospel.

We believe that these ordinances are : 1st, faith in the Lord Jesus Christ ; 2d, repentance ; 3d, baptism by the remission of sins ; 4th, laying on of hands by the gift of the Holy Spirit ; 5th, the Lord's Supper.

We believe that men must be called of God by inspiration and by laying on of hands from those who are duly commissioned to preach the Gospel and administer the ordinances thereof.

We believe in the same organization that existed in the Primitive church—viz., apostles, prophets, pastors, teachers, evangelists, etc.

We believe in the powers and gifts of the everlasting gospel—viz., the gift of faith, discerning of spirits, prophecy, revelation, vision, healing, and the interpretation of tongues, wisdom, charity, fatherly love, etc.

We believe the Word of God recorded in the "Book of Mormon," and in all other good books.

We believe all that God has revealed, all that He does now reveal, and we believe that He will reveal many more great and important things pertaining to the kingdom of God and Messiah's second coming.

We believe in the literal gathering of Israel and in the restoration of the ten tribes ; that Zion will be established on the Western Continent ; that Christ will reign personally on the earth a thousand years, and that the earth will be renewed and receive its paradisaical glory.

We believe in the literal resurrection of the body, and that the rest of the dead live not again until the thousand years are expired.

We claim the privilege of worshiping Almighty God according to the dictates of our conscience, unmolested, and allow all men the same privilege, let them worship how and where they may.

We believe in being subject to queens, presidents, rulers, and magistrates ; in obeying, honoring, and sustaining the law.

We believe in being honest, true, temperate, benevolent, virtuous, and upright, and in doing good to all men ; indeed, we may say that we follow the admonition of Paul, we "believe all things." Everything lowly, virtuous, praiseworthy, and of good report we seek after, looking forward "to the recompense of reward." But an idle or lazy person cannot be a Christian, neither have salvation. He is a drone, and destined to be stung to death and tumbled out of the hive.

THEIR MODE OF WORSHIP.

Their mode of conducting worship is to assemble at a particular hour, and the senior priest then indicates order by asking a blessing on the congregation and exercises, when a hymn from their own collection is sung, prayer made extempore, and another hymn sung, followed by a sermon from some one previously appointed to preach, which is usually continued by exhortations and remarks from those who feel moved to speak.

Then notices of the arrangement for tithe, labor for the ensuing week, and information on all secular matters interesting to them in a church capacity are read by the clerk of the council, and the congregation is dismissed by benediction. While the congregation is assembling and departing from the house, it is usual to have marches, waltzes, anthems, and the most brilliant music performed by a good band, to drive away all sombre feeling and to prepare the mind for exciting and eloquent preaching.

CHAPTER XIV.

The Josephites—Epitome of the faith and doctrines of the reorganized Church of Jesus Christ of Latter-Day Saints—David Whitmer—The debate at Kirtland, Ohio, in 1884, concerning the "Book of Mormon"—The revelation on celestial marriage, given to Joseph Smith in 1843.

The branch of Mormons calling themselves "Josephites" and "Latter-Day Saints of the Reorganized Church of Jesus Christ" number twenty thousand at the present time. Their spiritual leader is Joseph Smith, Jr. He is the son of Joseph Smith, the first Mormon prophet, and Emma, "the elect." Until within two years he has resided at Plano, Ill., but has removed to Laomi, Decatur Co., Iowa, where he edits two journals in the interests of his followers, called respectively *Zion's Hope* and *Saints' Herald*. He is a man of ability, is well educated, and a law-abiding citizen, as the Josephites are generally considered to be in their residence in several States of the Union, principally in Iowa, Missouri, and Illinois, but scattered throughout New England and the Middle States. When Brigham Young led the great body of Mormons to Utah, a few remained in the neighborhood of Nauvoo, and others, and in greater numbers, in Iowa. These were disaffected spirits, who would not yield to the rule of Brigham, and who naturally clustered about the young Joseph as the successor to the Prophet. The distinction between the Utah Mormons and the Josephites is, that the latter profess to be bitterly opposed to polygamy. In other particulars their creed bears a remarkable resemblance to that of the Mormons, although the Josephites contend that the Utah Mormons have departed from the original faith, and no longer live in agreement to its doctrines; that they are treasonable to the government, full of wiles and treachery, and a stain and blot on the history of our country. Brigham Young was the very consummation of evil, in their estimation, and his followers in office not a whit better. There is, in short, a deadly enmity between the Saints of Zion and the Josephites; yet both profess to believe the "Book of Mormon" divine, and that Joseph was "called of God to do the work, however he may have been led away in his latter years." This "led away" is a convenient expression to cover a multitude of sins in the Prophet's career toward its close. Joseph was fond of Emma, but his affections wandered to younger and fairer saints during the residence of the Mormons in Ohio, and he there began to talk of "celestial marriage," to the surprise, and, it is affirmed, "horror" of some of the brethren. His "revelation" on this subject, he said, was given to him at Nauvoo, July 12th, 1843. The Prophet's sons and his legal wife, Emma, have declared since his death that polygamy is a stain put upon his memory by Brigham Young and his followers.

Some attempts have been made (according to the written observations of several chroniclers of Mormonism) to heal the breach between the Utah Saints and the Josephites, which have only ended in a more open and active enmity on the part of either. Elder Smith attends the conferences, which are held quarterly or annually at some one of the appointed colonies of Josephites, where his preaching inspires his adherents, and makes new converts of those who gather through curiosity to see the show. The next great conference will be at Independence, Mo., beginning the 6th of April, 1885. Independence is closely connected with the early history of Mormonism. Josephite conferences have been held in Boston (where the Saints have had a place of worship for twelve or fourteen years), sometimes at Providence, Rhode Island, and at Dennisport, Cape Cod, where they have a flourishing colony.

David Whitmer, one of the original "witnesses," is still living at Richmond, Mo. He was asked not long ago if his testimony was the same now as it was originally published, regarding "the plates and the angel"— alluding to the golden plates and the angel Moroni, at the time "the word" was given to Joseph. "He rose to his feet, stretched out his hands, and said: 'These handled the plates, these eyes saw the angel, these ears heard the voice—I know it was of God,'" wrote one of the inquirers.

Whitmer has what he calls the original translation of the golden plates in manuscript. The Josephites state that the Utah Mormons sent a delegation, headed by Orley Pratt, to purchase it; and that when Whitmer declined to part with it Pratt reminded him of his poverty and the large sum he was willing, as a representative of his church, to pay for this coveted possession, and that he replied: "You have not money enough in Utah to purchase it." One of the most notable events among the Josephites was the recent debate at Kirtland, Ohio, concerning the "Book of Mormon." It lasted ten or twelve days. The discussion was carried on between Elder E. L. Kelly, of Kirtland, and Clark Braden, a Campbellite preacher of Minnesota, who has since published his arguments against the verity of the book. Mr. Kelly has also had his points of defence printed for circulation among the Josephites. The debate was an exhaustive one, apparently, every published article of the slightest importance on the subject being brought under the examination of the two men, both of whom are considered exceptionally intelligent. Whatever the present result of this controversy may be, its ultimate influence may lead to a still more serious inquiry into the Mormon delusion.

In the January number of a small monthly published at Laomi, Iowa, there is an editorial to prove that Joseph, the Seer, predicted that if Brigham Young ever became the head of the church, he " would lead it to hell." There is also a letter in the same number, which is interesting in connection with the evidence that Smith was a polygamist, as follows :

" SAN BERNARDINO, CALIFORNIA,
December 31, 1883.

" MRS. MARY RALPH, being duly sworn, deposes and says : I lived in Nauvoo, Illinois, close to the house of Joseph Smith, just across the road, some time. I also was present at a public meeting, and heard the Prophet Joseph Smith say while preaching, ' Here is Brother Brigham ; if he ever leads this church, he will lead it to hell ;' and I believe he was a true prophet of God. I was well acquainted with the two Partridge girls and the two Walker girls and their two brothers, William and Lorin Walker ; they were orphans, and all lived in the family of Joseph Smith ; but I never knew they were any of them his wives ; but I saw Susy Walker in 1847, and she had a young baby in her arms ; she told me she had been sealed to Joseph for eternity and to Heber C. Kimball for time, and Brother Heber was acting proxy for Brother Joseph. Dianthy Farr, daughter of Aaron Farr, told me she was sealed in the same way, and William Clayton was acting proxy for Brother Joseph with her. The first I ever heard of the proxy and sealing business was in 1846. Bathsheba Smith, wife of George A., told me of it then.

" MARY RALPH.

" Sworn to before me, this 31st day of December, 1883, W. J. Curtis, Notary Public in and for San Bernardino County, State of California."

'An article in the same paper, headed " Constitutional Law," is by " President Joseph Smith." After giving an extract from the editorial columns of the *Deseret News* of December 5th, 1884, he makes the following comments :

THE PERSECUTIONS IN ARIZONA.

" Another conviction has been obtained in Howard's Court in Arizona, for polygamy. Peter J. Christofferson is the victim. The evidence, it is stated, was as incomplete as in the case of Mr. Tenney. A despatch to the San Francisco *Chronicle* says : ' The Mormons threaten vengeance against the court.' That, of course, is a falsehood. The Prescott press despatcher has taken a leaf out of his Salt Lake confrère's book. The ' Mormons ' will naturally feel indignant at the course pursued, in committing without bail, pending an appeal, prisoners who have been convicted on hearsay. But they will neither threaten nor injure the court.

"Submission to the law is and has been one of the characteristics of the Latter-Day Saints, and they have not changed their principles nor their policy by moving over the line into another territory. Their non-obedience to the anti-polygamy enactments is well known to spring from their belief in the invalidity of those statutes, and it is acknowledged that with those exceptions the ' Mormons ' are exemplary in their submission to the laws of the land.

" Whatever opposition may proceed from our friends in Arizona to the verdicts of juries and the rulings of courts, no matter how unjust and arbitrary they may be, will be taken on legal grounds and pursued by lawful measures. Such proceedings as have been inaugurated may give temporary comfort to bigots, but patience is a ' Mormon ' virtue, and ' the end is not yet.' "

He says there are three points in the foregoing editorial worth a notice : 1, persecution in Arizona ; 2, constitutional law ; 3, submission to law. With an elaborate argument on these points, he adds :

" The church from 1830 to 1844 was law-abiding. Its utterances in theory, principle, dogma, faith, and practice were in keeping with the teaching of the Constitution. It was the claim of the elders that the discovery of America was foreseen and provided for by God, as the founding of a government to be the asylum for the oppressed of all nations. It was the belief of the leaders and the people that the struggle for independence was the baptism of the tree of Liberty in fire and blood, without which it could never flourish. It was taught as a heritage of the covenant made with Abraham, that the men who framed and wrote the Declaration and the Constitution were raised up by the Almighty for that purpose. Christ so stated it in His declarations to the church in the restoration of the gospel. Love of country was held and enjoined from father to son. This was enforced as a sacred duty, and more binding on the Saints because of the wondrous manifestations of God's providence, watch, care, and determination concerning the land, and the people who should live upon it. The church felt this. Joseph Smith boasted that he was a 'Green Mountain boy;' for in those Vermont hills patriots were born and raised. Obedience to law—the laws of the land—was a duty and a cardinal virtue. The laws of the States in which the church originated and appointed for the stakes of Zion were under the Constitution. They were good and sufficient for the establishment and continuation of the church until the Prophet and Patriarch were slain. There was up to that time no church tenet or practice that required a Saint to break or defy or evade the law of the land; and yet everywhere the Elders went or Saints settled there were laws forbidding more than one companion in wedlock.

"The Utah fragment sought a soil on which to develop the folly of Solomon and David anew—a land where the crime and abomination of the people to whom Jacob ministered the rebuke of God might be again re-enacted."

The close of the article is as follows:

"The law of 1862, prohibiting polygamy in Utah and other territories, passed by Congress, has been declared to be constitutional by the Supreme Court of the United States. Each successive enactment of Congress, had in respect to the same crime, has been but supplementary or auxiliary to that law, providing safeguards against those who have proposed to evade the law because 'they believed it to be invalid.' The Acts of Congress, under which the men 'persecuted' in Arizona were arrested, tried, and convicted, have been but enabling clauses of the same law in harmony with the first.

"The judge, under whose administration these men were tried, is the proper one to interpret the language of the Constitution in respect to his own court, which declares that 'the judges in every State shall be bound thereby (by the Constitution and all laws passed under it), anything in the Constitution or laws of any State to the contrary notwithstanding.'

" No Legislature of any State of the United States, nor any assembly of any territory belonging to the United States, has a right to enact provisions which make nugatory or inoperative the Constitution or the laws of the United States, made under it. Neither the State of Iowa nor the (state of Deseret) territory of Utah can rightfully pass and enforce enactments which estop the action of the courts of the United States from punishing men who have refused obedience to the laws declared to be constitutional by the Supreme Court, or who have violated statutes passed by Congress in pursuance of the general provisions of the Constitution, approved by the Supreme Court. The laws of the United States passed into being and operation upon territory belonging to the States *per se*. That which is a crime in the States, by virtue of the United States law, is a crime in the territories of the States. Not until territories merge into States are they relieved of such disabilities as are imposed by the special and direct jurisdiction of the United States.

" What the (state of Deseret) Utah Territory could not do as a Territory, she could not authorize the Church of Jesus Christ to do. Hence, marriage being a civil contract, according to the declaration of the church, founded under God under the divinely authorized provisions of the Constitution of the United States, while that church was within States whose laws were monogamic, and before the establishment of such territory of Utah, it must remain a civil contract still in all and every territory belonging to the United States, nor was it in the power of the Territorial Assembly to so endow the church in Utah by an incorporating charter with the right to violate the general rules of the States as to remove the right to regulate the domestic relations of husband and wife, parents and children from the province of Congress and the United States courts. And not until Utah shall be admitted as a State of the Union, with an express provision in its constitution providing for the practice of plural or polygamic marriage, can it become lawful, or the laws against it become invalid.

" Should Utah be admitted as a State without such express provision in its constitution at its admission, we believe that the Legislature could not then legalize polygamy, neither by direct enactment nor by the roundabout method adopted by the Legislature of Deseret, and approved by the Utah Territorial Assembly, by charter to the church, allowing it to control the marriage relations.

"Whether Congress may lawfully admit Utah with such a clause in the Constitution permitting plural marriage either as a civil contract or as a church sacrament we do not discuss, as such contingency is of doubtful occurrence. But it may be pertinent to say that bigamy or polygamy (plural marriage), being a crime in all other States of the Union, should Utah be admitted with such a clause in its constitution, 'full faith and credit' could not be given such 'public acts' in the other States, for persons plurally married in Utah could not legally live in those States."

From this quotation it will be seen how strongly the leader of the Josephites denounces the Utah Mormons and polygamy. He is still, however, a Mormon, teaching Mormon doctrines, the divine origin of the "Book of Mormon," and that Joseph Smith, his father, was a prophet. While the Josephites have not increased as rapidly as the Utah Mormons during the thirty odd years since the division in the church, or since Brigham Young led all save a remnant of the Saints to Deseret, it is astonishing to find this second body of "the chosen people" so numerous, and with places of worship in old New England towns. The attention of the civilized world has been startled into activity, regarding the Mormons of Utah, by their atrocities, by their plurality of wives, and acts of defiance toward the government, while very little has been known or written of the Josephites, who have meantime been increasing in numbers and wealth, and outwardly, at least, respecting the Federal law. They have also joined the great mass of people in throwing stones at their former neighbors and friends, forgetting how thin the material is of which their own habitation is made. A number of the Josephites are intelligent and fairly educated; these are the leaders of the mass, half-educated, credulous, and often illiterate men and women, with crude notions as to right and wrong, and ready to adopt a religious belief that is eloquently and persuasively preached in their hearing.

The following are extracts from a letter printed in the Boston *Evening Transcript* of June 7th, 1884. It is headed, "Down on the Cape—A Colony of Latter-Day Saints at Dennisport, Mass.:"

"Released from the vehicle, and standing in the porch of the hotel, we ventured to inquire of John in what part of Harwich the Mormon Colony is located.

"'Wa'll, now you've got me,' he replied. 'I guess you mean the "Latter-Day Saints." We don't call 'em Mormons down here.'

"'I suppose so. Will you answer some questions I may ask you of them?'

"'Sartain sure; but I won't tell a lie about them if I go under. They live right down to Dennisport, about a mile from here, and I'll take you down there after dinner.'

"West Harwich is a clean, lively little town, with good accommodations for summer boarders at moderate prices. This was quickly learned, and we started to see the 'Saints,' whose houses occupy two long streets, or roads, down to the Port. These dwellings are comfortable in appearance, and have gardens about them. A moderate-sized building, larger than the houses, we were told, 'is the place where the Saints have their meetings.'

"Our driver was true to his principle of reticence concerning the Mormons, but excused it with the promise to find Captain Howes, one of the most prominent of the 'Saints,' who would tell us all we wanted to know; and, suiting the action to the word, he drove on to the wharf and called out to an amphibious-looking individual sitting in a boat that was close to the deck:

"'Captain, here's some folks from ever so far; they want to see you.'

"The captain stared, and so did the dozen or so fishermen loitering about and talking of the morning's catch of three thousand mackerel that was to be sent to Boston; but after a moment he called out that he would come ashore. The sea was slightly ruffled with an east wind, but was of that deep blue that artists love to picture, and away out were the fishing-smacks coming into port with their burdens. We had turned and been driven under shelter by the time 'the captain' made his appearance, and closer observation proved him to be a hardy specimen of his peculiar calling : tall, lithe, keen-eyed, and of a rather intelligent visage. 'Yes,' said he, as if he had hastily made up his mind what to say, 'I am perfectly willing to talk of my religion. We are Mormons of the kind called "Josephites;" we are the true "Latter-Day Saints;" we do not believe in plurality—'

"'You mean polygamy?'

"'Yes, that is what I mean. When the Mormons separated, at the time of Joseph Smith's death, some of them went off to their destruction with Brigham Young ; but we don't countenance them. Joseph Smith, Jr., of Plano, Ill., is our leader—'

"'And his father, Joe Smith—'

"'We believe his father was a true prophet. We believe in immersion as the true baptism, because Christ was baptized in the river Jordan ; we believe that no one will be eternally lost, although they have to suffer for their sins, and we think Christ is coming in person to reign over us.'

"'How about your form of worship?'

"'Well, we have a Bible that Elder Pratt translated—it's like the King James Bible, only it explains things a good deal, makes them clear ; we sing and have prayer-meetings and a Sunday-school and Sunday services, just like other people.'

"'You have a good many religions mixed up in one.'

"'Yes ; the best of all of them put together.'

"'And the "Book of Mormon"?'

"'Well, that is a history of Mormon that Smith found written on some gold plates.'

"'Who wrote it?'

"'I don't know.'

"He went then on to state that he had always resided at Dennisport ; that he was converted by an elder, a Mormon missionary, and that Joe Smith, Jr., had attended one of their conferences, two of which are held in Ocean Hall at West Harwich each year ; that these meetings are largely attended by Mormons resident in New England, who are colonized in several places—at Fall River, Providence, Boston, and elsewhere.

"'I wish I had time to talk more of our people,' concluded the fisherman ; 'but you must go and see our elder,' and he turned away with a little twinkle in his gray eyes.

"The elder was ill, or forewarned of our coming, and we did not see him ; but from a less cautious person we gathered some significant statements respecting the 'Saints.' While they profess not to believe in 'plurality,' they act in numerous cases upon the principle of 'affinity.' Marriages among them have in this way been frequently broken and resumed. One woman went to Utah, was gone twenty years, and returned to her old marital relations. Our informer, when we expressed surprise at this and other statements of a like character, said :

"' Why, it's right enough ; people can't help liking each other if they are married.'

"The conferences this person mentioned as most enjoyable occasions, with 'good speaking from real smart men,' and a general attendance of the people in the neighborhood, some of whom, it is said, are generally made converts. It was impossible to learn just how many Mormons there were at Dennisport—really a part of West Harwich—but there are more than fifty of their dwellings, and over one hundred residents in them may fairly be estimated.

"The children of this colony attend the free school with the other children of Harwich, and there is a general tolerance of the 'Saints,' old and young, by the residents in the vicinity in a business, if not in a social, way. An intelligent man, born and brought up on the cape, in speaking of them, said : 'These Mormons are industrious, and behave very well ; but, of course, they've got some black sheep among them, like any other body of religious people.' Another said, in excuse for one of the 'Saints' who departed from the colony with an 'affinity,' 'Why, he came back and lives here now.'"

A Mormon elder, in speaking of this letter, remarked that the Captain Howes alluded to is a man who is much esteemed by his brethren. The statements made by several unprejudiced residents of Harwich regarding their neighbors of Dennisport show that there is an obliquity of vision in regard to the moral code among these fishermen, which comes either from lack of principle or defective training. The Mormon of Utah is a polygamist if he has the means to be so ; it is a precept of his faith ; the followers of Joseph the Second can have but one wife and an "affinity." It must, however, be added, that indisputably many of the Josephites lead peaceable, innocent, and inoffensive lives. This may be said of the greater proportion of them probably. The women have few of the trials of their sisters in Utah ; the men are toilers on the sea and land. They rejoice in their religious faith. It is pitiful that it has no better foundation than to have been stolen from an old romance.

EPITOME OF THE FAITH AND DOCTRINES OF THE REORGANIZED CHURCH OF JESUS CHRIST OF LATTER-DAY SAINTS.

"We believe in God the Eternal Father, and in His Son Jesus Christ, and in the Holy Ghost. Matt. 28 : 19. 1 John 1 : 3. St. John 11 : 26.

"We believe that men will be punished for their own sins, and not for Adam's transgression. Ecc. 12 : 14. Matt. 16 : 27. 1 Cor. 8 : 18. Rev. 20 : 12-15.

"We believe that through the atonement of Christ all men may be saved, by obedience to the laws and ordinances of the gospel. 1 Cor. 15 : 8. 2 Tim. 1 : 10. Rom. 8 : 1-6.

"We believe that these ordinances are:

"(1st) Faith in God and in the Lord Jesus Christ. Heb. 11 : 6. 1 Peter 1 : 21. 1 Tim. 4 : 10. John 3 : 16, 18, 36. Mark 11 : 22. John 14 : 1.

"(2d) Repentance. Matt. 3 : 2, 8, 11. Luke 13 : 3 ; 24 : 47. Ezek. 18 : 30. Mark 1 : 5, 15. Acts 2 : 38. Romans 2 : 4. 2 Cor. 7 : 10.

"(3d) Baptism by immersion, for the remission of sins. Matt. 3 : 13-15. Mark 1 : 4, 5. Luke 8 : 8. John 8 : 5. Acts 2 : 38 ; 22 : 16 ; 2 : 41 ; 8 : 12, 37, 38. Mark 16 : 16. Col. 2 : 12. Romans 6 : 4, 5. John 3 : 23. Acts 8 : 38, 39.

"(4th) Laying on of hands for the gift of the Holy Ghost. Deut. 34 : 9. John 20 : 21, 22. Acts 8 : 17 : 19 : 6. 1 Tim. 4 : 14. Acts 9 : 17. 1 Cor. 12 : 3. Acts 19 : 1-6.

"(5th) We believe in the Resurrection of the Body ; that the dead in Christ will rise first, and the rest of the dead will not live again until the thousand years are expired. Job 19 : 25, 26. Dan. 12 : 2. 1 Cor. 15 : 42. 1 Thess. 4 : 16. Rev. 20 : 6. Acts 17 : 31. Phil. 3 : 21. John 11 : 24. Isaiah 26 : 19. Ps. 17 : 15.

"(6th) We believe in the doctrine of Eternal Judgment, which provides that men shall be judged, rewarded, or punished according to the degree of good or evil they shall have done. Rev. 20 : 12. Ecc. 3 : 17. Matt. 16 : 27. 2 Cor. 5 : 10. 2 Peter 2 : 4, 13, 17.

"We believe that a man must be Called of God, and ordained by the Laying on of Hands of those who are in authority, to entitle him to preach the Gospel, and Administer in the Ordinances thereof. Heb. 5 : 1, 5, 6, 8. Acts 1 : 24, 25 ; 14 : 23. Eph. 4 : 11. John 15 : 16.

"We believe in the same kind of organization that existed in the primitive church—viz., apostles, prophets, pastors, teachers, evangelists, etc. 1 Cor. 12 : 28. Matt. 10 : 12. Acts 6 : 4. Eph. 4 : 11 ; 2 : 20. Titus 1 : 5.

"We believe that in the Bible is contained the word of God, so far as it is translated correctly. We believe that the canon of Scripture is not full, but that God, by His Spirit, will continue to reveal His word to man until the end of time. Job 32 : 8. Hebrews 13 : 8. Proverbs 29 : 18. Amos 3 : 7. Jeremiah 23 : 4 ; 31 : 31, 34 ; 33 : 6. Psalms 85 : 10, 11. Luke 17 : 26. Rev. 14 : 6, 7 ; 19 : 10.

"We believe in the powers and gifts of the everlasting gospel—viz., the gift of faith, discerning of spirits, prophecy, revelation, visions, healing, tongues, and the interpretation of tongues, wisdom, charity, brotherly love, etc. 1 Cor. 12 : 1-11 ; 14 : 26. John 14 : 24. Acts 2 : 8. Matt. 28 : 19, 20. Mark 16 : 16.

"We believe that Marriage is ordained of God ; and that the law of God provides for but one companion in wedlock, for either man or woman, except in cases where the contract of marriage is broken by death or transgression. Genesis 2 : 18, 21-24 ; 7 : 1, 7, 13. Proverbs 5 : 15-21. Malachi 2 : 14, 15. Matt. 19 : 4-6. 1 Cor. 7 : 2. Hebrews 13 : 4.

"We believe that the doctrines of a plurality and a community of wives are heresies, and are opposed to the law of God. Gen. 4 : 19, 23, 24 ; 7 : 9 ; 22 : 2, in connection Gal. 4th and 5th chapters. Gen. 21 : 8-10. Mal. 2 : 14, 15. Matt. 19 : 3-9.

"We believe that the religion of Jesus Christ, as taught in the New Testament Scriptures, will, if its precepts are accepted and obeyed, make men and women better in the domestic circle, and better citizens of town, county, and State, and consequently better fitted for the change which cometh at death.

"We believe that men should worship God in 'Spirit and in truth ;' and that such worship does not require a violation of the constitutional law of the land. John 4: 21-24. Doctrine and Covenants, sect. 58, par. 5.

"We claim the privilege of worshipping Almighty God according to the dictates of our conscience, and allow all men the same privilege, let them worship how, where, or what they may."

Please understand that the Reorganized Church* of Jesus Christ of Latter-Day Saints is in no way connected with Salt Lake Mormons. That polygamy never was and never can be a doctrine or practice among those who follow the teachings of Christ and the Holy Spirit. Hear what the "Book of Mormon" says on polygamy: "Wherefore, my brethren, hear me, and hearken to the word of the Lord; for there shall not any man among you have save it be one wife, and concubines he shall have none, for I, the Lord God, delight in the chastity of women," etc.

Polygamy originated with the leaders of the Utah Church, and that church has departed from the faith of the pure gospel system, as taught by the church of Christ, both of former and latter days, and the Utah Church has clearly fulfilled the prophecy of Paul, 1 Tim. 4 : 1, and Jer. 17 : 5, 6.

The Reorganized Church has done more to put down polygamy than any other denomination on the face of the earth.

[Any history of Mormonism would be incomplete without a copy of the "Revelation," which has played so important a part in the development of the church. It is here copied intact for the benefit of the historical student.]

CELESTIAL MARRIAGE.

A revelation on the patriarchal order of marriage, or plurality of wives, given to Joseph Smith, the seer, in Nauvoo, July 12th, 1843.†

"I. Verily, thus saith the Lord unto you, My servant Joseph, that inasmuch as you have inquired of my hand to know and understand wherein I, the Lord, justified my servants Abraham, Isaac, and Jacob,

---

* From a Josephite newspaper.
† From Stenhouse's "Rocky Mountain Saints," p. 176.

as also Moses, David, and Solomon my servants, as touching the principle and doctrine of their having many wives and concubines; behold, and lo! I am the Lord thy God, and will answer thee as touching this matter; therefore prepare thy heart to receive and obey the instructions which I am about to give unto you; for all those who have this law revealed unto them must obey the same; for, behold! I reveal unto you a new and an everlasting covenant; and if ye abide not that covenant, then are ye damned; for no one can reject this covenant, and be permitted to enter into my glory; for all who will have a blessing at my hands shall abide the law which was appointed for that blessing, and the conditions thereof as was instituted from before the foundation of the world; and as pertaining to the new and everlasting covenant, it was instituted for the fulness of my glory; and he that receiveth a fulness thereof must and shall abide the law or be damned, saith the Lord.

"II. And verily I say unto you, that the conditions of this law are these: All covenants, contracts, bonds, obligations, oaths, vows, performances, connections, associations, or expectations, that are not made, and entered into, and sealed by the Holy Spirit of promise of him who is anointed, both as well for time and for all eternity, and that, too, most holy by revelation and commandment, through the medium of mine anointed, whom I have appointed on the earth to hold this power (and I have appointed unto my servant Joseph to hold this power in the last days, and there is never but one on the earth at a time, on whom this power and the keys of this priesthood are conferred), are of no efficacy, virtue, or force in and after the resurrection from the dead; for all contracts that are not made unto this end, have an end when men are dead.

"III. Behold! mine house is an house of order, saith the Lord God, and not a house of confusion. Will I accept an offering, saith the Lord, that is not made in my name? Or will I receive at your hands that which I have not appointed? And I will appoint unto you, saith the Lord, except it be by law, even as I and my Father ordained unto you before the world was! I am the Lord thy God, and I give unto you this commandment, that no man shall come unto the Father but by me or by my word, which is my law, saith the Lord; and everything that is in the world, whether it be ordained of men by thrones, or principalities, or powers, or things of name, whatsoever they may be, that are not by me, or by my word, saith the Lord, shall be thrown down, and shall not remain after men are dead, neither in nor after the resurrection, saith the Lord your God; for whatsoever things are not by me shall be shaken and destroyed.

"IV. Therefore, if a man marry him a wife in the world, and he marry her not by me, nor by my word, and he covenant with her so long as he is in the world, and she with him, their covenant and marriage is not of force when they are dead, and when they are out of the world; therefore, they are not bound by any law when they are out of the world; therefore, when they are out of the world, they neither marry, nor are given in marriage; but are appointed angels in heaven, which angels are ministering servants to minister to whose who are worthy of a far more and eternal weight of glory; for these angels did not abide my law; therefore they cannot be enlarged, but remain separately and singly without exaltation, in their saved condition to all eternity, and from henceforth are not gods; but are angels of God forever and ever.

"V. And again, verily I say unto you, if a man marry a wife, and make a covenant with her for time and for all eternity, if that covenant is not by me or by my word which is my law, and is not sealed by the Holy Spirit of promise through him whom I have anointed and appointed unto this power, then it is not valid, neither of force when they are out of the world, because they are not joined by me, saith the Lord, neither by my word; when they are out of the world, it cannot be received there, because the angels and the gods are appointed there, by whom they cannot pass; they cannot, therefore, inherit my glory, for my house is an house of order, saith the Lord God.

"VI. And again, verily I say unto you, if a man marry a wife by my word, which is my law, and by the new and everlasting covenant, and it is sealed unto them by the Holy Spirit of promise, by him who is anointed, unto whom I have appointed this power, and the keys of this priesthood; and it shall be said unto them, ye shall come forth in the first resurrection, and if it be after the first resurrection, in the next resurrection, and shall inherit thrones, kingdoms, principalities, and powers of dominions, all heights, and depths, then it shall be written in the Lamb's Book of Life, that he shall commit no murder whereby to shed innocent blood; and if ye abide in my covenant, and commit no murder whereby to shed innocent blood, it shall be done unto them in all things whatsoever my servant hath put upon them in time and through all eternity, and shall be full of force when they are out of the world; and they shall pass by the angels, and the gods which are set there, to their exaltation and glory in all things, as hath been sealed upon their heads, which glory shall be a fulness and a continuation of the deeds forever and ever.

"VII. That they shall be gods, because they have no end; therefore they shall be from everlasting to everlasting, because they continue; then shall they be above all, because all things are subject unto them. Then shall they be gods, because they have all power, and the angels are subject unto them.

"VIII. Verily, verily I say unto you, except ye abide my law, ye cannot attain to this glory; for straight is the gate, and narrow the way that leadeth unto the exaltation and continuation of the lives, and few there be that find it, because ye receive me not in the world, neither do ye know me. But if ye receive me in the world, then shall ye know me, and shall receive your exaltation that where I am ye shall be also. This is eternal lives, to know the only true and wise God, and Jesus Christ, whom He hath sent. I am He. Receive ye therefore my law. Broad is the gate, and wide the way, that leadeth to the death; and many there are that go in thereat, because they receive me not, neither do they abide in my law.

"IX. Verily, verily I say unto you, if a man marry a wife according to my word, and they are sealed by the Holy Spirit of promise according to mine appointment, and he or she shall commit any sin or transgression of the new and everlasting covenant whatever, and all manner of blasphemies, and if they commit no murder wherein they shed no innocent blood, yet they shall come forth in the first resurrection, and enter into their exaltation; but they shall be destroyed in the flesh, and shall be delivered unto the buffetings of Satan, unto the day of redemption, saith the Lord God.

"X. The blasphemy against the Holy Spirit which shall not be forgiven in the world, nor out of the world, is in that ye commit murder wherein ye shed innocent blood, and assent unto my death, after ye have received my new and everlasting covenant, saith the Lord God; and he that abideth not in this law can in nowise enter into my glory, but shall be damned, saith the Lord.

"XI. I am the Lord thy God, and will give unto thee the law of my holy priesthood, as was ordained by me, and my father before the world was. Abraham received all things, whatsoever he received by revelation and commandment by my word, saith the Lord, and hath entered into his exaltation, and sitteth upon his throne.

"XII. Abraham received promises concerning his seed, and of the fruit of his loins—from whose loins ye are—namely, my servant Joseph—which were to continue so long as they were in the world; and as touching Abraham and his seed, out of the world, they should continue; both in the world and out of the world should they continue as innumerable as the stars; or, if ye were to count the sand upon the seashore, ye could not number them. This promise is yours also, as ye are of Abraham, and the promise was made to Abraham; and by this law are the continuation of the works of my Father, wherein He glorifieth Himself. Go ye therefore and do the works of Abraham; enter ye into my law, and ye shall be saved. But if ye enter not into my law, ye cannot receive the promise of my Father, which He made unto Abraham.

"XIII. God commanded Abraham and Sarah, gave Hagar to Abraham to wife. And why did she do it? Because this was the law, and from Hagar sprang many people. This, therefore, was fulfilling among other things the promises. Was Abraham, therefore, under condemnation? Verily, I say unto you, *nay*; for I, the Lord, commanded it. Abraham was commanded to offer his son Isaac; nevertheless, it was written, Thou shalt not kill. Abraham, however, did not refuse, and it was accounted unto him for righteousness.

"XIV. Abraham received concubines, and they bare him children; and it was accounted unto him for righteousness, because they were given unto him, and he abode in my law, as Isaac also, and Jacob did none other things than that which they were commanded; and because they did none other things than that which they were commanded, they have entered into their exaltation, according to the promises, and sit upon thrones, and are not angels, but are gods. David also received many wives and concubines, as also Solomon and Moses, my servants, as also many others of my servants, from the beginning of creation until this time; and in nothing did they sin, save in those things they did not receive of me.

"XV. David's wives and concubines were given unto him of me, by the hand of Nathan, my servant, and others of the prophets, who had the keys of this power, and in none of these things did he sin against me, save in the case of Uriah and his wife, and therefore he hath fallen from his exaltation, and received his portion, and he shall not inherit them out of the world, for I gave them unto another, saith the Lord.

"XVI. I am the Lord thy God, and I gave unto thee my servant Joseph an appointment and restore all things; ask what ye will, and it shall be given unto you, according to my word; and as he have asked concerning adultery—verily, verily, I say unto you, if a man receive a wife in the new and everlasting covenant, and if she be with another man, and I have not appointed her by the holy anointing, she hath committed adultery, and shall be destroyed. If she be not in the new and everlasting covenant, and she be with another man, she hath committed adultery; and if her husband be with another woman, and he was under a vow, he hath broken his vow and hath committed adultery; and if she hath not committed adultery, but is innocent, and hath not broken her vow, and she knoweth it, and I reveal it unto you my servant Joseph, then shall you have power, by the power of my holy priesthood, to take her, and give her unto him that hath not committed adultery, but hath been faithful, for he shall be made ruler over many ; for I have conferred upon you the keys and power of the priesthood, wherein I shall restore all things, and make known unto you all things in due time.

"XVII. And verily, verily I say unto you, that whatsoever you seal on earth, shall be sealed in heaven ; and whatsoever you bind on earth in my name and by my word, saith the Lord, it shall be eternally bound in the heavens ; and whosesoever sins ye shall remit on earth, shall be remitted eternally in the heavens ; and whosesoever sins ye retain on earth, shall be retained in heaven.

"XVIII. And again, verily I say, whomsoever you bless, I will bless, and whomsoever you curse, I will curse, saith the Lord ; for I the Lord am thy God.

"XIX. And again, verily I say unto you my servant Joseph, that whatsoever you give on earth, and to whomsoever you give any one on earth, by my word, and according to my law, it shall be visited with blessing, and not cursings, and with my power, saith the Lord, and shall be without condemnation on earth and in heaven, for I am the Lord thy God, and will be with thee, even unto the end of the world, and through all eternity ; for verily I seal upon you your exaltation, and prepare a throne for you in the kingdom of my Father, with Abraham your father. Behold, I have seen your sacrifices, and I will forgive all your sins ; I have seen your sacrifices in obedience to that which I have told you ; go therefore, and I make a way for your escape, as I accepted the offering of Abraham, of his son Isaac.

"XX. Verily I say unto you, a commandment I give unto my handmaid Emma Smith, your wife, whom I have given unto you, that she stay herself, and partake not of that which I commanded you to offer unto her ; for I did it, saith the Lord, to prove you all, as I did Abraham, and that I might require an offering at your hand, by covenant and sacrifice ; and let my handmaid Emma Smith receive all those that have been given unto my servant Joseph, and who are virtuous and pure before me ; and those who were not pure, and have said they were pure, shall be destroyed, saith the Lord God ; for I am the Lord thy God, and ye shall obey my voice ; and I give unto my servant Joseph that he shall be made ruler over many things, for he hath been faithful over a few things, and from henceforth I will strengthen him.

"XXI. And I command mine handmaid Emma Smith to abide and cleave unto my servant Joseph, and to none else. But if she will not abide this commandment she shall be destroyed, saith the Lord; for I am the Lord thy God, and will destroy her if she abide not in my law; but if she will not abide this commandment, then shall my servant Joseph do all things for her, even as he hath said; and I will bless him, and multiply him, and give unto him an hundred-fold in this world of fathers and mothers, brothers and sisters, houses and lands, wives and children, and crowns of eternal lives, in the eternal worlds. And again, verily I say unto my handmaid, forgive my servant Joseph his trespasses, and then shall she be forgiven her trespasses, wherein she hath trespassed against me, and I the Lord thy God will bless her and multiply her, and make her heart to rejoice.

"XXII. And again I say unto my servant Joseph, put his property out of his hands, lest an enemy come and destroy him; for Satan seeketh to destroy; for I am the Lord thy God, and he is my servant; and behold! and lo, I am with him, as I was with Abraham thy father, even unto his exaltation and glory.

"XXIII. Now, as touching the law of priesthood, there are many things pertaining thereunto. Verily, if a man be called of my Father, as was Aaron by mine own voice, and by the voice of Him that sent me; and I have endowed him with the keys of the power of this priesthood, if he do anything in my name, and according to my law, and by my word, he will not commit sin, and I will justify him. Let no one therefore set on my servant Joseph; for I will justify him; for he shall do the sacrifice which I require at his hands for his transgressions, saith the Lord your God.

"XXIV. And again, as pertaining to the law of the priesthood; if any man espouse a virgin, and desire to espouse another, and the first give her consent; and if he espouse the second, and they are virgins, and have vowed to no other man, then he is justified; he cannot commit adultery, for they are given unto him; for he cannot commit adultery with that that belongeth unto him, and no one else; and if he have ten virgins given unto him by this law, he cannot commit adultery, for they belong to him, and they are given unto him, therefore is he justified. But if one or either of the ten virgins, after she is espoused, shall be with another man, she hath committed adultery, and shall be destroyed; for they are given to him to multiply and replenish the earth, according to my commandment, and to fulfil the promise which was given by my Father before the foundation of the world, and for their exaltation in the eternal worlds, that they may bear the souls of men ; for herein is the work of my Father that he may be glorified.

" XXV. And again, verily, verily I say unto you, if any man have a wife who holds the keys of this power, and he teaches unto her the law of my priesthood as pertaining these things, then shall she believe, and administer unto him, or she shall be destroyed, saith the Lord your God ; for I will destroy her ; for I will magnify my name upon all those who receive and abide in my law. Therefore it shall be lawful in me, if she receive not this law, for him to receive all things whatsoever I, the Lord his God will give unto him, because she did not administer unto him according to my word ; and she then becomes the transgressor ; and he is exempt from the law of Sarah, who administered unto Abraham, according to the law, when I commanded Abraham to take Hagar to wife. And now, as pertaining to this law, verily, verily I say unto you, I will reveal more unto you hereafter ; therefore let this suffice for the present. Behold, I am Alpha and Omega. Amen."

Elder W. W. Phelps said, in Salt Lake Tabernacle, in 1862, that while Joseph was translating the "Book of Abraham" in Kirtland, Ohio, in 1835, from the papyrus found with the Egyptian mummies, the Prophet became impressed with the idea that polgyamy would yet become an institution in the Mormon Church. Brigham Young was present, and was much annoyed at the statement made by Phelps ; but it is highly probable that it was the real secret which was then divulged. There cannot be a doubt that Joseph went into polygamy at a venture.

The following extract is from the pen of an unknown reviewer of a bound volume of "The True Latter-Day Saints Herald"—sold with other books relating to Mormonism—the ten years' gatherings of Charles L. Woodward, in New York, January 19th, 1880.

"' The True Latter-Day Saints Herald.' Vols. 1 to 22, 8vo. Vols. 1–16, bound in 3 vols. sheep. Vols. 17–22 unbound, uncut. Cincinnati, O., and Plano, Ill., 1860–1875, $40.

"This is the organ of Joseph Smith, the son of the Prophet, who, trading on antipolygamy, is said to have a following of not less than thirty thousand fools, known as 'Young Josephites.' Nothing better proves the truth of the old saying that 'a lie well stuck to is as good as the truth,' than the success of Joseph II. in making people believe that his father did not promulgate the polygamy 'revelation.' Knowing full well that even to-day there are women in Utah known by hundreds still living to have been Joe's 'plurals,' but relying upon the fact that the witnesses have told so many lies that they cannot be believed, even when they speak the truth, he calls for the progeny, with an air that settles it. Fortunately—all fortunately—Joe did have no little prophets by his numerous polygamous wives. Only by religious lunatics would this fact be accepted as disproof of marriage, whether to one or one hundred. The cry, 'Show us the progeny,' seems to be regarded by Joseph II. and his addle-brained adherents as a socdollager. Joseph I. never dared openly practise nor advocate polygamy. Nor did any of the Mormons until they were safe beyond the white settlements."

APPENDIX.

[*From Scribner's Monthly, August,* 1880.]

No. 1.

Mrs. Matilda Spaulding McKinstry's Statement Regarding "The Manuscript Found."

WASHINGTON, D. C., April 3, 1880.

So much has been published that is erroneous concerning "The Manuscript Found," written by my father, the Rev. Solomon Spaulding, and its supposed connection with the book called the Mormon Bible, I have willingly consented to make the following statement regarding it, repeating all that I remember personally of this manuscript, and all that is of importance which my mother related to me in connection with it, at the same time affirming that I am in tolerable health and vigor, and that my memory, in common with elderly people, is clearer in regard to the events of my earlier years rather than those of my maturer life.

During the war of 1812 I was residing with my parents in a little town in Ohio called Conneaut. I was then in my sixth year. My father was in business there, and I remember his iron foundry and the men he had at work, but that he remained at home most of the time, and was reading and writing a great deal. He frequently wrote little stories, which he read to me. There were some round mounds of earth near our house which greatly interested him, and he said a tree on the top of one of them was a thousand years old. He set some of his men to work digging into one of these mounds, and I vividly remember how excited he became when he heard that they had exhumed some human bones, portions of gigantic skeletons, and various relics. He talked with my mother of these discoveries in the mound, and was writing every day as the work progressed. Afterward he read the manuscript which I had seen him writing, to the neighbors, and to a clergyman, a friend of his who came to see him.

Some of the names that he mentioned while reading to these people I have never forgotten. They are as fresh to me to-day as though I heard them yesterday. They were "Mormon," "Maroni," "Lamenite," "Nephi."

We removed from Conneaut to Pittsburg while I was still very young, but every circumstance of this removal is distinct in my memory. In that city my father had an intimate friend named Patterson, and I frequently visited Mr. Patterson's library with him, and heard my father talk about books with him. In 1816 my father died at Amity, Penn., and directly after his death my mother and myself went to visit at the residence of my mother's brother, William H. Sabine, at Onondaga Valley, Onondaga Co., N. Y. Mr. Sabine was a lawyer of distinction and wealth, and greatly respected. We carried all our personal effects with us, and one of these was an old trunk, in which my mother had placed all my father's writings which had been preserved. I perfectly remember the appearance of this trunk, and of looking at its contents. There were sermons and other papers, and I saw a manuscript about an inch thick, closely written, tied with some of the stories my father had written for me, one of which he called "The Frogs of Wyndham." On the outside of this manuscript were written the words, "Manuscript Found." I did not read it, but looked through it, and had it in my hands many times, and saw the names I had heard at Conneaut, when my father read it to his friends. I was about eleven years of age at this time.

After we had been at my uncle's for some time my mother left me there and went to her father's house at Pomfret, Conn., but did not take her furniture nor the old trunk of manuscripts with her. In 1820 she married Mr. Davison, of Hartwicks, a village near Cooperstown, N. Y., and sent for the things she had left at Onondaga Valley, and I remember that the old trunk, with its contents, reached her in safety. In 1828 I was married to Dr. A. McKinstry, of Monson, Hampden Co., Mass., and went there to reside. Very soon after my mother joined me there, and was with me most of the time until her death, in 1844. We heard, not long after she came to live with me—I do not remember just how long—something of Mormonism, and the report that it had been taken from my father's "Manuscript Found;" and then came to us direct an account of the Mormon meeting at Conneaut, Ohio, and that, on one occasion, when the Mormon Bible was read there in public, my father's brother, John Spaulding, Mr. Lake, and many other persons who were present, at once recognized its similarity to "The Manuscript Found," which they had heard read years before by my father in the same town. There was a great deal of talk and a great deal published at this time about Mormonism all over the country. I believe it was in 1834 that a man named Hurlburt came to my house at Monson to see my brother, who told us that he had been sent by a committee to procure "The Manuscript Found," written by the Rev. Solomon Spaulding, so as to compare it with the Mormon Bible. He presented a letter to my mother from my uncle, William H. Sabine, of Onondaga Valley, in which he requested her to loan this manuscript to Hurlburt, as he (my uncle) was desirous " to uproot " (as he expressed it) " this Mormon fraud." Hurlburt represented that he had been a convert to Mormonism, but had given it up, and through "The Manuscript Found" wished to expose its wickedness. My mother was careful to have me with her in all the conversations she had with Hurlburt, who spent a day at my house. She did not like his appearance, and mistrusted his motives ; but having great respect for her brother's wishes and opinions, she reluctantly consented to his request. The old trunk, containing the desired " Manuscript Found," she had placed in the care of Mr. Jerome Clark, of Hartwicks, when she came to Monson, intending to send for it. On the repeated promise of Hurlburt to return the manuscript to us, she gave him a letter to Mr. Clark to open the trunk and deliver it to him. We afterward heard that he did receive it from Mr. Clark at Hartwicks, but from that time we have never had it in our possession, and I have no present knowledge of its existence, Hurlburt never returning it or answering letters requesting him to do so. Two years ago I heard he was still living in Ohio, and with my consent he was asked for "The Manuscript Found." He made no response, although we have evidence that he received the letter containing the request. So far I have stated facts within my own knowledge. My mother mentioned many other circumstances to me in connection with this subject which are interesting, of my father's literary tastes, his fine education, and peculiar temperament. She stated to me that she had heard the manuscript alluded to read by my father, was familiar with its contents, and she deeply regretted that her husband, as she believed, had innocently been the means of furnishing matter for a religious delusion. She said that my father loaned this " Manuscript Found " to Mr. Patterson, of Pittsburg, and that, when he returned it to my father, he said : " Polish it up, finish it, and you will make money out of it." My mother confirmed my remembrances of my father's fondness for history, and told me of his frequent conversations regarding a theory which he had of a prehistoric race which had inhabited this continent, etc., all showing that his mind dwelt on this subject. "The Manuscript Found," she said, was a romance written in biblical style, and that while she heard it read she had no especial admiration for it more than for other romances he wrote and read to her. We never, either of us, ever saw, or in any way communicated with the Mormons, save Hurlburt, as above described; and while we had no personal knowledge that the Mormon Bible was taken from "The Manuscript Found," there were many evidences to us that it was, and that Hurlburt and others at the time thought so. A convincing proof to us of this belief was that my uncle, William H. Sabine, had undoubtedly read the manuscript while it was in his house, and his faith that its production would show to the world that the Mormon Bible had been taken from it, or was the same with slight alterations. I have frequently answered questions which have been asked me by different persons regarding "The Manuscript Found," but until now have never made a statement at length for publication.

(Signed) M. S. McKINSTRY.

Sworn and subscribed to before me this 3d day of April, A.D. 1880, at the city of Washington, D. C.

CHARLES WALTER, Notary Public.

No. 2.

Letter from Joseph Miller, of Amity, Penn.

TEN MILE, PA., February 13, 1882.

MRS. ELLEN E. DICKINSON:

I rec. yours of the 1st of Feb., contents duly noted you state you wished to get all the information in my possession in regard to Solomon Spaulding. I knew the man very well, was intimately acquainted often heard him read from what he called his MS., he came to our house and wanted me to go with him and bail him for 50 Dollars as he needed the money and while on the road he told some of his history, he said while living in Ohio he lost his health and in looking over the Country where he lived he discovered some mounds, they appeared to be the work of an ancient race of people and he concluded he would write their history or a fictitious novel of the people that built the mounds, after living there, he told me he moved to Pittsburg and while there he applied to Mr. Patterson to have his novel printed for the purpose as he stated to help him take care of his family. Patterson said he, Patterson would publish it, if he, Spaulding, would write a title page. He told me he kept a little store in Pittsburg, he then moved to Amity, leaving a coppy of the manuscript in Patterson's hands, after being at Amity some time he went back to Pittsburg took his title page he called it the lost manuscript found when he went to Pittsburgh the manuscript could not be found, he said there was or had been a man by the name of Sidney Rigdon had stole it, Spaulding did not die at my house as you have it but died at a house he had rented in Amity and kept as a Public house or tavern, he was a man fully six feet high rather stooped forward a little of sober visage, very reserved in conversation and very candid apparently in all his dealings and I think a very good man, it used to be very common at that day for to gather in at the Public house in the evenings and often Mr. Spaulding would read from his MS. to entertain us. I had the Book of Mormon in my house for about six months for the purpose of comparing it with my recollection of the Lost Manuscript found," and I unhesitatingly say that a great part of the historical part of the Book of Mormon is identical with the MS. and I fully believe that the MS. is the foundation of the whole concern.

Yours truly
JOSEPH MILLER.
TEN MILE WASHINGTON CO. PA.

To MRS. ELLEN E. DICKINSON.

No. 3.

Mrs. Ann Treadwell Redfield's Statement.

SYRACUSE, June 17, 1880.

In the year 1818 I was principal of the Onondaga Valley Academy, and resided in the house of William H. Sabine, Esq. I remember Mrs. Spaulding, Mr. Sabine's sister, perfectly, and of hearing her and the family talk of a manuscript in her possession, which her husband, the Rev. Mr. Spaulding, had written somewhere in the West. I did not read the manuscript, but its substance was so often mentioned, and the peculiarity of the story, that years afterward, when the Mormon Bible was published, I procured a copy, and at once recognized the resemblance between it and Mrs. Spaulding's account of "The Manuscript Found." I remember also to have heard Mr. Sabine talk of the romance, and that he and Mrs. Spaulding said it had been written in the leisure hours of an invalid, who read it to his neighbors for their amusement.

Mrs. Spaulding believed that Sidney Rigdon had copied the manuscript while it was in Patterson's printing-office, in Pittsburg.

She spoke of it with regret. I never saw her after her marriage to Mr. Davison, of Hartwick.

ANN TREADWELL REDFIELD.

No. 4.

Statement of John Spaulding.

Solomon Spaulding was born in Ashford, Conn., in 1761, and in early life contracted a taste for literary pursuits. After he left school he entered Plainfield Academy, where he made great proficiency in study, and excelled most of his classmates. He next commenced the study of law, in which he made little progress, having in the mean time turned his attention to religious subjects. He soon after entered Dartmouth College, with the intention of qualifying himself for the ministry, where he obtained the degree of A.M., and was afterward regularly ordained.

After preaching three or four years he gave it up, and removed to Cherry Valley, N. Y., and commenced the mercantile business, in company with his brother Josiah. In a few years he failed in business, and removed to Conneaut, Ohio, in 1809. The year following I removed to Ohio, and found him engaged in building a forge. I made him a visit three years after, and found he had failed, and was considerably involved in debt. He told me he had been writing a book, which he hoped to have printed, the avails of which he thought would enable him to pay all his debts. The book was entitled "Manuscript Found," of which he read to me many passages. It was an historical romance of the first settlers of Americans, endeavoring to show that the American Indians are descended from the Jews, or the lost tribes. It gave a detailed account of their journey from Jerusalem by land and sea, till they arrived in America under the command of Nephi and Levi. They afterward had contentions and quarrels, and separated into two distinct nations, one of which he denominated Nephites, and the other Lamanites. Cruel and bloody wars ensued, in which great multitudes were slain. They buried their dead in large heaps, which caused the mounds so common in this country. Their arts, sciences, and civilization were brought into view, in order to account for all the curious antiquities found in various parts of North and South America. I have recently read the "Book of Mormon," and to my great surprise I find nearly the same historical matter, names, and so, as they were in my brother's writings. I well remember that he wrote in the old style, and commenced about every sentence with "And it came to pass," or "Now it came to pass," the same as in the "Book of Mormon;"

and according to the best of my recollection and belief, it is the same as my brother Solomon wrote, with the exception of the religious matter. By what means it has fallen into the hands of Joseph Smith, Jr., I am unable to determine.   JOHN SPAULDING.

No. 5.

Henry Lake's Statement.

CONNEAUT, ASHTABULA Co., OHIO, September, 1883.

I left the State of New York late in the year 1810, and arrived in this place about the 1st of January following. Soon after my arrival I formed a copartnership with Solomon Spaulding, for the purpose of rebuilding a forge, which he had commenced a year or two before. He frequently read to me from a manuscript which he was writing, and which he entitled " Manuscript Found," which he represented as being found in this town. I spent many hours in hearing him read said writings, and became well acquainted with its contents. He wished me to assist him in getting it printed, alleging that a book of that kind would meet with a ready sale. This book represented the American Indians as the lost tribes, gave an account of their leaving Jerusalem, their contentions and wars, which were many and great. One time, when he was reading to me the tragic account of Laban, I pointed out to him what I considered an inconsistency, which he promised to correct ; but by referring to the " Book of Mormon," I find, to my surprise, it stands there just as he read it to me then. Some months ago I borrowed a Golden Bible, put it in my pocket, and carried it home, and thought no more of it. About a week after my wife found the book in my coat pocket as it hung up, and commenced reading it aloud as I lay on the bed. She had not read twenty minutes before I was astonished to find the same passages in it that Spaulding had read to me more than twenty years before from his " Manuscript Found." Since that I have more fully examined the said Golden Bible, and have no hesitation in saying that the historical part of it is principally, if not wholly, taken from " The Manuscript Found." I well recollect telling Mr. Spaulding that the so frequent use of the words, "And it came to pass," " Now it came to pass," rendered it ridiculous.

Spaulding left here in 1812, and I furnished him with the means to carry him to Pittsburg, where he said he would get the book printed and pay me. But I never heard any more from him or his writings, till I saw them in the " Book of Mormon."

          (Signed)   HENRY LAKE.

No. 6.

Copy of George Clark's Letters.

FIRST LETTER.

SONOMA, CALIFORNIA, December 30, 1880.

MRS. ELLEN E. DICKINSON.

DEAR MADAM: Your letters of December 13th and 16th came to hand yesterday. I remember very well that Mrs. Davison spent a winter at my father's house, nearly, if not quite, fifty years ago. I think she left our house in the spring or summer after to go to Massachusetts. Some time after (perhaps one or two years) she wrote to my father to sell her effects, consisting of an old bureau, feather bed, and linen, and remit to her the proceeds, which he did. The old trunk still remained in the garret when I sold the farm, and was given away, to whom I do not remember. It was an old rickety, moth-eaten hair trunk, and entirely worthless. There was nothing whatever in it. My wife remembers that Mrs. Davison gave her the manuscript to read during her stay with us, and that she read a part of it and returned it to Mrs. D.; also that Mrs. Davison told her that it was written by Mr. Spaulding as a pastime to while away the days of sickness. My father died January 7th, 1864; my mother about thirty years since. Regretting that I cannot give you a more satisfactory answer, I remain respectfully yours,

GEORGE CLARK.

SECOND LETTER.

MRS. ELLEN E. DICKINSON.

DEAR MADAM: Yours of January 10th received. My wife does not remember the words Mormon, Maroni, etc., nor anything else of the contents of the manuscript in question. She remembers perfectly that it looked soiled and worn on the outside. She thought it rather dry reading, and after reading a few pages laid it aside. She remembers perfectly what Mrs. Davison said about it as being the origin of the Mormon Bible, and she thought it would die out in a few years. My wife (then Miss Brace) came to our house on a visit in 1831, and it was at that time Mrs. Davison was there. Mrs. Davison left our house to go to her (adopted) daughter's in Munson in the spring of that year (1831). Mr. Sabine was an uncle of my mother's. I do not remember of Mr. Hurlburt's being at our house at any time, or of his sending for the manuscript.

Yours respectfully,

SONOMA, CALIFORNIA, January 24, 1881. GEORGE CLARK.

APPENDIX. 245

No. 7.
Oscar Kellogg's Statement.

I accompanied Mrs. Dickinson on her visit to D. P. Hurlburt, at his residence near Gibsonburg, Sandusky Co., Ohio, November 13th, 1880, and was present at the entire interview. I have just heard Mrs. Dickinson's narrative of that interview read. I think it is as complete and truthful as could be written. We carefully listened to every word said, and watched Mr. Hurlburt's countenance and arrived at the same conclusion—that Hurlburt knows more than he told. O. E. KELLOGG.

NORWALK, OHIO, November 15, 1880.

No. 8.
Hurlburt's Statement.

GIBSONBURG, OHIO, January 10, 1881.

To all whom it may concern : In the year eighteen hundred and thirty-four (1834) I went from Geauga Co., Ohio, to Munson, Hampden Co., Mass., where I found Mrs. Davison, late widow of the Rev. Solomon Spaulding, late of Conneaut, Ashtabula Co., Ohio. Of her I obtained a manuscript, supposing it to be the manuscript of the romance written by the said Solomon Spaulding, called " The Manuscript Found," which was reported to be the foundation of the " Book of Mormon." I did not examine the manuscript until I got home, when, upon examination, I found it to contain nothing of the kind, but being a manuscript upon an entirely different subject. This manuscript I left with E. D. Howe, of Painesville, Geauga Co., Ohio, now Lake Co., Ohio, with the understanding that when he had examined it he should return it to the widow. Said Howe says the manuscript was destroyed by fire, and further the deponent saith not.

(Signed) D. P. HURLBURT.

No. 9.
Author's Letter from Palmyra.
EARLY MORMON HAUNTS.

PALMYRA, WAYNE CO., N. Y., June, 1882.

DEAR EVANGELIST : As is pretty widely known, this remarkably active and pretty town is connected with the early history of Mormonism. It was here that Joseph Smith, Jr., the first Prophet of the "Church of the Latter-day Saints," lived when he was a dull-eyed, flaxen-haired boy, and long after he had entered upon his "mission" and received "the golden plates," whereon was written "the new faith." This story seems but a legend to those little interested in or acquainted with the facts—one that has grown into present proportions by the accretions of many years. But not so. A little way up the main street, or rather in a side street leading from the principal thoroughfare of the town, resides John H. Gilbert (usually called Major Gilbert), a venerable, well-preserved man of eighty odd years, who in his youth was actively employed in the type-setting and presswork incident to the issue of the first edition of the "Book of Mormon." He allowed the writer to handle a copy of this edition, which he has carefully preserved. His description of the manuscript of the book, brought to him by "Hyrum" (as the Smiths spelled this name), brother of Joseph, is very interesting. The major got up from his chair, and taking a leaf or two of the book (unbound), he showed me how these early Mormons guarded their precious "translations" under their coats from a curious and unbelieving community, day by day, as they brought it, a few pages at a time, to be printed. The spelling and grammar were defective; and as for punctuation, there was none. The major pointed out these rather uninspired defects to the scribes employed by the Prophet, and he assures us that they kindly allowed him to make the necessary alterations, only, however, after they had become convinced of the necessity of something approaching literary accuracy—a matter not at all apparent to them.

A large number of modern Mormons have visited Major Gilbert, to whom he has related these and other recollections of their "Golden Bible." It would seem that they must leave him wiser if not better men, if they at all credit his very clear and positive statements, his memory and judgment being as yet untouched by age.

Mr. Seth W. Chapman owns the former home of the Smiths, and the land they cultivated after their fashion. It is two or three miles out of Palmyra, and at the present time is very attractive in its vernal beauty. The portion of the present farmhouse which was once the humble dwelling of Joseph, Sr., and his numerous family is composed of a single room of fair dimensions, over a cellar, with two small garret rooms above. Later, and after the sons and daughters were grown, a small bedroom was added to the main apartment. Here the Smiths lived for twelve years, making baskets and brooms, and raising vegetables, when they were not peddling beer and gingerbread at general trainings, or robbing hen-roosts or clothes-lines, or engaged in some other nocturnal calling. It has been said that the Prophet Joseph once returned from Nauvoo to view the place where he had dwelt before he became rich and famous, and where he had taken his first lessons in craft and dissimulation ; but this report rests on no sufficient basis. The present race of Mormons frequently visit the Chapman farm—the room above described, and the field now so beautifully green, where "the diggers," as they were called, consisting of a band of genuine vagabonds, with Joe as their leader, turned up the soil to find gold. Only the day previous to the visit of the writer, James H. Hart, a Mormon from Bloomington, Idaho, had inspected the premises. He circulated a pamphlet in the interest of the "Saints" and their peculiar institution, polygamy, during his stay in Palmyra. Mr. Cannon, son of the well-known Mormon of that name, has also recently visited the early abiding-place of Joseph and his brethren.

The spot where the famous "Peek Stone" was discovered on the property of Clark Chase, in the year 1819, is now marked by a gray slab, which stands close to a well—*the* well which was being dug when this white stone, in the shape of a child's foot, was turned up, and appropriated by the future "seer." The tradition is that Joseph ran home across lots, some two miles, to show his mother this new possession, which was like most, if not all, of his later possessions, unlawfully gained ; and that from this date he saw wonders through the "Peeker," it being employed by himself, and perhaps others in the neighborhood, to find any or everything they desired. The slight elevation where Clark Chase resided, and for whom the well was excavated, is now bare of any tenement, the former dwelling having been either burned or torn down a long time ago. Just beyond the well, a quarter of a mile or so, is the "Miner Farm," on which is shown a cave, or excavation, that was used by Smith and his close followers while engaged in deciphering the golden plates. It was originally boarded in, but is in a dilapidated condition at present. The same family own this farm now that owned it in Joe Smith's time. The elder members have passed away, but the present occupants are quite familiar with the events.

"Hill Cummorah," a conical elevation several hundred feet in height, and which, in its isolation and peculiar shape, bears a certain resemblance to an extinct volcano, is also of special interest. Just where Joseph found the box containing the golden plates is not known ; but it was somewhere near the dizzy top of this hill, that an angel was standing over him while he examined the contents. An old picture represents him as kneeling on the steep incline of the hill, the wind blowing his long hair out in all directions, his eyes big with surprise, and the placid, winged creature above him in a cloud, but not so dense as to prevent a good view of the future Prophet eagerly taking his credentials (which had been buried some fourteen hundred years) from the cemented chest—the sword of Laban, the Urim and Thummim (or spectacles), and the golden plates. Out of the cloud are zigzags of lightning playing around the angel and Joseph, which neither appears to notice.

The "Hill Cummorah" is three miles from where Joseph lived when this remarkable incident occurred, and his return to his domicile must have been a weary journey, after the excitement consequent upon such a distinction. The true Mormon of to-day venerates this locality as a sacred spot, and travels from afar to see its quiet but not remarkable beauty.

The farm owned by Martin Harris, the man who mortgaged his property to print the "Book of Mormon," is in an opposite direction to the "Hill" from Palmyra. A niece of Mrs. Harris resides in the town, and gives interesting remembrances of what she heard in her youth of the Mormons. It is but just to say that this lady has a more exalted estimation of the character of her relative than the world in general.

Sidney Rigdon, the real instigator and brains of the original Mormon swindle — the man who read and copied the romance called "Manuscript Found," written by the Rev. Solomon Spaulding, at Conneaut, Ohio, in 1812—is well remembered by a few of the older residents of Palmyra. It was Rigdon who preached the first Mormon sermon in the third story of a building, in what is now called Exchange Row. He introduced himself as the "Messenger of God," to the very few people who attended this meeting, telling them that the Bible and the "Book of Mormon" should be equally precious to the true Christian. His "sermon" was not agreeable to those who heard it, or the Palmyrians in general, and he did not repeat it, nor did any other "Saint" give a regular discourse there afterward. He might have fared worse if his audience had been acquainted with Mr. Spaulding's romance, which he had plagiarized so freely, and copied verbatim in many instances, in the "Book" which he introduced to them.

No. 10.

Statement of J. W. Gilbert, sent to the author by Hon. Diedrich Villers, Jr., with letter from the Rev. Diedrich Villers, and statement by the same.
(Copy.)

PALMYRA, WAYNE Co., N. Y., December 29, 1880.

DEAR SIR: Although I was the principal typesetter of the first Mormon Bible, I had no acquaintance with any of the originators of this great humbug, except Martin Harris. Jo. Smith I never saw but once. If you see fit to pay me a visit I shall be very glad to meet you and will show you a copy of the original edition of the Mormon Bible in sheets as I folded them from the press, besides a great number of articles cut from newspapers.

I am in my seventy-ninth year and in good health.

Yours truly,

J. H. GILBERT.

Hon. DIEDRICH VILLERS, JR., VARICK.

(VARICK) FAYETTE P. O., SENECA Co., N. Y., January 19, 1882.

DEAR MADAM: Your letter of the 7th inst. came duly to hand. I enclose a few recollections and traditions of Mormonism in Seneca County, with a copy of a letter, which may be of some service to you. At my great age (eighty-four years) I can remember but little of events which transpired over fifty years ago, and as the neighborhood in which Smith conducted his operations was some eight or nine miles from my residence, I was not even at that time much conversant with the facts. There is yet living in this county (besides Mr. Shiley, to whom I refer), a member of the Schott family, closely related to some of that family who became apostates to Mormonism.

(Signed) DIEDRICH VILLERS.

Rev. Diedrich Villers's Statement.

RECOLLECTIONS OF THE MORMONS IN SENECA CO., N. Y.

I infer that you desire information as to the early history of Mormonism in Seneca Co., N. Y., more than fifty years ago, when the present powerful Mormon organization was in its infancy, and its doctrines advocated hereabouts by Joseph Smith and other adventurers.

I will give you such data as occurs to me. As it is always right to give to every one his due, I may say that polygamy was unheard of in connection with Mormonism in those days, and its introduction was left to a later day—by Latter-Day Saints.

When I came to Seneca County as pastor of a number of congregations of the (German) Reformed Church, in April, 1821, I found among the members of a remote congregation, Zion's Church (afterward known as Jerusalem Church), in West Fayette, a plain, unassuming farmer of the name Peter Whitmer, a native of Pennsylvania, of the class of settlers known as Pennsylvania Germans. He was a quiet, unpretending, and apparently honest, candid, and simple-minded man. On the fifth day of April, 1822, at my first confirmation services of a class after instruction in the Heidelberg Catechism, I find among the names of the thirty-eight young persons then confirmed by me those of John Whitmer, Christian Whitmer, and Jacob Whitmer. My recollection is, that I baptized one or more of the Whitmer family as adults, according to the custom of the Reformed Church.

I may state here, that I never met or had any acquaintance with Joseph Smith, Hiram Page, Cowdrey, or Sidney Rigdon, nor, in fact, with any of the persons connected with them, except the Whitmers and the Jolly family. I am informed by Mr. Jacob Shiley, an old gentleman, aged seventy-nine years, now a resident of Fayette (who fifty or more years ago occupied a farm adjoining the residence of the Whitmers and Jollys), that the five persons of the name Whitmer, whose names appear in the "Testimony of three witnesses" and the "Testimony of eight witnesses," appearing at the end of the Mormon Bible, to wit: the three above-named, Christian, John, and Jacob Whitmer, and Peter Whitmer, Jr., and David Whitmer were all sons of Peter Whitmer, Sr.

Hiram Page, who is described to me as an itinerant botanic or root doctor, married a daughter of Peter Whitmer. It was said at the time of the marriage of Page to Miss Whitmer, that her father was opposed to the marriage until convinced by Page that Miss Whitmer was consumptive, and that he (Page), by the extraction of a certain tooth, the location of which he alone knew, could effect a cure. As there was doubtless a previous understanding between Page and the young lady, the pretended cure was reputed to have been effected through Page's agency, and the marriage took place.

One of the sons of Mr. Whitmer (as I am informed by Mr. Shiley) married a Miss Jolly, whose mother, the wife of William Jolly, of West Fayette, was a baptized convert to Mormonism, and with her husband removed with the Mormons to Ohio. Mr. Jolly, however (as Mr. Shiley informs me), declined to contribute the proceeds of the sale of his property to the common stock of Mormonism, and eventually withdrew from them, and died in Ohio, near Cleveland.

Two other sons of Mr. Whitmer (as Mr. Shiley informs me) married ladies of the name Schott, of West Fayette, near Waterloo, one of whom is said to have returned to Seneca County upon the death of her husband.

My informant (Mr. Shiley) says that he has attended the services held at the houses of Peter Whitmer and William Jolly, and heard, among others who spoke (or preached), Joseph Smith, Sidney Rigdon, and Hiram Page. The baptisms were performed by immersion in Thomas' Creek and Kendig Creek, in the town of Fayette. Mr. Jacob Shiley and his brother George Shiley, also still living in West Fayette, were present, and witnessed the immersion in baptism of Mrs. William Jolly. When it became known to me that Peter Whitmer and his family were becoming the dupes of Smith and his co-workers, I called upon Mr. Whitmer, in order to remonstrate with him and to warn him of the errors and delusions and the false doctrines promulgated by these men. My conversation, however, apparently made no impression upon him, his only reply to my arguments being the repeated quotation in the German language of the words : " Jesus Christ, yesterday, to-day, and forever."

As an illustration, to show how easily the Whitmers were duped, it is related, that by some contrivance of Smith and his associates a wooden image or representation was placed in a tree in a field where one of Whitmer's sons was engaged in ploughing, and that when interrogated as to whether he had not seen an angel, he answered in the affirmative. " Then," said Smith, " this is the place where the ' Book of Mormon ' must be completed, since the angel has already appeared eleven times, and it has been revealed to me that at the place of the twelfth appearing of the angel, the book must be completed." Hence Whitmers', in West Fayette, became the resort of Smith and his fellow-impostors during the progress of this work.

As for a time a number of persons besides the Whitmers were inclined to favor the Mormons, I preached a sermon in Zion's (Jerusalem) Church on June 13th, 1830, from the text, Galatians 1 : 8. So far as I know, no other persons in that vicinity except the Whitmers, the Jolly family, and several members of the Schott family became adherents.

A history of Seneca Co., N. Y., published in 1876 by Everts, Ensign & Everts, Philadelphia, Penn., contains some reference to Mormonism, from the recollection of Hon. Daniel S. Kendig, still living at Waterloo, who was born in Fayette in 1802, and lived there in the early years of his life. French's *New York Gazetteer*, published by R. Pearsall Smith, at Syracuse, New York, in 1860, also contained some data concerning Mormonism, and states that the first Mormon society was formed in the town of Fayette, Seneca County, in 1830. In this gazetteer Martin Harris is reported to have mortgaged his farm to defray the expense of printing the Mormon Bible. It was generally reported hereabouts, however, that Peter Whitmer had become surety for paying the cost of printing this Bible, and it may be difficult now to ascertain the exact facts in regard thereto; but as Smith was engaged in preparing the Bible for publication at Whitmer's house, it is probable that Whitmer also became involved in the expense of publication.

It is conceded, I think, that when Mr. Whitmer disposed of his property in this county he contributed what remained to the Mormon fund, and followed the fortunes of Mormonism. The edition printed of the "Book of Mormon" was, I am told, three thousand copies.

I have a copy of the "Book of Mormon," by "Joseph Smith, Jr., Author and Proprietor," bearing the imprint, "Palmyra. Printed by E. B. Grandin for the Author, 1830." This is doubtless one of the original copies.

The price of the Mormon Bible when issued was said to have been fixed in the first instance at $1.50 or $1.75 per copy; as the sale at that price was very slow, the price was reduced from time to time by Smith, under instructions from "the angel of the Lord," until at last copies were offered, I have been told, as low as fifty cents per copy, and even as low as twenty-five cents each.

There is yet living at Palmyra, N. Y., an octogenarian, Mr. J. H. Gilbert, who set type upon the original edition of the Mormon Bible.

[I have taken the liberty of copying for your confidential information a portion of a letter written by him to my son, Diedrich Villers, Jr., who has taken considerable interest in collecting early local history; and should you wish to use any of the facts therein contained, he will doubtless grant permission, should you write to him stating generally that you are advised that he possesses certain information as to Mormonism.]

No. 11.

The following was written by R. Patterson, of the Presbyterian Banner, Pittsburg—an extract from a letter written to him by Mr. Rudolph, in 1881, to Mrs. E. E. Dickinson.

Mr. Z. Rudolph, father of Mrs. General Garfield, knew Sidney Rigdon very well, and has stated that during the winter previous to the appearance of the "Book of Mormon," Rigdon was in the habit of spending weeks away from his home, going no one knew where ; and that he often appeared very preoccupied, and would indulge in dreamy, imaginative talks, which puzzled those who listened. When the "Book of Mormon" appeared, and Rigdon joined in the advocacy of the new religion, the suspicion was at once aroused that he was one of the framers of the new doctrines, and probably was not ignorant of the authorship of the "Book of Mormon."

[*Published in the New York Evangelist, December* 23, 1880.]

No. 12.

Author's visit at Mentor, Ohio.

GENERAL AND MRS. GARFIELD IN THEIR FARM HOME AT MENTOR, OHIO.

It may interest the readers of *The Evangelist* to learn something of the experience of one of its contributors, who has recently received the hospitality of the President-elect in his farm-house at Mentor, Ohio, without betraying the spirit of his kindliness and cordial entertainment.

The writer had been visiting in the vicinity of Cleveland, and had heard much of the democratic style of living of General Garfield, but was quite unprepared for the reality. Having a letter of introduction for the occasion, and another in my possession, written for me for another purpose by Dr. Henry M. Field, who is a personal friend of General Garfield, the way was made easy to follow a natural desire to see the incoming President at his own home, as well as to see Mrs. Garfield.

Mentor is a very small village, twenty miles east of Cleveland ; and quite at the west end of its one long street is the plain frame house, painted white, which is destined to be known in the history of our country. It is two stories high, irregular in shape, but has a comfortable, substantial appearance. Like most farm-houses, it is near the road, for convenience, and possibly for cheerfulness. Driving toward it from the station, the contrast between this unpretentious, simple home and that of Washington, at Mount Vernon, was very marked. It was very cold and snowing, and the question from the driver did not seem impertinent, "How long will you be here?" as we reached the side steps of the piazza. The reply, "It is impossible for me to say ; possibly I shall not remain at all," was met with, "Oh, yes, you will ; for the General is at home, and they are very hospitable."

A servant maid ushered me into a square corridor, heated by a large stove, where the furniture made it apparent that it is a kind of general reception-room or office. A tall Dutch clock is in one corner, which looks as though it might be an heirloom, and with its loud ticking keeps me company until a gentleman entered, whom the writer instantly recognized, from his resemblance to his pictures, as General Garfield. Let me pause to say that he is a far handsomer man than his photographs represent him, they failing, as all photographs do, to catch his genial, pleasant expression. His height is rather above the medium, figure good, rather inclined to stoutness ; his hair brown and full, eyes blue, complexion clear and fair, and his features regular. He is, in short, one of those persons we call good-looking, without knowing exactly why, as it is the whole appearance that impresses one favorably. After cordial greetings, and the letters referred to had been read, the General went up-stairs and called his wife " to come down, as they had visitors."

The parlor opening to the right from the corridor is a large square room, with an open fireplace, and two long windows. The woodwork is oak, varnished, which makes a pretty contrast with the white walls. The mantel is of oak, and has two shelves above it, which are filled with vases and plaques. To one side of the fireplace is an open cabinet, also of oak, that is filled with artistic effects and books. The floor is covered with matting, over which large Turkey rugs are laid. There is a piano, low easy-chairs, window draperies, plenty of books, some good pictures, and an entire air of refinement and tastefulness, without the slightest attempt at luxury. Between the windows is a little picture of some purple pansies enclosed in a gilt frame, on which is written or painted a verse from Whittier. It is the recent gift of a Bay State girl. This apartment is one of those living-rooms which at once gives a visitor the impression that joyful, contented hours are passed in it ; that children's voices have echoed within its walls, and bedtime stories have been told beside the hearth ; that books have been read by the shaded lamp, and music has added its charms to the home scene. A second room opens from this parlor, a pretty room, all in blue, where beside the east window is a low rocking-chair, having a cover made of dainty patchwork. It is the bed-chamber of the mother of the President elect, who shall be introduced to the reader later on.

Mrs. Garfield at once responded to her husband's request, and came down to welcome the two chance visitors—the writer and a member of Congress, on his way to Washington from San Francisco. An invitation was immediately given to remain to dinner, and soon after our outer garments were removed a bell was rung in the hall. The General led the way to the dining-room—a bright, cheerful room with an open fire. The table was long, and as though set for several persons, and the table-service was plain, but tasteful—white porcelain, flowered with green. Oak cabinets with glass doors, on either side of the fireplace, displayed an abundance of handsome dishes, glassware, and silver.

Mrs. Garfield sat at one end of the long table, and the General at the other. Two elderly ladies came in, who seated themselves one on either side of the General, whom he introduced to us as " My mother and my aunt, Mrs. ——." The elder Mrs. Garfield is a sweet-faced old lady, who resembles her distinguished son, and showing in every look her pride in his success. She is contented to be an elderly person, wearing a cap, and otherwise evincing her excellent sense in not attempting to appear young by the accessories of the toilet. Major Swain, the General's private secretary ; Mr. ——, the telegraph operator (who resides at the house) ; and a neighbor whom they called "Doctor," with the guests mentioned, made up the number at table—nine in all.

The dinner, which was plain, substantial, and well cooked, once under way (the host and hostess helping every one), the General at once opened a very pleasant conversation, and told anecdotes with infinite zest. The Western gentleman spoke of some recent political annoyances in San Francisco, the Chinese, the Rev. Starr King's career in that city, etc. ; but the General led the talk back to some incidents nearer home ; told us that his farm of one hundred and sixty acres was settled by the Mormon of whom he purchased it ; that Mentor was the first place where the Mormons gathered in Ohio, and that the wonderful temple they built at Kirtland is only two or three miles from his house. He told us something of Joe Smith, and of Rigdon (a Mormon preacher), of whom his wife's father took lessons in Latin and Greek. The General and Mrs. Garfield both distinctly remembered this man, who abjured his faith in Joe Smith and became a wandering expounder of the doctrines of the Disciples, or Campbellites. They had heard him preach, and considered him a man of ability and good education. He informed us also that a good many Mormons still reside in that neighborhood—believers in the "Book of Mormon," but not in polygamy. Some of these people are very old, but have a full remembrance of the early excitement in regard to Mormonism and Joe Smith's departure for "pastures new" in the far West.

After dessert, with tea and coffee, but no wine, we returned to the parlor. The Doctor reminded the General that the next day would be his birthday, and asked Mrs. Garfield, senior, how old he would be. She turned toward her son with a beaming smile, and responded, "He will be forty-nine years old."

"Not thirty-nine, as some people say, mother?" laughingly asked the General.

"I think I ought to know," she replied, with some dignity.

"Yes, yes," said the Doctor; "sure *you* should know." He then chatted a little, said something about eating two dinners, having his at home at noon, and not being accustomed to such fashionable hours (between one and two o'clock), and made his familiar adieu, being evidently an intimate of the family. The Western gentleman also soon took his departure; said he had stopped to pay his respects to the General and Mrs. Garfield, and must catch the next train for the East. The door was ajar into "mother's room," and the old lady came in to bring some papers she had been reading, asking Mrs. Garfield, junior, how she liked one or two articles she pointed out. The General sat down in a low seat by one of the windows, and while chatting was interrupted once or twice by his clerk bearing telegrams for his inspection.

Until now I have written nothing especial of Mrs. Garfield, the lady of the White House for the next four years. She seems slightly careworn; is of medium height and slender figure; has dark, wavy, brown hair; small, regular features, and dark eyes. She is evidently intelligent, well read, and a decided character. I could readily believe all I had heard as to her care for her five children, her supervision of their studies and personal wants. She is a dignified woman, kindly, cordial, and utterly void of the airs and graces of a fashionable-society woman, which she might have become in her long residence in Washington. I could believe, too, in what is said of the domestic life in this household, the happy relations between husband and wife, and the beautiful respect and honor shown to the venerable mother of the President-elect. Mrs. Garfield is more reticent than the General—quieter, less free in conversation, but pleasing. That she is a sensible woman was proved by a trifling circumstance. She had on a simple morning dress, for which she did not once apologize. She came down from her chamber when called, and did not wait to make a toilet, which was also proof of her excellent breeding.

The writer wishes she could remember all the talk of the hour—of the joking remark of the General that his wife resembles a caricature in an illustrated paper, where she is represented as ready to sweep some feminine politicians out of her parlor, who are teasing the new President for office. This was all the better, that the lady in question will not have her picture taken by ambitious photographers. The General told, too, of an aged man in his vicinity, Mr. E. D. Howe, who was the first publisher of the Cleveland *Herald*, in 1819, and sold it himself, riding on horseback to deliver it ; and much beside of interest.

But it was growing darker, and snowing still, and the writer suddenly remembered the driver (who had so confidently predicted a prolonged visit), and the necessary departure by the afternoon train. Accompanied to the door by both the host and hostess, the General ran ahead, and catching up a broom lying on the piazza, brushed aside the snowflakes with the *abandon* of a boy. I could not but remark laughingly, " I never expected a President of the United States to sweep the steps for me ; so I fancy some politicians will feel the influence of your broom, sir." He waved the broom slightly as he replied, " Possibly," and " Good-by."

And so this (to me) memorable visit to Mentor was over, and something in the past to recall with pleasure ; and in dwelling upon it afterward in my journey, and upon the testimony of all those whom I met in Ohio who have a personal acquaintance with the General and Mrs. Garfield, I could come to but one conclusion as to the result of the recent Presidential election—a favorable conclusion, as you may imagine.

I may add that I heard that the elder Mrs. Garfield is to go to Washington with the General ; and she will be, it is said, the first mother of a President who has resided at the White House.

Mrs. E. E. Dickinson.

New York, December 10; 1880.

No. 13.

John Spaulding's statement.   (See No. 4 in the Appendix.)

[*Published in Scribner's Magazine of October,* 1881.]

No. 14.

Hiram Lake's and Lorin Gould's statements.

Conneaut, Ashtabula Co., Ohio, December 23, 1880.

I am sixty-nine years of age, and have lived all my life in Conneaut, Ashtabula Co., Ohio. My father, Henry Lake, was partner with Solomon Spaulding, in 1811 and 1812, in a forge in Conneaut (then Salem). About 1834, when I was about twenty-three years of age, I remember that there was a great excitement concerning Mormonism in Conneaut. My father read the "Book of Mormon," or heard it read, and was familiar with its contents, and he told me it was unquestionably derived from a manuscript written by his former partner, Solomon Spaulding, called "Manuscript Found; or, the Lost Tribes." I believe my father, about this time, made an affidavit to the same effect, which was published. Since 1834 I have conversed with Aaron Wright, John N. Miller, and Nathan Howard, old residents here, now deceased, all of whom lived here in 1811 and 1812, and who had heard Spaulding's manuscript read, and they told me they believed the "Book of Mormon" was derived from Spaulding's "Manuscript Found." Some or all these persons made affidavits to this effect, which were published in a book called "Mormonism Unveiled," edited by E. D. Howe, of Painesville, Ohio.

HIRAM LAKE.

CONNEAUT, ASHTABULA CO., OHIO, December 23, 1880.

I have resided in the neighborhood of Conneaut, Ashtabula Co., Ohio, sixty-six years. During all that period I have known Hiram Lake, whose statement [given below], dated December 23d, 1880, I have read. This statement I believe to be true. I was acquainted with Henry Lake, Aaron Wright, John N. Miller, and Nathan Howard, the persons named in Hiram Lake's statement, and about 1834-35, the time of the excitement concerning Mormonism, I heard them all say that the "Book of Mormon" was undoubtedly taken from a manuscript written by Solomon Spaulding, which they had heard Spaulding read in 1811 or 1812, called "The Manuscript Found; or, the Lost Tribes."

LORIN GOULD.

No. 15.

MONROE, December 18, 1880.

MRS. ELLEN E. DICKINSON:

Your letter of the 6th inst. is received, but I fear I shall be unable to give you any new information on the subject of your inquiry. My father settled in Vermont when a young man, where he remained until 1823, when he came to this country. I was then seventeen years of age. His brother John was living here, the first and only one of his father's family whom I ever saw. Uncle Solomon left Salem (as it was then called) 1814, and died about two years after. When the Mormon Bible was published some of his acquaintances recognized in it much which they were quite sure they had heard him read in his "Manuscript Found." In Henry Howe's "History of Ohio," page 285, is an article taken from a work published by E. D. Howe, called a "History of Mormonism," in which he gives what evidence he could gather, that the historical part of the "Book of Mormon" was written by Solomon Spaulding. He gives the testimony of Uncle John Spaulding and Mr. Henry Lake.

In our "Spaulding Memorial" is a letter to the publisher from Uncle Josiah Spaulding, who visited his brother, and gives what recollections he had of his writings. But perhaps you have the book or have seen it; if not, and you wish to do so, I think you can obtain it by sending to Rev. Samuel J. Spaulding, Newburyport, Mass.

These are all the sources of knowledge I have of my uncle's writings, and doubtless you have as much or more. There will probably never be any new light gained on the subject, as all his associates have passed away.

MRS. URANIA HAVILAND.

SOUTH RIDGE, ASHTABULA COUNTY, OHIO.

No. 16.

Copied by Hurlburt's permission.

PAINESVILLE, OHIO, August 7, 1880.

D. P. HURLBURT.

DEAR SIR: Just received your line, calling my attention to an article in *Scribner*, on the origin of that old Mormon Bible. Hardly a year passes that I do not receive more or less inquiries, some of which seem to reflect on your honesty in regard to the manuscript obtained from that wonderful old trunk, that was all explained truthfully in the book I published, as I then believed, and have ever since, that Spaulding's "Manuscript Found" was never found or received by you; I have no manner of doubt, but altogether a different manuscript on a very different subject. It was in my possession till after the publication of "Mormonism Unveiled," and then disappeared and lost, I suppose, by fire. I suppose this is all I need say on that subject. I was glad to hear that you are still in the form. I am now eighty-two years old, enjoying very good health. Hoping never to hear any more about that old Mormon imposition,

Yours very truly,

E. D. HOWE.

No. 17.

Statement of D. P. Hurlburt.

GIBSONBURG, OHIO, August 19, 1879.

I visited Mrs. Matilda (Spaulding) Davison at Munson, Mass., in 1834, and never saw her afterward. I then received from her a manuscript of her husband's, which I did not read, but brought home with me, and immediately gave it to Mr. E. D. Howe, of Painesville, Ohio, who was then engaged in preparing his book—"Mormonism Unveiled." I do not know whether or not the document I received from Mrs. Davison was Spaulding's "Manuscript Found," as I never read it entire, and it convinced me that it was not the Spaulding manuscript; but whatever it was, Mr. Howe received it under the condition on which I took it from Mrs. Davison—to compare it with the "Book of Mormon," and then return it to her. I never received any other manuscript of Spaulding's from Mrs. Davison, or any one else. Of that manuscript I made no other use than to give it, with all my other documents connected with Mormonism, to Mr. Howe. I did not destroy the manuscript nor dispose of it to Joe Smith, or to any other person. No promise was made by me to Mrs. Davison that she should receive any portion of profits arising from the publication of the manuscript, if it should be published. All the affidavits procured by me for Mr. Howe's book, including all those from Palmyra, N. Y., were certainly genuine.

D. P. HURLBURT.

No. 18.

Mr. Thurlow Weed's statement.

NEW YORK, April 12, 1880.

In 1825, when I was publishing the Rochester *Telegraph*, a man introduced himself to me as Joseph Smith, of Palmyra, N. Y., whose object, he said, was to get a book published. He then stated he had been guided by a vision to a spot he described, where, in a cavern, he found what he called a golden Bible. It consisted of a tablet, which he placed in his hat, and from which he proceeded to read the first chapter of the "Book of Mormon."

I listened until I became weary of what seemed to me an incomprehensible jargon. I then told him I was only publishing a newspaper, and that he would have to go to a book publisher, suggesting a friend who was in that business. A few days afterward Smith called again, bringing a substantial farmer with him, named Harris.

Smith renewed his request that I should print his book, adding that it was a divine revelation, and would be accepted, and that he would be accepted by the world as a prophet. Supposing that I had doubts as to his being able to pay for the publishing, Mr. Harris, who was a convert, offered to be his security for payment. Meantime I had discovered that Smith was a shrewd, scheming fellow, who passed his time at taverns and stores in Palmyra, without business, and apparently without visible means of support. He seemed about thirty years of age, was compactly built, about five-feet eight inches in height, had regular features, and would impress one favorably in conversation. His book was afterward published in Palmyra. I knew the publisher, but cannot at this moment remember his name. The first Mormon newspaper was published at Canandaigua, New York, by a man named Phelps, who accompanied Smith as an apostle to Illinois, where the first Mormon city, Nauvoo, was started.

(Signed) THURLOW WEED.

No. 19.

Statement by J. L. Howgate, formerly of Wayne County, N. Y., copied from the Salt Lake Tribune.

Spaulding had a nephew named King, who got a printer to copy the Spaulding manuscript, and then told Hale, a school-teacher, he could start a new religion and make money out of it, outlining his plan, which was to put some metallic covers and gold clasps on it—to afterward dig up—and with a big flourish proclaim it as a new religion from on high. Hale declined the proposition. Joe Smith then took kindly to the plan, and the two, pretending to have visions, then exhumed the book.

No. 20.

Letter from E. S. Gilbert, giving some incidents of early Mormonism.

CANASERAGA, N. Y., August 1, 1880.

MRS. ELLEN E. DICKINSON.

DEAR MADAM: Your interesting paper in *Scribner*, entitled "The Book of Mormon," has recalled the following anecdote to my mind, related by my aunt, Mrs. Orill Fuller, who was converted to the Mormon faith in the first days, and emigrated from this State to join the Mormon congregation, located, I think, at Kirtland, Ohio.

It appears that a certificate or affidavit, signed by the three witnesses—David Whitmer, Oliver Cowdrey, and Martin Harris—was appended to the "Book of Mormon" to this effect: "We, the undersigned, have *seen* and *hefted* the book of plates." Arrived at her destination, my aunt became acquainted with David Whitmer, who lived there; and wishing to be edified by the account of a reliable eye-witness concerning the appearance and peculiarities of the wonderful plates, she took early opportunity to converse with him on the subject, when, to her amazement, the veracious Whitmer assured her that he never had seen them.

"Suppose," said he, "that you had a friend whose character was such that you knew it impossible that he could lie; then if he described a city to you which you had never seen, could you not, by the eye of faith, see the city just as he described it?" She answered that, however that might be, the certificate attached to the Mormon Bible had given rise to the belief that the three witnesses had actually seen and handled the book of plates.

Thereupon he went on to relate the bottom facts, which formed the basis of his faith, to this effect: That he went into the woods after some maple sap, and having filled two large pails, he set out to return home. The pails of sap were so heavy that he was obliged to stop and rest at short intervals, and the sharp roots and stubs hurt his bare feet so badly that he had great difficulty in getting along at all. So sitting alone in the woods, he fell to thinking of Smith and of the plates he claimed to have found, and finally, to ease his doubts, he knelt and prayed that if Joseph Smith was a true prophet, and the plates a genuine revelation from God, that the sap might be made lighter as a token thereof. The prayer being ended, he arose, and lifted the sap, which now had apparently no weight whatever, and he went the remaining distance—I think a half mile—without setting it down once, getting over the ground easier than if empty-handed. Whether Cowdrey and Harris had such convincing proof, I do not know. I believe I read in the *Latter-Day Saints Herald*, that an angel appeared to them, holding the book of plates in his hands. My aunt's family did not remain at Kirtland long; they seceded and went to Michigan, under the leadership of James G. Strong; if I remember rightly, renounced Mormonism some time after, and are now living somewhere in the West. David Whitmer is still living, though very aged. These details, perhaps unimportant in themselves, derive a possible significance in connection with Mrs. McKinstry's narrative, showing how miracles and visions were, of necessity, substituted for ocular demonstration of the existence of the plates. You are at liberty to make any use of these statements that you choose, and I remain,

Yours truly,   E. S. GILBERT.

No. 21.

Statement of Oliver Smith, found in an old book in the Astor Library.

CONNEAUT, OHIO, August, 1833.

When Solomon Spaulding first came to this place, he purchased a tract of land, surveyed it out, and commenced selling it. While in this business he boarded at my house six months. All his leisure hours were occupied in writing an historical novel founded upon the first settlers of this country. He said he intended to trace their journey by land and sea till their arrival in America, give an account of their arts, sciences, civilization, wars, and contentions. In this way he would give a satisfactory account of the old mounds, so common to this country. During the time he was at my house he read one hundred or more pages to me; Nephi and Levi were by him represented as leading characters, etc. When the "Book of Mormon" came in the neighborhood, and I heard the historical part of it related, I at once said it was the writing of Solomon Spaulding.

No. 22.

Rev. N. C. Lewis, of the Methodist Episcopal Church, of Susquehannah Co., Penn., in 1834, made a sworn statement to the effect that he had "been acquainted with Joseph Smith, Jr., for some time; being a relative of his wife's, and residing near him, have frequent opportunities of conversation with him. He is not a man of veracity, and his general character in this part of the country is that of an impostor, hypocrite, and liar."

No. 23.

RANDOLPH, N. Y., November 9, 1881.

ELLEN E. DICKINSON:

DEAR MADAM: I have read with interest your letters on the "Book of Mormon," in the October number of *Scribner's Monthly*, and take the liberty to offer another source of information. There was living three years ago, near the town of Gilroy, Santa Clara Co., California, a Mrs. Monroe, who claims that Joe Smith was living in her father's house when he discovered the golden plates on which the "Book of Mormon" was inscribed, and that the translation was made then. I do not remember very much of her story, not being interested in the matter at that time; but I am certain you can obtain some very interesting particulars, if you can reach her.

I am very truly yours,

ALICE GREY COWAN.

No. 24.

Extracts from an old book on Mormonism found at the Astor Library.

Eleven male residents of Manchester, Ontario Co., N. Y., November 3d and 4th, 1833, made an affidavit that the family of Joseph Smith, Sr., with whom the Gold Bible originated, are a lazy, indolent, intemperate set, and their word is not to be depended on. The same day, in the same year, fifty-one other men of standing in the same vicinity state: We, the undersigned, have been acquainted with the Smith family for a number of years, while they resided near this place, and have no hesitation in saying that we consider them destitute of that moral character which ought to entitle them to the confidence of any community. Joseph Smith, Sr., and his son Joseph, in particular, were considered entirely destitute of moral character, and addicted to vicious habits.

No. 25.

Testimony of an army officer.

From an army officer for several years familiar with Mormon habits we learn some facts which show their animus toward the government. In 1865 they began and persistently followed up the practice of arresting soldiers who were in Salt Lake City from Camp Douglass, and fining them for nominal offence which they induced them to commit, such as giving them spirits, and then arresting them, and fining them under special orders. No Mormon would swear in their behalf, and the officers had no remedy. On one occasion troops were sent to rescue the imprisoned men, and a serious conflict was imminent when Brigham Young disavowed the action of officers, acting under his orders, to escape the dilemma.

The Indians of Arizona, Montana, Wyoming, and Dakota found ready market with Mormon agents for government horses, and any stolen, so that at one time thirty branded horses, fully recognized, were found in Salt Lake City, in Mormon stables, within two weeks after they had been stolen by Indians. The same was true of clothing and other supplies, which were not carried to the tribes by the plunderers, but sold to the Mormons by systematic arrangement. This was one reason why the Mormons themselves were rarely disturbed by Indians. They excited the Indians against the building of the railroad and of forts and settlements, thus to preserve their isolation as long as possible. By systematic false swearing they covered their agents, and by presents and supply of arms and powder fomented Indian hostilities for years.

APPENDIX.   265

No. 26.

The following letter from Rev. W. H. Rice, of Addison, Steuben Co., N. Y., tells its own story. There is a possibility that L. L. Rice, of Honolulu, S. I., may have a Spaulding manuscript in his possession; but unquestionably it is not the original "Manuscript Found," from which the "Book of Mormon" was constructed, as all the evidence given in these pages will show. AUTHOR.

ADDISON, N. Y., February 21, 1885.

MRS. ELLEN E. DICKINSON:

Yours of the 18th is received. When my father went to Honolulu, he took some documents which had not been examined for many years. A few months since he began to look them over, and found one marked "Conneaut Story." He found it to be a story in Scripture narrative style, purporting to be written by Rev. Solomon Spaulding. It must have been unnoticed in his hands forty-five years or more, and he writes me that he has no recollection as to its origin or how it came into his possession. His age is eighty-four. It has been examined by all the best scholars in Honolulu, including Rev. Dr. Hyde, Judge McCully of the Supreme Court, and none of them has expressed a doubt that it is an original manuscript from the pen of Solomon Spaulding. It is similar in style to the "Book of Mormon," but is not identical with it in any part. It is signed by several "witnesses," all of whom, as I have learned, actual residents of Conneaut or its vicinity—now all dead. Hurlburt is, I believe, one of the names. This is the substance of all I know about it. I should think there could be no doubt that Mr. Spaulding wrote it; but whether he also wrote other stories in similar style is an important question.   Yours truly,
                                        W. H. RICE.

No. 27.

COPY OF THE TITLE-PAGE OF THE ORIGINAL EDITION OF THE "BOOK OF MORMON."

A copy of the original edition of the "Book of Mormon" is, without doubt, the scarcest book published in the nineteenth century which has obtained any reputation. As an evidence of this, a gentleman was in search of a copy for a great many years, and always unsuccessful, until a copy came into his possession by accident in New York, among a lot of old school books, which, by the by, in external appearance it strongly resembles.

The following is an exact copy of the title-page of this book:

"The) *Book of Mormon*). An account written by the hand of Mormon from plates taken from the plates of Nephi. Wherefore it is an abridgement of the Record of the people of Nephi; and also of the Lamenites; written to the Lamenites which are a remnant of the House of Isreal; and also to Jew and Gentile; written by way of commandment and also of the spirit of Prophesy and of Revelation, written and sealed up, and hid up unto the Lord, that they might not be destroyed; to come forth by the gift and power of God unto the interpretation thereof; sealed by the hand of Morini and hid up unto the Lord to come forth in due time by the way of Gentiles, the interpretation thereof by the gift of God; an abridgement taken from the Book of Ethen. Also which is a record of the people of Jared which were scattered at the time, the Lord confounded the language of the people when they were building a tower to get to Heaven; which is to show unto the remnant of the House of Isreal how great things the Lord hath done for their fathers, and that they may know the covenants of the Lord, that they are not cast off forever; and also to the convincing of the Jew, and Gentile that Jesus is the Christ the *Eternal God*, manifesting Himself unto all nations. And now if there be fault, it be the mistake of man; wherefore condemn not the things of God, that ye may be found spotless at the Judgment seat of Christ.

By JOSEPH SMITH, JUNIOR,

Author and Proprietor.

PALMYRA.

Printed by E. D. GRANDIN,

For the Author.

1830."

Camp Douglas is situated on a hill overlooking the city. It is occupied by several regiments of Federal troops, under command of United States officers. While the troops are a nominal safeguard to the Gentiles of Salt Lake Valley, they would be quite inadequate in number to protect them in case of a conflict between the Mormons and Gentiles.

The Rev. Joseph Cook predicts a civil war in Utah within a few years; in fact, at almost any time, as a natural sequence to the events now transpiring among the Saints. He affirms that every male Mormon is trained and ready for the conflict. He also asserts that Mormonism without polygamy is so dread an evil, that it should be exterminated at any cost. Every Mormon he considers a sworn enemy to the Federal Government, and that Mormonism is a political as well as spiritual hierarchy, and without immediate and stringent measures are used, in a few years the Mormon leaders will rule every State west of the Mississippi.

INDEX.

B.

"Book of Commandments" for the government of the Church, published while at Independence, Mo., 91.

"Book of Mormon," copy of the title-page of the original edition, 266.

C.

Celestial marriage, the text of Joseph Smith's pretended revelation on the subject at Nauvoo in 1843, 228.

Clark, George, copy of his letter bearing on the Spaulding manuscript, 244.

Clay, Henry, his correspondence with Joseph Smith while at Nauvoo, 99.

Conneant, O., visit to by the author and reminiscences of Sam. Spaulding and the first Mormon conference held there in 1834, 77.

Cowan, Alice Grey, important testimony, 263.

D.

Dickinson, Mrs. Ellen E., letter from Palmyra in New York *Evangelist* on the "Early Mormon Haunts," 245.

G.

Garfield, President, account of the author's visit to Mentor in 1880, and Mr. and Mrs. Garfield's statements concerning Joe Smith and Rigdon and the Mormons while at Kirtland, only three miles from Mentor, 253.

Gilbert, J. W., statement of one of the type-setters of the "Book of Mormon," 249.

Gould, Lorin, statement in relation to Hiram and Henry Lake, and others, 258.

H.

Haviland, Mrs. Urania, statement in regard to the Spaulding family, 259.

Howe, E. D., who aided Hurlburt in getting possession of the Spaulding manuscript; a thrilling interview with him by the author in 1880 described, 72; on the origin of the old Mormon Bible, 259.

Howgate, J. L., statement in regard to starting a new religion, 261.

Hurlburt, D. P., who purloined Spaulding's manuscript; sketch of him, 62; a thrilling interview with him by the author and Oscar E. Kellogg in November, 1880, 62; statements in relation to his connection with the lost manuscript, 245, 260.

J.

Josephites, The, a branch of Mormons calling themselves "Josephites," and "Latter-Day Saints of the Reorganized Church of Jesus Christ," 215; their present number; Joseph Smith, Jr., their spiritual leader, 215; description of a colony of "Latter-Day Saints" at Dennisport, Mass., 223; epitome of their faith, 226.

K.

Kellogg, Oscar E., statement in reference to the author's interview with Dr. Hurlburt, 245.

L.

Lake, Henry, statement of his business and social relations with Spaulding, who often read to him from the "Manuscript Found," 243.

Lake, Hiram, concerning Mormonism in Connecticut, 257.

M.

Mormonism, founded by Joseph Smith in 1830 at Palmyra, N. Y., 28; the "Book of Mormon," printed in Palmyra in 1830; Mormon Church organized soon after, 42; first Mormon conference held at Fayette, N. Y., 43; Sidney Rigdon preaches the first Mormon sermon, 43; the first missionaries sent out, 44; removal to Kirtland, O., 44; rapid spread of the delusion, 45, 51; the name of "Mormons" repudiated and that of "Latter-Day Saints" adopted, 51; in 1835 the first missionaries sent out to foreign lands, 52; history of the Mormons at Kirtland, 54; description of the temple built there, 56; the Mormons in Missouri, 82; what led to the arrest of Smith, Rigdon, and other leaders, and their imprisonment and the expulsion of their followers from Independence after incredible sufferings, which they had provoked, 89; "Book of Commandments," published in 1833, 91; the Mormons at Nauvoo, 94; the Mormon temple there, 101; a "revelation" establishing polygamy, 103; brings on a crisis of affairs at Nauvoo in 1844; the conflict and death of the "Prophet," 108; Brigham Young's election to the presidency, 113; sketch of his early years and career as one of the "Twelve Apostles," 114; elected to be the "first president," 115; exodus from Nauvoo, 116; re-establishment of the Saints in Utah, 125; conflict with the Government, the "Minute Men," the "Danites," the "Mountain Meadow Massacre," 133; death of Brigham Young, 158; number of Mormons at the present day, 184; character of the converts and whence drawn, 185; the "doctrines" of Mormonism, 200; analysis of the Mormon faith, 202; hierarchical organization, 205; the "Book of Mormon," 206; Church polity, 209; the faith of the "Latter-Day Saints," 212; their mode of worship, 213; a grand conference to be held at Independence, Mo., in April, 1885, 217; extracts from an old book on Mormonism found in the Astor library, 264; testimony of an army officer, 264.

Miller, Joseph, letter to the author in regard to what he knew of Solomon Spaulding, 240.

N.

Nauvoo, Ill., the capital of Mormondom, 95; description of it and of the leaders while there, 95; description of the city after the Mormons abandoned it, 117; the temple burnt in 1848, 121.

P.

Patterson, R., of the *Presbyterian Banner*, an extract from a letter written to him by Mr. Rudolph, the father of Mrs. General Garfield, 252.

Polygamy in Utah was established by Smith in Nauvoo, 140; Brigham Young, immediately after the settlement of the Saints in Zion, had a "revelation" about "celestial marriage," and did his utmost to promote polygamy, both by his teaching and example, 140; his official sanction and the ceremony he used in forming such marriages, 143; the degrading and awful effects of the practice, 146; copy of the "Edmunds bill" for the suppression of polygamy, 150; copy of a bill introduced into the House of Representatives, June 19, 1884, and ordered to be printed, 153; trial of Rudger Clawson for polygamy by Judge Zane, 172; John Taylor's testimony, 172; Varian's speech in behalf of the prosecution, 174; the Judge's sentence, 178; his charge to the jury in the same case, 182.

R

Redfield's, Mrs. Ann Treadwell, statement in reference to the Spaulding manuscript, 241.

Rice, W. H., of Honolulu, and Rice, W. H., of Addison, N. Y., important testimony concerning the Spaulding manuscript, 265.

Rigdon, Sidney, sketch of his early life, gifts, and character, 47; meets Smith, and enters into all his schemes, 48; becomes a Campbellite preacher, 48; his power as an advocate of the new faith, 50; a great number of converts at Kirtland, and wonderful scenes, 51; he establishes numerous societies in Canada, Missouri, Illinois, Virginia, New York, and in nearly all the Northern, Middle, and in several of the Southern States, 52; Smith the tool of Rigdon in formulating the "Book of Mormon" from the "Manuscript Found," which he copied while a printer in Patterson's office, 53; president of a "wild-cat" bank at Kirtland, 52; tricked out of the leadership by Brigham Young when Smith was killed, 52; expelled from Nauvoo; becomes a vagrant, and dies in obscurity and poverty, 53.

S.

Salt Lake City, its population, climate, and natural features and surroundings, 187; its institutions, regulations, society matters, etc., 189.

Smith, Joseph, the founder of Mormonism and author of the Mormon Bible; his birth and some account of his father's family; removal to Palmyra, N. Y., 28; his mother's influence over him, 30; "Joe Smith" becomes the head of a band, whose business was to sleep all day and search for hidden treasures at night, 30; how he lived and spent his time during several years, 31; becomes a religious fanatic during a revival, claims to work miracles, etc., and gathers a few dissolute followers, 34; "Gold Bible Hill," where he claimed to discover the plates of the Mormon Bible, 35; his own account of the discovery, and what succeeded, 37; he inveigles a rich farmer, Martin Harris, who furnished him with money, 39; Thurlow Weed declines to print the Bible, 40; the book is at last published, and creates intense excitement in Central and Western New York, 41; the Mormon Church organized with six members, 42; the "First Hegira" made in 1831, 44; immense success at the West, 45; Smith's unsavory reputation in Palmyra, 46; on his going to Missouri he first organizes a military command, and assumes the prerogatives of his high military as well as spiritual mission, 84; his career at Independence, Mo., 83; his career at Nauvoo, Ill., 94; his "revelation" concerning polygamy precipitates a crisis and an armed conflict, and Smith and his brother are killed, 108; his influence over his wife, who after his death published a statement that she had no faith in his prophetic power or pretended revelations, 111.

Smith, Joseph, Jr., the leader of the Josephites, 215; his account of the persecutions endured in Arizona, 219; he strongly and bitterly denounces the Utah Mormons and polygamy, 222.

Smith, Oliver, letter to author, 261.

Spaulding, John, his testimony about the Spaulding romance, 242.

Spaulding, Mrs. Matilda Spaulding McKinstry's statement regarding the "Manuscript Found," 237.

Spaulding, Samuel, sketch of his life, 13; circumstances leading to his writing the original of the Mormon Bible, 15; the romance known as the "Manuscript Found," 16; attempt to get it published, 17; reasons for believing that Rigdon made a copy of it while in Patterson's printing-office, 17; Spaulding's death, 17.

Spaulding, Mrs. Samuel, her relations and friends among the leading men of Central New York, 19; her residence with "Squire Sabine," her brother, a lawyer of distinction and wealth, 19; the famous "hair-covered trunk," containing sermons, essays, novels, and the famous romance which has played so conspicuous a part in the Mormon history, 20; marries Mr. Davison, 22; the Spaulding trunk of manuscripts is placed in the custody of a cousin, Jerome Clark, 22; removes to Munson, Mass., and becomes greatly excited over what she hears of the Mormons, and the report that it was founded on her husband's romance, 23; the manuscript stolen from her trunk, and traced to one Hurlburt, who figures in these pages, 27.

T.

Taylor, John, elected as successor to Brigham Young; early life and great abilities, 167; founded a Mormon school in Paris, called "L'Étoile de Deseret;" translated the "Book of Mormon" into French and German; has written school books to enlighten the Mormons on spiritual matters, 168; his remarkable testimony in the polygamy case of Rudger Clauson, 172.

U.

Utah Territory, boundary, resources, possibilities, etc., 194.

V.

Villers, Rev. Diedrich, recollections of the Mormons in Seneca Co., N. Y., 249.

W.

Weed, Thurlow, statement of his personal knowledge of Joseph Smith while he lived in Palmyra, 260.

Whitmer, David, one of the original "witnesses" of Joe Smith, 217.

Y.

Young, Brigham, early years, 113; becomes one of the "Twelve Apostles," 114; elected "First President," and invested with the "Keys," 115; conflict with the State authorities and repeal of the charter of Nauvoo in 1845, 115; the exodus from Nauvoo in 1846, 116; the famous journey through the wilderness, 125; the arrival of the advance company of the Saints in Utah, 125; a territory organized and Young made governor in 1849, 127; he defies the power of the United States Government, and Judge Drummond is driven from his bench by an armed Mormon mob, 128; the day of Young's arrival at Salt Lake City is still observed (July 24th) instead of July 4th, 132; the "Minute Men" and the "Danites," which he organized for military purposes; the "Mountain Meadow Massacre," 133; John D. Lee, who was tried and executed by our Government for his part in this butchery, was Brigham Young's tool, 137; his efforts in favor of polygamy, 140; grants woman's suffrage in 1871, to strengthen Mormonism, 148; death of Brigham Young in 1877, 158; outline of his personal traits and of his life and intercourse with his people and wonderful influence over them, 161; the number of his wives and children, 156.

www.ingramcontent.com/pod-product-compliance
Lightning Source LLC
Chambersburg PA
CBHW031958230426
43672CB00010B/2195